# THE STATE OF
# BLACK AMERICA 1996

Published by **National Urban League, Inc.**
January 1996

# THE STATE OF BLACK AMERICA 1996

## Editors

*Audrey Rowe*
*John M. Jeffries*

Copyright© National Urban League, Inc., 1996
Library of Congress Card Catalog Number 77-647469

ISBN 0-9632071-5-6

Price $24.95

# National Urban League, Inc.

The Equal Opportunity Building • 500 East 62nd Street • New York , New York 10021

# TABLE OF CONTENTS

# BUILDING A 21ST CENTURY COMMUNITY: THE STATE OF BLACK AMERICA 1996

By Hugh B. Price
President
The National Urban League

In three years the 21st Century will be here. Is America awake to it inevitability and aware of its possibilities? Is Black America? Are both prepared for the demands of the rigorous economic and social environment it will usher in?

These are the fundamental questions posed by the disparate essays of this volume of *The State of Black America 1996.*

"Global competitiveness" has already shown the power it has to disrupt long held business practices, drive some companies under and threaten the viability of numerous others that had once seemed invulnerable, bump millions of people into lower-paying jobs, or throw them out of work altogether—and thus, destabilize ar entire society. Every indication is that the economic winds of change will be blowing at gale force during a the next decade and beyond. In a post big-government era, can American society build a 21st Century Community strong enough to not merely withstand those winds but use them for its own source of energy?

In other words, if America is to do well in the competition, all the groups in American society must be in good social and economic health. All Americans must be equipped—and encouraged—to contribute to our nation's economic well-being.

Unfortunately, as the essays in *The State of Black America 1996* eloquently attest, neither the former nor, the latter conditions are now true.

Our authors paint a disturbing portrait of a society irrationally at odds with its ever more insistent need to utilize all of its resources: They show that this is a society which tolerates double-digit unemployment among blacks, and even higher rates of underemployment. One which permits high rates of residential segregation that traps blacks (and Latinos) in inner cities far from jobs in the suburbs. One which in great measure ignores the obvious necessity of harnessing the positive energy of all our youth. One in which the physical and mental health of African-Americans is sapped by the illnesses, diseases and behavioral disorders which afflict them at rates far greater than they do whites. One which has largely turned away from fashioning a comprehensive public-sector housing program, and which likewise stubbornly resists addressing the issue of child-care. One in which African-Americans and Latino-Americans often rightly feel that they must protect themselves not only from criminals, but from a criminal justice system which too often treats them unjustly.

And one in which African-Americans's lack of access to the capital that would lead to greater private home ownership and help spur a greater private-sector economic development has left them with a stake in the American economy that is far too small for the country's own good.

The thrust of these essays is not a matter of merely focusing on the negative. Neither the authors nor the Urban League wish to slight the striking progress African-Americans have forged during the past three decades, a growth evident in the expansion of the black middle class and stable working class, the consistent achievement of an annual one million-plus enrollment of our young people in higher education, and the exponential increase in the number of black elected officials.

Indeed, we at the Urban League are devoting more of our time and efforts to accentuating the positive. For example, in September we held our first "Doing The Right Thing" celebration of youngsters who are excelling in school, doing better than they had been, and sending their communities. We did so because we want to emphasize to our children what we value and convey a message to society that it tends to ignore and needs to hear loud and clear: that our children are an asset, not a liability, to America. We will stage our "Doing the Right Thing" celebration every year from now on.

Nonetheless, we have no intention of ignoring the problems that confront us-and America. For these are problems which sap the nation's strength and confidence that it can not merely survive, but thrive in the first decades of the 21st Century. They will not be resolved merely by casting our fate to the wind and hoping the market treats us well. The essays presented here show that would be a foolish choice, indeed.

For example, contrary to the once-fashionable, facile assertions of their declining importance, the economic well-being of the America's cities is now even more crucial to the nation's competitive strength. James Stewart shows how a continued high unemployment and underemployment of African-Americans and Latino-Americans in the nation's ghettos and barrios will undermine the economic productivity the society needs, and offers several cogent recommendations on how to bring these neglected potential contributors of economic strength into the loop of productivity.

America will have to overcome major obstacles to do so. One of those may be the provocative point Timothy Bates asserts in his essay: that living costs in urban areas with thriving business districts are held down by low-wage service industries and businesses which draw heavily upon a low-skilled and unskilled, primarily black and brown labor force. Bates' contention raises the most profound issues for how the society can raise the skill-level of its entire labor force; and he himself suggests how the problem this presents can be overcome.

In addition, the labor market must find a way to eliminate the old "tradition" which has always assured that blacks will earn significantly less than whites for doing the same job and having the same credentials and experience. That continues. In fact, such economic gaps are increasing, according to John M. Jeffries's and Richard L. Schaffer's essay on the economy and the labor market participation of African-Americans.

They show that as real earnings have dropped and income inequality has increased for all American workers in the last decade, both the hourly earnings gap between whites and blacks, and the economic divide between higher- and lower-income black families has widened. This distressing reality, on top of the "usual" double-digit black unemployment rate, is a sobering reminder that, despite the gains achieved, Black America still faces difficult challenges.

One of the most pressing is in improving the health of African-Americans. Dr. June Jackson Christmas provides the stark details of the breadth of the health crisis among black Americans. Different age cohorts endure different afflictions—from high rates of infant mortality, to high rates of teenage pregnancy and unwed fatherhood, drug addiction (and a resulting epidemic of people infected with AIDS) and homicide, to significant rates of breast, prostate, lung and liver cancer. Any one of these health crises by themselves is a cause for alarm. It is a measure of Dr. Christmas's broad scope that even as she urges us to intensify our efforts in each of these fields, she also declares that positive "changes will not ensure better health unless attention is given also to alleviating poverty and discrimination...."

Thus, we return to the twin issues which have plagued Black America—and, indeed, all of America throughout the Twentieth Century. Can America, spurred by the prospect of the dire consequences of failure, finally resolve them?

We should know the answer to that question soon as we approach the 21st Century: It will be evident in what American society decides to do about our modern day Great Depression—the one in America's inner cities.

The "downsizing" which has become a household word for most Americans only recently struck urban neighborhoods with a vengeance a generation ago when factories began closing in droves. Now, with jobless rates three to four times the national average and with labor force participation rates even worse, inner cities are well into the third decade of economic and social despair that matches the depths of the depression of the 1930s.

That catastrophe, in turn, has produced a bitter, deadly surge in crime in these impoverished areas. In his essay Christopher E. Stone describes in poignant detail some of the valiant efforts African-American and Latino-American residents of these neighborhoods have mounted to fight crime. Those efforts are all the more courageous and poignant because of the injustice law-abiding blacks and Latinos often endure from the criminal justice system. Stone makes clear that reducing the crime problem in these neighborhoods—and reducing the distrust blacks stnd Latinos have for the system of law enforcement— is ultimately dependent on building up the number of residents in them who have jobs and a decent wage.

Thus, with all of America's economic future hanging in the balance, it's imperative to end the Great Depression in America's ghettos.

We believe the urban policy must have a laser-like focus on jobs for the inner-city poor. No fancy master plans. No complex urban policies with dozens of components. We need public policies which make work economically worthwhile. We've been content for far too long with a low-wage economy that locks hard-working Americans into poverty. Boosting the minimum wage helps a bit, as does protecting the Earned Income Tax Credit from continuous assault by Congress.

The missing piece of the benefits puzzle is guaranteed health care and affordable child care, a point Evelyn K. Moore makes in cogent detail. Decent paying jobs with basic benefits will draw idle workers into the labor force and lift them out of poverty.

Make no mistake. Inner city folk want to work. We've got to spread the job action around if inner city folk are to work — and if cities are to work. There is no macro-economic policy, no economic growth scenario, no Model Cities approach, no black capitalism strategy and no enterprise zone experiment imaginable that can match the Depression-era Works Progress Administration in jumpstarting hope by driving unemployment down in a hurry.

There's nothing un-American about spending public money to help fill gaping holes in the labor market. It is what our national government has done over the years to generate jobs where they are in short supply. The Economic Development Administration under President Eisenhower breathed economic life into the rural south with its investments in labor intensive construction projects like highways that helped pave the way for that region's long-term recovery. Rural towns, once terrified of escaped convicts, now compete feverishly for new prisons, built, of course, with public dollars, to capture the jobs for their young men, the purchasing power for their shops and the business activity for their tax base. Communities and Congressmen stubbornly resist military base closings because of the local economic impact. And they compete fiercely for aerospace and defense contracts local firms for the same reasons.

An urban jobs policy aimed at putting inner-city people back to work wouldn't differ in principle from such past efforts as the WPA and the Eisenhower-era EDA programs, only in their output and primary beneficiaries. To keep this from becoming a patronage cookie jar for politicians, let community groups like the Urban League and community development corporations employ these workers. Or perhaps we could enlist the National Guard to operate the jobs program funded jointly by the federal and state governments. The military certainly has the credibility, the operating systems and the capacity to run a large-scale jobs program. That sounds like the Army to me, only with a different mission.

Can society afford a jobs program for the poor? Let me pose the question a different way. Can we afford all the homelessness and anger that will result if mothers and children, cut off of welfare and without work, land on the streets? Can states such as California, propelled by draconian and unwise mandatory sentencing schemes, afford to see their prison expenditures soar? Are these dire possibilities the best way to build 21st Century communities in the United States which will enable the country to thrive in the new world a-coming?

No, of course not. Our best hope is to help all our citizens become more skilled and more able to quickly grasp the new technical skills that workers in the 21st Century will have to have. It won't do to pretend otherwise. For, what is required to do well in the new world won't be achieved without having fixed the pressing social as well as economic problems of American society. The global force of economic interdependence which has bound nations more tightly to each other has also bound groups within nations more tightly to each other.

That means that just as a nation cannot hope to have social peace if it is not on a sound economic footing, so, too, a multi-ethnic society like America's which lacks social cohesion—in which ethnic groups are at odds, for example; or in which enormous disparities in opportunity and income exist between groups—will be at a great, perhaps fatal disadvantage in the new game of global economic competition.

America can do better than that and be better than that. The 21st Century will demand that it must be.

# CHANGES IN THE ECONOMY AND LABOR MARKET STATUS OF BLACK AMERICANS

JOHN M. JEFFRIES AND RICHARD L. SCHAFFER

# ABSTRACT

The restructuring of the American economy from goods to services production continues to have a significant impact on economic opportunity and labor market outcomes for black Americans. Since the 1980s, real earnings have declined and income inequality has increased for American workers. Although the black middle-class has grown substantially, the real earnings of blacks have declined, and the economic divide has widened between lower- and higher-income black households. The black-white hourly earnings gap that narrowed during the 1970s expanded in subsequent years. Persistent disparities remain in the labor market status of black and white Americans: for over 30 years the black unemployment rate has been twice that of whites, and it has not dropped below 10 percent since the mid-1970s; 56 percent of blacks 16 and older are employed compared with 64 percent of whites; and the rate of black poverty is three times that of whites. We offer four broad categories of policy recommendations to improve economic opportunity and labor market outcomes for black Americans: (1) supply-side policies to enhance the human capital of current and future workers and their ability to achieve more favorable labor market outcomes, (2) demand-side policies to stimulate the creation of employment opportunities, (3) policies which match labor supply and demand, and (4) policies to make work pay. Although the federal budget deficit and lack of political consensus constrain action, the needs are clear. Addressing them is a matter of national priorities and political will.

During the last quarter of the 20th century, America has been engaged in a significant redeployment of its resources, human and otherwise. The economy's shift from goods to services production has been well-documented. More recently, those who track, analyze, and forecast the economy's performance have been particularly struck by several developments that appear to signal important changes associated with how the national economy operates. These recent macroeconomic developments provide the context for our discussion of the labor market and employment status of black Americans in the 1990s.

Following the nation's longest "peacetime" economic expansion, from December 1982 to June 1990, the U.S. economy entered a recession that "officially" began in July 1990 and ended eight months later in March 1991. Compared to previous recessionary periods, economists generally agree that the 1990-91 recession was mild, i.e., it "was shorter than most of the previous postwar recessions and characterized by proportionately fewer job losses." (Singleton, 1993)

However, the character of economic and income growth immediately preceding and following the 1990-91 recession strongly suggests that the traditional, mutually reinforcing relationship between productivity growth and the economic well-being of the nation's labor force has been altered. In effect, the benefits from the economy's performance have been decidedly less uniform relative to previous periods. Upon closer examination of the most recent business cycle's idiosyncrasies, there is a growing acknowledgment of the 1990-91 downturn's somewhat unique and residual impact on employment in particular industrial segments and occupational groups. These newly emerging macroeconomic trends significantly impact the current and future labor market status of black Americans.

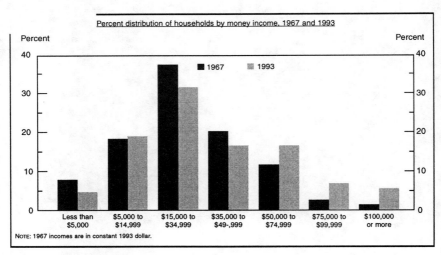

Percent distribution of households by money income, 1967 and 1993

NOTE: 1967 incomes are in constant 1993 dollar.

Source: Ryscavage, Paul. "A Surge In Growing Income Inequality" *Monthly Labor Review*, August 1995, page 51.

## I. America's Changing Distribution of Income and Economic Growth

Among the most frequently discussed economic topics in recent years is the changing income distribution in America. While there are varying opinions regarding the causes and normative judgments that ought to be associated with such changes, there is a consensus that the level and distribution of household and earned incomes have changed since the late 1960s, with significant developments occurring during the 1980s. As a result, the socioeconomic distance between the country's low-, middle-, and upper-income classes has widened.

Chart 1 and Table 1 and Table 2 represent slightly modified versions of data presented in an article published in the U.S. Bureau of Labor Statistics' *Monthly Labor Review* in August 1995, the title of which aptly captures the essence of the debate, "A Surge in Growing Income Inequality?". (Ryscavage, 1995) In sum, the author concludes from the data presented in Chart 1:

- Among households having incomes of $50,000 or more, there was a larger share in 1993 than in 1967 (an increase from 17 percent to 29 percent);

- Among households with incomes between $15,000 and $50,000, there was a smaller proportion in 1993 compared to 1967 (a decrease from 39 percent to 31 percent);

- The share of households with incomes below $15,000 also declined slightly over the period (falling from 25 percent to 23 percent);

- Overall, median real income grew from $28,434 to $33,685 between 1967 and 1989, but then fell to $33,241 in 1993. (Ryscavage, 1995).

With respect to the shares of aggregate household income received by different income classes presented in Table 1:

- Over the two decades between 1973 and 1993, the top 20 percent of households increased their share of income;

- The share of income going to households in the middle and lower segments of the income distribution declined or changed very little over the period; and

- The income gap separating the top of the fourth quintile and the bottom of the fifth quintile increased from $47,136 in 1967 to $60,280 in 1993 (in 1993 dollars). (Ryscavage, 1995)

Table 1

## Shares of Aggregate Household Income Received by Each Fifth and Top 5 Percent of Households, 1967-1993

{In percent}

| Year | Lowest Fifth | Second Fifth | Third Fifth | Fourth Fifth | Highest Fifth | Top 5 percent |
|------|--------------|--------------|-------------|--------------|---------------|---------------|
| 1967 | 4.0 | 10.8 | 17.3 | 24.2 | 43.8 | 17.5 |
| 1968 | 4.2 | 11.1 | 17.5 | 24.4 | 42.8 | 16.6 |
| 1969 | 4.1 | 10.9 | 17.5 | 24.5 | 43.0 | 16.6 |
| 1970 | 4.1 | 10.8 | 17.4 | 24.5 | 43.3 | 16.6 |
| 1971 | 4.1 | 10.6 | 17.3 | 24.5 | 43.5 | 16.7 |
| 1972 | 4.1 | 10.5 | 17.1 | 24.5 | 43.9 | 17.0 |
| 1973 | 4.2 | 10.5 | 17.1 | 24.6 | 43.6 | 16.6 |
| 1974 | 4.3 | 10.6 | 17.0 | 24.6 | 43.5 | 16.5 |
| 1975 | 4.3 | 10.4 | 17.0 | 24.7 | 43.6 | 16.6 |
| 1976 | 4.3 | 10.3 | 17.0 | 24.7 | 43.7 | 16.6 |
| 1977 | 4.2 | 10.2 | 16.9 | 24.7 | 44.0 | 16.8 |
| 1978 | 4.2 | 10.2 | 16.9 | 24.7 | 44.1 | 16.8 |
| 1979 | 4.1 | 10.2 | 16.8 | 24.7 | 44.2 | 16.9 |
| 1980 | 4.2 | 10.2 | 16.8 | 24.8 | 44.1 | 16.5 |
| 1981 | 4.1 | 10.1 | 16.7 | 24.8 | 44.4 | 16.5 |
| 1982 | 4.0 | 10.0 | 16.5 | 24.5 | 45.0 | 17.0 |
| 1983 | 4.0 | 9.9 | 16.4 | 24.6 | 45.1 | 17.1 |
| 1984 | 4.0 | 9.9 | 16.3 | 24.6 | 45.2 | 17.1 |
| 1985 | 3.9 | 9.8 | 16.2 | 24.4 | 45.6 | 17.6 |
| 1986 | 3.8 | 9.7 | 16.2 | 24.3 | 46.1 | 18.0 |
| 1987 | 3.8 | 9.6 | 16.1 | 24.3 | 46.2 | 18.2 |
| 1988 | 3.8 | 9.6 | 16.0 | 24.3 | 46.3 | 18.3 |
| 1989 | 3.8 | 9.5 | 15.8 | 24.0 | 46.8 | 18.9 |
| 1990 | 3.9 | 9.6 | 15.9 | 24.0 | 46.6 | 18.6 |
| 1991 | 3.8 | 9.6 | 15.9 | 24.2 | 46.5 | 18.1 |
| 1992 | 3.8 | 9.4 | 15.8 | 24.2 | 46.9 | 18.6 |
| 1992 | 3.8 | 9.4 | 15.8 | 24.2 | 46.9 | 18.6 |
| 1993 | 3.6 | 9.1 | 15.3 | 23.8 | 48.2 | 20.0 |
| 1993 | 3.6 | 9.0 | 15.1 | 23.5 | 48.9 | 21.0 |

Source: Ryscavage (1995), p.54.

Table 2

## Mean Income of Each Fifth and Top 5 Percent
## of the Household Income Distribution,
## 1979, 1989, 1991, 1992, and 1993

{In 1993 dollars}

| Year | Lowest Fifth | Second Fifth | Third Fifth | Fourth Fifth | Highest Fifth | Top 5 percent |
|------|--------------|--------------|-------------|--------------|---------------|---------------|
| 1979 | $7,823 | $19,457 | $32,079 | $47,076 | $84,484 | $128,847 |
| 1989 | 8,182 | 20,278 | 33,707 | 50,966 | 99,669 | 161,030 |
| 1991 | 7,706 | 19,255 | 31,984 | 48,758 | 93,501 | 145,913 |
| 1992 | 7,506 | 18,725 | 31,548 | 48,429 | 93,837 | 148,937 |
| 1993 | 7,411 | 18,647 | 31,260 | 48,572 | 98,589 | 163,228 |

Annual rare of change (percent):

| | | | | | | |
|------|------|------|------|------|------|------|
| 1979-89 | 0.4 | 0.4 | 0.5 | 0.8 | 1.7 | 2.2 |
| 1989-91 | -3.0 | -2.6 | -2.6 | -2.2 | -3.2 | -4.9 |
| 1991-92 | -2.1 | -2.2 | -0.8 | -0.2 | 0.8 | 2.5 |
| 1992-93 | -1.3 | -0.4 | -0.9 | 0.3 | 5.1 | 9.6 |

Source:  Ryscavage (1995), p.55.

17

Finally, the particular patterns of change in the nation's distribution of income during the 1980s and early 1990s are presented in Table 2, which shows the real (i.e., corrected for inflation) average incomes for each quintile in 1979, 1989, 1991, 1992, and 1993. The bottom half of Table 2 shows the annual rates of change of mean incomes between 1979 and 1989, and each succeeding pair of years thereafter. In summary:

- The incomes of the richest 20 percent of households increased 1.7 percent a year, while the poorest 20 percent of households decreased 0.4 percent annually between 1979 and 1989;

- Between 1989 and 1991, all households across the income distribution suffered losses in income. In effect, the losses of income kept income inequality from increasing;

- Only households in the top 5 percent of the income distribution experienced income growth between 1991 and 1992 — in all other households mean income remained virtually the same;

- Between 1992 and 1993, the top 5 percent of households continued to benefit from mean income increases, rising 10 percent from $149,000 to $163,000, while those in the top 20 percent saw increases of roughly 5 percent from $91,000 to $99,000. (Ryscavage, 1995)

Increases in mean income growth between 1992 and 1993 among households at the very top of the distribution were the largest single-year increases since the statistical series on income inequality was begun.

The 1980s were also characterized by a decline in real earnings. Chart 2 shows the precipitous decline in weekly earnings that occurred between 1979 and 1982, and the consistent fall throughout the remainder of the decade. Chart 3 illustrates the decline in average hourly earnings. According to the AFL-CIO's Department of Research, real average weekly and hourly earnings have fallen by 12 percent and 9 percent, respectively, since 1979. (AFL-CIO, Department of Research, 1996)

The peacetime expansion that preceded the 1990-91 recession paradoxically resulted in the growth of both income and earnings inequality, while generating employment growth at an impressive annual rate between 1979 and 1989. Table 3, also modified from "A Surge in Growing Income Inequality?", shows the distribution of labor-force participants with some work experience between 1979 and 1989, cross-classified by their average hourly earnings and the annual income of the households in which they lived. Because the table refers to all workers, it includes those who worked very little or only intermittently at part-time jobs, as well as those who worked full time throughout the year. Over the course of that ten-year period, employment grew rapidly at a pace of 1.8 million jobs a year. Based on the data presented in Table 3, Ryscavage, a senior labor economist in the U.S. Census Bureau's Housing and Household Economic Statistics Division, explains how the character of job generation in the 1980s resulted in earnings and income inequality:

> *Much of the increase in average annual employment was taking place among* persons with middle to high earnings who lived in high income households.... Employment in this earnings-income category was rising, on average, by about 921,000 persons a year during the 1980s. *Employment was also growing...at the other end of the earnings distribution. The employment of workers with low hourly earnings...increased* by about 494,000 persons per year. *But among workers with middle-level earnings who were from middle-income households, employment growth was meager at best* — 35,000 persons a year. [our emphasis] (Ryscavage, 1995)

**Chart 2**

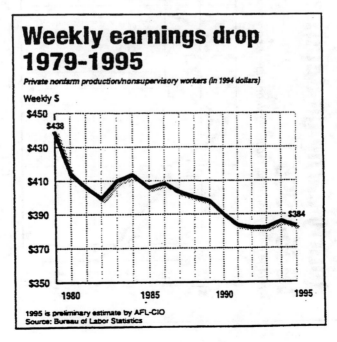

Source: AFL-CIO, Department of Economic Research, "America Needs A Raise" February 1996

**Chart 3**

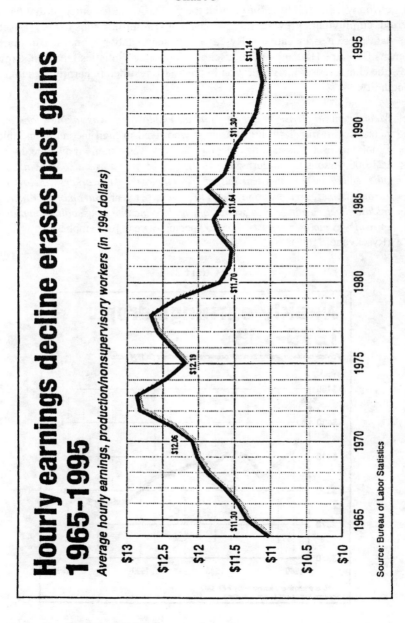

# Hourly earnings decline erases past gains 1965–1995

*Average hourly earnings, production/nonsupervisory workers (in 1994 dollars)*

Source: Bureau of Labor Statistics

Source: AFL-CIO, Department of Economic Research,
"America Needs A Raise" February 1996

20

In sum, during the 1980s year-to-year employment growth was significant. However, the distribution of the jobs created over the period resulted in increased earnings and income inequality between high- and low-income workers, and an erosion of the country's share of middle-income earners and households.

The impact of the shifting income distribution on the economic status of black Americans, in particular, is empirically difficult to ascertain due to limitations in the data series on which analysts typically rely. Fortunately, due to the attention that the shifting income distribution has drawn, two recent attempts to assess the specific movements of blacks within the overall income distribution, and their movements relative to whites, are especially illuminating. Andrew Hacker, in his 1995 revised edition of *Two Nations: Black and White, Separate, Hostile and Unequal,* presents data that show the share of high-income earners, within both the black and white income distributions, increased from 1970 to 1992. During this period, "the proportion of black households with incomes over $50,000 expanded by 56.9 percent [from 10 percent of all black households in 1970, to 16 percent in 1992], while the share of whites at that level rose by 45.7 percent [from 25 percent in 1970 to 38 percent in 1992]." (Hacker, 1995)

Table 3

**Annual Average Net Change in Persons with Work Experience, by Hourly Earnings and Household Income, 1979-89**

| NUMBERS IN THOUSANDS | | HOUSEHOLD INCOME | | | | |
|---|---|---|---|---|---|---|
| Hourly Earnings | Total | Less than $14,000 | $14,000 to $27,999 | $28,000 to $41,999 | $42,000 to $55,999 | $56,000 or more |
| Total | 1,756 | 116 | 187 | 132 | 74 | 1,248 |
| Less than $7.00 | 602 | 152 | 217 | 125 | 39 | 68 |
| $7.00 to $13.99 | 361 | -28 | -9 | 58 | 82 | 258 |
| $14.00 to $20.99 | 340 | -6 | -16 | -48 | -22 | 433 |
| $21.00 to $27.99 | 201 | 0 | -3 | -2 | -26 | 232 |
| $28.00 or more | 252 | -3 | -2 | -1 | 1 | 256 |

Source: Ryscavage (1995), p.59.

21

Hacker notes further that although changes in the two income distributions have moved in the same direction, there are revealing differences between them. The changing income distribution among white households has been characterized by a narrowing of the middle-income household share, coupled with an expansion of the top earners that has significantly outpaced the growth in low-income households. In contrast, the shifting black income distribution reflects *both the growth of the black middle class and the widening gap between higher- and lower-income earners and households.* (Hacker, 1995)

In a recent, somewhat unique, analysis, two economists in the U.S. Bureau of Labor Statistics constructed a dataset explicitly designed to assess more accurately "the *mobility* of individuals, families, and households over time ... the extent to which these economic units change positions in the income distribution over a given time period." [ authors' emphasis] (Gittleman and Joyce, 1995) By pulling together samples drawn from the Annual Demographic Files of the Current Population Survey (CPS) from 1968 to 1992, the authors analyzed "the positions and movements of various demographic groups within the earnings distribution of the entire nation." (Gittleman and Joyce, 1995) Among the conclusions drawn from the analysis, the following are of particular interest:

- Women were much more likely than men to be in the bottom 20 percent of the earnings distribution, and much less likely to be in the top quintile;

- Blacks were much more likely to be in the lowest quintile, and much less likely to be in the top quintile, than whites were; and
- White men were the least likely to be at the bottom and the most likely to be at the top, whereas the tendency for black women was just the opposite.

With specific reference to mobility patterns within the overall distribution, the authors found:

- Women were more likely to *stay* in the bottom quintile than men;

- *The ability to maintain one's position at the top of the overall earnings distribution appeared to be more elusive for blacks than for whites — even for black men relative to white women; and*

- *Significant differences by race in the likelihood of moving out of the bottom quintile existed only for men, with 52 percent of white men leaving the bottom 20 percent of the distribution, compared with 43 percent of black men.*

## II. The 1990-91 Recession and Its Implications for America's Labor Markets in the Nineties

Two factors, in particular, distinguished the 1990-91 recession from its predecessors: (1) the especially lethargic labor market performance immediately preceding and following the downturn, and (2) the breadth of employment decline across major industrial sectors and occupational groups.

Employment growth, prior to and immediately following the 1990-91 recession, was especially sluggish when compared to previous downturns. Columbia University's Center for International Business Cycle Research labeled the period beginning in the Spring of 1989 a "growth recession," due to the national economy's 1 percent growth rate during the 12 months leading up to the "official" beginning of the 1990-91 recession. Historically, the average rate of employment growth during the 12 months preceding recessionary periods has been approximately 2.5 percent. (Singleton, 1993)

Perhaps even more devastating, from the point of view of the nation's labor force, was that *nonagricultural payrolls did not begin to expand until 12 months after the recession's end was officially declared.* Even though the first quarter of 1991 registered productivity gains and an increase in the nation's output, as measured by the Gross Domestic Product, employment failed to grow. (Singleton, 1993)

In the past, job losses during economic contractions were concentrated in, if not limited to, the goods-producing sector of the nation's economy. Prior to the last slowdown, many economists argued that one of the services sector's distinguishing characteristics was its tendency to be "recession resistant." The employment declines in the 1990-91 downturn were atypical because the services sector did not offset losses in the goods-producing sector. In fact:

> Five of the six major industry groupings within the services-producing sector were significantly weaker ... [compared to previous postwar recessions] ... rather than growing at the average of 0.5 percent, employment in the service-producing industries fell by 0.2 percent. This decline translated into 140,000 job losses, in sharp contrast to *growth* of 425,000 that would have occurred had the recession been "typical." [author's emphasis] (Singleton, 1993)

Private services-producing employment losses in Transportation, Communications, and Public Utilities (TCPU), Wholesale and Retail Trade, and Finance, Insurance and Real Estate (FIRE) firms were especially severe. Consequently, many white-collar workers across the occupational distribution were involuntarily separated from their jobs in record numbers during the 1990-91 downturn. (Singleton, 1993; and Gardner, 1994)

In the postwar recessions prior to the 1990s, adult men accounted for 80 percent of job losers, due primarily to their concentration in goods-producing industries and blue-collar occupations. During the 1990-91 contraction, "adult women's employment experienced its first recessionary decline in three decades" as "a larger-than-usual proportion of the job cutbacks...occurred in service-producing industries where adult women most often work." (Gardner, 1994) With respect to race and ethnicity: "Hispanics were more severely affected than were blacks, while job cutbacks continued to be relatively mild for whites." (Gardner, 1994)

The uncharacteristically sluggish recovery also affected the success and speed with which workers were re-employed following unemployment that was directly attributable to the 1990-91 recession. Comparisons of the early 1980s and the early 1990s reveal that the replacement rates — the rate at which displaced workers regain employment — of blacks continue to lag behind that of whites. And based on data gathered through the displaced worker survey conducted in 1994, Hispanics accounted for the smallest proportion of the re-employed following the 1990-91 recession. (Gardner, 1994) Gardner's calculation of "re-employment rates," presented in Table 4, illustrates these trends clearly.

### III. Post-Recession Employment Growth: A Double-Edged Sword

The character of the net job growth that took place four quarters after the recession's end, between 1992 and 1993, is in many ways analogous to the trends that became evident during the 1980s — significant year-to-year additions to employment and gains in labor productivity, accompanied by a growing earnings and income inequality between high- and low-wage workers.

### Table 4
## RE-EMPLOYMENT RATES, BY RACE

|  | Remployment Rates | |
|  | 1981-82 | 1991-92 |
|---|---|---|
| **Whites** | 66.9% | 76.4% |
| **Blacks** | 46.4% | 66.6% |
| **Hispanics** | 55.7% | 64.9% |

Source: Gardner (1995), p. 49.

24

Analysis of the data in Table 5, which presents the annual average net change in the number of people working between 1992 and 1993, shows that the 1.5 million jobs were distributed across all earners and households in the following manner:

- Significant employment growth of persons with middle- to high-earnings from high-income households (an increase of 949,000);

- Only modest employment growth among low-wage earners from low- to middle-income households (an increase of roughly 300,000); and

- No employment growth among those in the middle earnings and income group (a *decline* of over 50,000 jobs);

**Table 5**

**Annual Average Net Change in Persons with Work Experience, by Hourly Earnings and Household Income, 1992-93**

| NUMBERS IN THOUSANDS | | HOUSEHOLD INCOME | | | | |
|---|---|---|---|---|---|---|
| Hourly Earnings | Total | Less than $14,000 | $14,000 to $27,999 | $28,000 to $41,999 | $42,000 to $55,999 | $56,000 or more |
| Total | 1,459 | -21 | 290 | 545 | -721 | 1,366 |
| Less than | 421 | -183 | 380 | 120 | -425 | 530 |
| $7.00 to $ | 510 | 86 | -77 | 699 | -85 | -113 |
| $14.00 to | -424 | 38 | -45 | -316 | -299 | 199 |
| $21.00 to | 246 | 23 | 0 | -25 | 25 | 222 |
| $28.00 or | 706 | 16 | 33 | 66 | 63 | 528 |

Source: Gardner (1995), p. 49.

Consistent with the conclusions drawn earlier:

> ... the pattern of employment growth in the 1992-93 period represented not only a return to the pattern seen in the 1980s, but an *exaggeration* of that pattern. While the ratio of employment growth at the top of the distribution to that at the bottom end averaged 1.88- to-1 in the 1980s, in the 1992-93 period it was 2.99- to-1. [author's emphasis] (Ryscavage, 1995)

Ryscavage (1995) offers the following by way of explanation:

> This development may have been the result of the combined effect of the return to the work force of many highly paid workers who were laid off in the early 1990s along with the resumption of the secular trend toward job creation at both ends of the wage distribution with little growth in the middle.

A more recent analysis of the responses to the 1994 displaced-worker survey provides insight into which workers were fortunate enough to have returned to work following the early 1990s downturn. (Gardner, 1995) The labor market outcomes of the different demographic groups, summarized in an abbreviated form in Table 5, are taken from Gardner's (1995) analysis. The displaced worker survey (Table 6) conducted in February 1994, found that:

- Seventy-five percent of those displaced in 1991 and 1992 had found new jobs by the time they were surveyed in 1994 (one in five were either unemployed or not in the labor force);

- Less than one-third of those re-employed held jobs paying wages equal to or more than the job that had been lost;
- Median weekly real earnings of the jobs lost in 1991 and 1992 were $515; in early 1994, earnings were 8 percent lower ($473);

- Only workers between the ages of 25 and 34 did not see their earnings eroded after re-employment;

- In general, men suffered greater earnings losses than women;

- For whites, the median earnings on the new job were 9 percent less than the earnings on the job that was lost; for black and Hispanic workers the earnings losses were 4 and 8 percent, respectively;

- However, re-employed white workers still had much higher weekly earnings ($484) in 1994 than their black ($398) and Hispanic ($375) counterparts.

Table 6

**Median Weekly Earnings of Displaced Full-time Wage and Salary Workers On Their Lost Jobs and On Jobs Held in February 1994 by Age, Sex, Race, and Hispanic origin**

| Age, Sex, Race, and Hispanic Origin | Displaced Full-time Wage and Salary Workers (1) | Re-employed in Full-time wage and salary jobs in February 1994 Total | Median weekly earnings on: | | |
|---|---|---|---|---|---|
| | | | Lost Job | Job held in February 1994 | Percent Change |
| **TOTAL** | | | | | |
| Total, 20 years and older | 2,519 | 1,515 | $515 | $473 | -8.2 |
| 25 to 54 years | 2,000 | 1,317 | 518 | 477 | -7.9 |
| 25 to 34 years | 606 | 424 | 432 | 441 | 2.1 |
| 35 to 44 years | 818 | 556 | 566 | 505 | -10.8 |
| 45 to 54 years | 576 | 336 | 546 | 464 | -15.0 |
| 55 to 64 years | 392 | 162 | 568 | 488 | -14.1 |
| Men, 20 years and older | 1,595 | 1,029 | 576 | 523 | -9.2 |
| Women, 20 years and older | 924 | 486 | 413 | 384 | -7.0 |
| **White** | | | | | |
| Total, 20 years and older | 2,172 | 1,315 | 530 | 484 | -8.7 |
| Men | 1,400 | 908 | 589 | 534 | -9.3 |
| Women | 771 | 407 | 426 | 388 | -8.7 |
| **Black** | | | | | |
| Total, 20 years and older | 246 | 136 | 415 | 398 | -4.1 |
| Men | 132 | 78 | 488 | 451 | -7.6 |
| Women | 114 | 58 | (2) | (2) | (2) |
| **Hispanic origin** | | | | | |
| Total, 20 years and older | 198 | 101 | 409 | 375 | -8.3 |
| Men | 141 | 76 | 456 | 395 | -13.4 |
| Women | 56 | 25 | (2) | (2) | (2) |

(1) Data refer to persons who had 3 or more years of tenure on a full-time wage and salary job they had lost or left between January 1991 and December 1992 because their plant or company closed or moved, there was insufficient work for them to do, or their positions or shifts were abolished.

(2) Data not shown where base is less than 75,000.

Source: Gardner (1995) p.49.

The other significant characteristic of the post-recession job growth in the early 1990s was the recovery's contribution to the nation's growing share of part-time and contingent work. A widely-cited source estimates that 20 percent of the private-sector jobs created in the 1992-1993 expansion were temporary jobs. (Mishel and Bernstein, 1994) The creation of either temporary or part-time jobs, in and of itself, is not an undesirable labor-market outcome. Some workers prefer the flexibility associated with part-time and temporary employment because it allows them to devote time to other important aspects of their lives — such as family obligations, pursuing education, and leisure — which compete with hours spent at work. However, recent surveys of employees in part-time and temporary jobs consistently reveal that a growing proportion of those workers would prefer full-time work. According to economists at the Economic Policy Institute,

"... the share of total employment made up by full-timers declined steadily from 1973 to 1989. At the same time, the share of jobs that are part-time increased from 16.6 percent in 1973 to 18.1 percent in 1989 and to 18.8 percent in 1993. This increase in the proportion of workers working part-time since 1973, has been due almost entirely to the increased rate at which workers are working part-time *involuntarily*." [authors' emphasis] (Mishel and Bernstein, 1994, p.219.)

Part-time and temporary work results in less income due to fewer hours worked; relative to full-time employment in the contemporary American economy, part-time jobs are concentrated in particularly low-paying occupations *and* in industries where competitive advantage is very closely associated with minimizing the cost of labor. (Mishel and Bernstein, 1994) Workers who are employed less than full time are also less likely to have employer-paid health insurance and other benefits.

The shifting income distribution over the past two decades has proven to be a mixed blessing for black labor force participants. On the one hand, more blacks have moved into the middle- and upper-income segments of the earnings distribution. At the same time, however, higher-income earning blacks, relative to their white counterparts, occupy a more tenuous position within those upper-income brackets, especially during periods of economic instability and corporate downsizing. Recent research suggests further that the hourly earnings gap between blacks and whites narrowed in the 1970s. However, in the midst of the changes in the 1980s discussed above, "blacks generally lost ground relative to whites ... the wage gap actually grew faster for those black males with more education." These income trends, along with the economy's performance and patterns of employment growth, strongly indicate that there is a growing economic chasm between blacks at the lower end of the earnings distribution and those moving from the low-to-middle and middle-to-high income classes.

## IV. The Labor Market Status of Black Americans: Disparities Persist

The most recent labor market data for individuals and demographic groups show that, relative to whites, blacks have twice the unemployment rate, earn less income, and suffer rates of poverty that are three times greater.

### A. Employment and Unemployment

Table 7 shows annual white and black unemployment rates over the past three decades. Black adult unemployment has remained twice as high as white unemployment for over 30 years, and has not fallen below 10 percent since the mid-1970s.

Based on the recently released March 1995 Current Population Survey (CPS), Table 8 indicates that blacks comprise roughly 12 percent of the 198 million individuals 16 years and older in the nation. Their share (11 percent) of the nation's civilian labor force is slightly smaller. Among the nation's 123 million employed persons, blacks are underrepresented at 10.5 percent. In contrast, blacks are overrepresented among those not in the labor force (accounting for roughly 13 percent of 67 million), and they constitute an even greater share — 20 percent — of the nation's 7.7 million unemployed.

In March 1995, 56 percent of the black population 16 years and older was employed, compared to a 64 percent employment-to-population ratio for whites. As one would expect, the employment-to-population ratio is greater for men than for women, although the ratios for black men and women are much closer than the ratios for white men and women.

### B. Poverty

The latest figures on poverty in the United States reveal that over 10 million of the 33 million blacks in the nation were living in poverty in 1994; of 193 million whites, 18 million were living in poverty. Stated differently, one in three black Americans were living in poverty in 1994; for whites the share was less than one in 10. There were just under 226 million blacks and whites in the nation. The black and white population shares were 15 percent and 85 percent, respectively. In total, there were 28 million blacks and whites living in poverty. In sharp contrast to its proportion of the total population, the black share of the poverty population was almost 40 percent.

Table 9 disaggregates the poverty population. In general, the data show that blacks suffer rates of poverty at least two-and-half times those of whites across every demographic and other descriptive category reported by the CPS. For both populations, the share of women in poverty greatly exceeds the proportion of men

# Table 7

## White and Black Unemployment Rates: 1960-1993

| Year | (a)<br>White | (b)<br>Black | Black/White<br>Ratio a/b |
|---|---|---|---|
| 1960 | 4.9 | 10.2 | 2.08 |
| 1961 | 6.0 | 12.4 | 2.07 |
| 1962 | 4.9 | 10.9 | 2.22 |
| 1963 | 5.0 | 10.8 | 2.16 |
| 1964 | 4.6 | 9.6 | 2.09 |
| 1965 | 4.1 | 8.1 | 1.98 |
| 1966 | 3.3 | 7.3 | 2.21 |
| 1967 | 3.4 | 7.4 | 2.18 |
| 1968 | 3.2 | 6.7 | 2.09 |
| 1969 | 3.1 | 6.4 | 2.06 |
| 1960s Average | 4.3 | 9.0 | 2.09 |
| 1970 | 4.4 | 8.2 | 1.86 |
| 1971 | 5.4 | 9.9 | 1.83 |
| 1972 | 5.0 | 10.0 | 2.00 |
| 1973 | 4.3 | 8.9 | 2.07 |
| 1974 | 5.0 | 9.9 | 1.98 |
| 1975 | 7.8 | 14.8 | 1.90 |
| 1976 | 7.0 | 13.1 | 1.87 |
| 1977 | 6.2 | 13.1 | 2.11 |
| 1978 | 5.2 | 11.9 | 2.29 |
| 1978 | 5.1 | 11.3 | 2.22 |
| 1970s Average | 5.5 | 11.1 | 2.02 |
| 1980 | 6.3 | 14.3 | 2.27 |
| 1981 | 6.7 | 14.2 | 2.12 |
| 1982 | 8.6 | 18.9 | 2.20 |
| 1983 | 8.4 | 19.5 | 2.32 |
| 1984 | 6.5 | 15.9 | 2.45 |
| 1985 | 6.2 | 15.1 | 2.44 |
| 1986 | 6.0 | 14.5 | 2.42 |
| 1987 | 5.3 | 12.0 | 2.45 |
| 1988 | 4.7 | 11.7 | 2.49 |
| 1989 | 4.5 | 11.4 | 2.53 |
| 1980s Average | 6.3 | 14.9 | 2.37 |
| 1990 | 4.7 | 11.3 | 2.40 |
| 1991 | 6.0 | 12.4 | 2.07 |
| 1992 | 6.5 | 14.1 | 2.17 |
| 1993 | 6.0 | 12.9 | 2.15 |
| 1994 | 5.3 | 11.5 | 2.17 |
| 1995 | 4.7 | 10.3 | 2.19 |

Source: U.S. Bureau of Labor Statistics, Employment and Earnings, various years, and Hacker (1995), p.109.

# Table 8

Selected Economic Characteristics of Persons and Families, by Sex and Race: March 1995

(Numbers in thousands.)

| Characteristic | All Races | Black | White, not Hispanic |
|---|---|---|---|
| CIVILIAN LABOR FORCE STATUS | | | |
| Both sexes, 16 years and over | 198,022 | 23,146 | 150,248 |
| In civilian labor force | 131,108 | 14,529 | 100,536 |
| *Percent in civilian labor force* | *66.2* | *62.8* | *66.9* |
| Employed | 123,429 | 13,033 | 95,778 |
| Unemployed | 7,679 | 1,496 | 4,759 |
| *Percent unemployed* | *5.9* | *10.3* | *4.7* |
| Not in labor force | 66,914 | 8,617 | 49,712 |
| | | | |
| Males, 16 years and over | 94,894 | 10,364 | 72,302 |
| In civilian labor force | 70,570 | 7,003 | 54,201 |
| *Percent in civilian labor force* | *74.4* | *67.6* | *75* |
| Employed | 66,181 | 6,248 | 51,387 |
| Unemployed | 4,390 | 755 | 2,814 |
| *Percent unemployed* | *6.2* | *10.8* | *5.2* |
| Not in labor force | 24,324 | 3,362 | 18,101 |
| | | | |
| Females, 16 years and over | 103,128 | 12,781 | 77,946 |
| In civilian labor force | 60,538 | 7,526 | 46,335 |
| *Percent in civilian labor force* | *58.7* | *58.9* | *59.4* |
| Employed | 57,248 | 6,785 | 44,391 |
| Unemployed | 3,289 | 741 | 1,944 |
| *Percent unemployed* | *5.4* | *9.9* | *4.2* |
| Not in labor force | 42,590 | 5,255 | 31,611 |

## Employment-to-Population Ratios

| | |
|---|---|
| All races | 0.62 |
|     Males | 0.70 |
|     Females | 0.56 |
| | |
| Black | 0.56 |
|     Males | 0.60 |
|     Females | 0.53 |
| | |
| White, not Hispanic | 0.64 |
|     Males | 0.71 |
|     Females | 0.57 |

## Black to White Unemployment Ratios

| | |
|---|---|
| Both sexes | 2.19 |
|     Males | 2.08 |
|     Females | 2.36 |

Source: U.S. Census Bureau, March 1995 Current Population Survey.

# Table 9

**Selected Characteristics of the Population Below the Poverty Level in 1994, by Region and Race**

**UNITED STATES**

**Below the Poverty Level**

| Age by Sex | Black (%) | White (%) |
|---|---|---|
| Total Persons | 30.6 | 9.4 |
| Under 18 | 43.8 | 12.5 |
| 18 to 64 | 23.4 | 8.2 |
| 55 and over | 26.0 | 9.0 |
| 65 and over | 27.4 | 9.6 |
| **Male** | 27.0 | 8.0 |
| Under 18 | 43.3 | 12.2 |
| 18 to 64 | 17.4 | 6.8 |
| 55 and over | 19.0 | 6.4 |
| 65 and over | 20.6 | 5.4 |
| **Female** | 33.7 | 10.7 |
| Under 18 | 44.3 | 12.7 |
| 18 to 64 | 28.5 | 9.5 |
| 55 and over | 30.8 | 11.2 |
| 65 and over | 31.7 | 12.6 |
| **Metropolitan-Nonmetropolitan Residence** | | |
| Total | 30.6 | 9.4 |
| All metropolitan areas | 29.8 | 8.4 |
| Inside central cities | 34.2 | 11 |
| Outside central cities | 22.3 | 7.3 |
| Nonmetropolitan areas | 35.4 | 12.8 |

Source: U.S. Census Bureau, March 1995 Current Population Survey.

# Table 9 (continued)

**Selected Characteristics of the Population Below the Poverty Level in 1994, by Region and Race**

Civilian NonInstitutionalized Work
Experience in 1994

|  | Black (%) | White (%) |
|---|---|---|
| Both sexes, 15 years and over | 25.0 | 8.5 |
|  |  |  |
| Worked | 13.7 | 5.1 |
| 50 to 52 weeks | 6.7 | 2.6 |
| 49 weeks or less | 28.9 | 11.4 |
|  |  |  |
| Duration of unemployment |  |  |
| 1 to 4 weeks | 31.2 | 9.8 |
| 5 to 14 weeks | 26.8 | 10.3 |
| 15 to 26 weeks | 26.3 | 16.6 |
| 27 weeks or more | 44.6 | 26.1 |
|  |  |  |
| Did not work | 44.2 | 16.5 |
|  |  |  |
| Males, 15 years and over | 19.4 | 6.8 |
|  |  |  |
| Worked | 9.6 | 4.4 |
| 50 to 52 weeks | 4.6 | 2.4 |
| 49 weeks or less | 22.1 | 10.8 |
|  |  |  |
| Duration of unemployment |  |  |
| 1 to 4 weeks | 19.3 | 7.3 |
| 5 to 14 weeks | 23.0 | 8.1 |
| 15 to 26 weeks | 19.7 | 14.6 |
| 27 weeks or more | 33.5 | 23.6 |
|  |  |  |
| Did not work | 38.7 | 14.7 |
|  |  |  |
| Females, 15 years and over | 29.5 | 10.2 |
|  |  |  |
| Worked | 17.4 | 5.9 |
| 50 to 52 weeks | 8.8 | 2.9 |
| 49 weeks or less | 34.1 | 12.0 |
|  |  |  |
| Duration of unemployment |  |  |
| 1 to 4 weeks | 40.6 | 12.1 |
| 5 to 14 weeks | 30.7 | 13.3 |
| 15 to 26 weeks | 35.1 | 19.4 |
| 27 weeks or more | 56.1 | 30.4 |
|  |  |  |
| Did not work | 48.0 | 17.5 |

Source: U.S. Census Bureau, March 1995 Current Population Survey

who are poverty-stricken, and those under the age of 18 are more likely to be poor than those 18 and over. The same relative proportions hold for metropolitan vs. non-metropolitan residents (especially for those residing in central cities), female household heads with no spouse present vs. other family types, and among those not working vs. those working.

The poverty figures are entirely consistent with the previous discussion of the shifting income distribution and its impact on black and white labor-force participants. Among the white and black poor with some civilian work experience in 1994, 5 percent of whites and 14 percent of blacks worked. In fact, 3 percent of whites and 7 percent of blacks who were poor worked between 50 and 52 weeks during the year.

## C. Income, Earnings, Education, and Occupational Status

The March 1995 CPS data on black Americans revealed that:

- Almost three-quarters of blacks aged 25 and over were high school graduates;

- 13 percent of black adults had a bachelor's degree;

- Black men working year-round, full-time earned a median income of $25,350 in 1994, 72 percent of the income of non-Hispanic white men; and

- Black females earned $20,610 in 1994, 85 percent of the income of non-Hispanic white women.

The income and earnings of blacks continue to lag behind those of whites. Although the differences are often less pronounced when comparing the earnings of black and white women, the income and earnings disparities between blacks and whites persist across all levels of education and occupational status.

Tables 10 and 11 show the total money earnings in 1994 of blacks and whites, 15 years and older, for all persons and only those who worked year-round, full-time, respectively. For all persons (Table 10), black median earnings were $4,623 less than the white median, resulting in a 1.3 ratio of white-to-black earnings. For every dollar earned by blacks, whites earned $1.30. The earnings disparity between black and white men was the largest, a ratio of 1.48, while the gap between the earnings of men and women was less for blacks than for whites.

The data in Table 10 also show the concentrations of earners across the income distribution. Sixty-eight percent of black persons aged 15 years and older earned less than $22,500. For whites the comparable share was 55 percent. Almost 8 percent of whites earned $60,000 or more, compared to less than 3 percent of blacks.

Among blacks and whites who worked year-round, full-time (Table 11), the median earnings of whites were higher for all race and gender groups. Over a third (36.9 percent) of year-round, full-time black workers earned less than $17,500; for whites the share was 22.7 percent. At the other end of the income distribution, 15 percent of whites, compared to 3 percent of blacks, had incomes over $60,000.

Tables 12, 13, 14, and 15 disaggregate the national data discussed above for the southern and northern/western regions of the country. Based on comparisons of total money earnings of all persons in the even-numbered Tables 10, 12 and 14, earnings are lower in the South (see Table 12) for whites and blacks of both sexes than in other regions (see Table 14). The ratio of white-to-black earnings, for both sexes, is slightly higher in the South when compared to the nation as a whole, and significantly higher than the ratio in the composite northern/western region. In stark contrast, the white-to-black ratio for both sexes in the northern/western region shows significantly less disparity at 1.16 (see Table 14). The median earnings of black women in the northern/western region are slightly higher than those of their white counterparts. Among year-round, full-time workers (in the odd-numbered Tables 11, 13, and 15), the exact same patterns hold, with the exception that black women in the northern/western region who work year-round, full-time still earn less than their white counterparts.

In Appendix A, the March 1995 CPS data on total money earnings for adults (25 years old and over) in 1994, by race, sex, and region are presented in Tables 10A, 11A, 12A, 13A, 14A, and 15A (the all persons data in Tables 10A, 12A, and 14A; and the year-round, full-time data in Tables 11A, 13A, and 15A). The only significant departure from the trends and patterns discussed above is that among black adults, a slightly greater proportion had earnings, 67 percent, compared with 63 percent of all blacks 15 years and older. The comparable proportion for adult whites remained at roughly 70 percent.

Differences in the level of earned income between blacks and whites exist among workers with the same levels of educational attainment. Table 16 compares the median earnings of blacks and whites by level of education, and Table 17 disaggregates the all-persons data (in Table 16) to focus specifically on those who worked year-round, full-time. With respect to the latter group of earners, the median earnings of blacks were consistently lower than whites with the same level of education.

For those black labor force participants who work year-round, full-time, increased education translates into increased earnings. However, the labor market returns to additional years of educational attainment provide a premium to whites relative to blacks and to men relative to women. Black women and white men realize greater earnings from increased education relative to other race and gender groups.

35

Table 10

**Total Money Earnings in 1994 of Persons 15 Years Old and Over, by Sex and Race**

| UNITED STATES | Black | | | | | | ALL PERSONS | | | | White, not Hispanic | | | |
| --- | --- | --- | --- | --- | --- | --- | --- | --- | --- | --- | --- | --- | --- | --- |
| | Both Sexes | Cumul.% | Male | Cumul.% | Female | Cumul.% | Both Sexes | Cumul.% | Female | Cumul.% | Male | Cumul.% | Female | Cumul.% |
| Total (000's) | 23,922 | | 10,825 | | 13,097 | | 153,490 | | | | 74,238 | | 79,252 | |
| Total with earnings (000's) | 15,105 | | 7,195 | | 7,910 | | 107,280 | | | | 57,485 | | 49,795 | |
| Percent | 100 | | 100 | | 100 | | 100 | | | | 100 | | 100 | |
| $1 to $2,499 or less | 12.2 | 12.2 | 9.6 | 9.6 | 14.5 | 14.5 | 10.6 | 10.6 | 14.5 | 14.5 | 8.1 | 8.1 | 13.5 | 13.5 |
| $2,500 to $4,999 | 6.9 | 19.1 | 5.9 | 15.5 | 7.8 | 22.3 | 6.3 | 16.9 | 7.8 | 22.3 | 4.7 | 12.8 | 8.2 | 21.7 |
| $5,000 to $7,499 | 7.0 | 26.1 | 6.6 | 22.1 | 7.3 | 29.6 | 6.1 | 23.0 | 7.3 | 29.6 | 4.4 | 17.2 | 8.0 | 29.7 |
| $7,500 to $9,999 | 6.5 | 32.6 | 5.8 | 27.9 | 7.1 | 36.7 | 4.9 | 27.9 | 7.1 | 36.7 | 3.5 | 20.7 | 6.6 | 36.3 |
| $10,000 to $12,499 | 9.0 | 41.6 | 8.4 | 36.3 | 9.4 | 46.1 | 6.7 | 34.6 | 9.4 | 46.1 | 5.1 | 25.8 | 8.5 | 44.8 |
| $12,500 to $14,999 | 6.3 | 47.9 | 6.0 | 42.3 | 6.7 | 52.8 | 4.3 | 38.9 | 6.7 | 52.8 | 3.3 | 29.1 | 5.4 | 50.2 |
| $15,000 to $17,499 | 8.0 | 55.9 | 7.4 | 49.7 | 8.6 | 61.4 | 6.2 | 45.1 | 8.6 | 61.4 | 5.5 | 34.6 | 7.0 | 57.2 |
| $17,500 to $19,999 | 5.5 | 61.4 | 5.2 | 54.9 | 5.7 | 67.1 | 4.3 | 49.4 | 5.7 | 67.1 | 3.8 | 38.4 | 5.0 | 62.2 |
| $20,000 to $22,499 | 6.4 | 67.8 | 6.8 | 61.7 | 6.1 | 73.2 | 6.0 | 55.4 | 6.1 | 73.2 | 5.8 | 44.2 | 6.2 | 68.4 |
| $22,500 to $24,999 | 3.8 | 71.6 | 3.9 | 65.6 | 3.7 | 76.9 | 3.8 | 59.2 | 3.7 | 76.9 | 3.7 | 47.9 | 4.0 | 72.4 |

Table 10

(continued)

**Total Money Earnings in 1994 of Persons 15 Years Old and Over, by Sex and Race**

**UNITED STATES**

**ALL PERSONS**

|  | Black | | | | | | Both | | White, not Hispanic | | | |
|---|---|---|---|---|---|---|---|---|---|---|---|---|
|  | Both Sexes | Cumul.% | Male | Cumul.% | Female | Cumul.% | Sexes | Cumul.% | Male | Cumul.% | Female | Cumul.% |
| $25,000 to $29,999 | 7.9 | 79.5 | 8.7 | 74.3 | 7.1 | 84.0 | 8.3 | 67.5 | 8.6 | 56.5 | 8.1 | 80.5 |
| $30,000 to $34,999 | 6.0 | 85.5 | 6.6 | 80.9 | 5.4 | 89.4 | 7.0 | 74.5 | 8.0 | 64.5 | 5.9 | 86.4 |
| $35,000 to $39,999 | 4.3 | 89.8 | 5.2 | 86.1 | 3.4 | 92.8 | 5.5 | 80.0 | 6.9 | 71.4 | 4.0 | 90.4 |
| $40,000 to $44,999 | 2.9 | 92.7 | 3.5 | 89.6 | 2.3 | 95.1 | 4.7 | 84.7 | 6.2 | 77.6 | 3.0 | 93.4 |
| $45,000 to $49, 999 | 1.9 | 94.6 | 2.6 | 92.2 | 1.2 | 96.3 | 3.0 | 87.7 | 4.0 | 81.6 | 1.9 | 95.3 |
| $50,000 to $59,999 | 2.6 | 97.2 | 3.7 | 95.9 | 1.6 | 97.9 | 4.5 | 92.2 | 6.6 | 88.2 | 2.1 | 97.4 |
| $60,000 to $74,999 | 1.5 | 98.7 | 2.0 | 97.9 | 1.1 | 99.0 | 3.3 | 95.5 | 5.1 | 93.3 | 1.3 | 98.7 |
| $75,000 and over | 1.3 | 100.0 | 2.0 | 100.0 | 0.7 | 100.0 | 4.4 | 100.0 | 7.2 | 100.0 | 1.2 | 100.0 |
| Median earnings ($'s) | 15,659 | | 17,621 | | 13,910 | | 20,282 | | 26,096 | | 14,920 | |
| Stardard error ($'s) | 205.0 | | 407.0 | | 338.0 | | 97.0 | | 145.0 | | 146.0 | |

**White-Black Ratios**
**Median Earnings**

| | Male | Female |
|---|---|---|
| | 1.48 | 1.07 |

| Both Sexes | |
|---|---|
| 1.30 | |

**Male-Female Ratios**
**Median Earnings**

| Both Sexes | White, Not Hispanic |
|---|---|
| 1.27 | 1.75 |

Table 10A

## Total Money Earnings in 1994 of Persons 25 Years Old and Over, by Sex and Race

**UNITED STATES**

**ALL PERSONS**

| | Black | | | | | | Both Sexes | Cumul.% | White, not Hispanic | | | |
|---|---|---|---|---|---|---|---|---|---|---|---|---|
| | Both Sexes | Cumul.% | Male | Cumul.% | Female | Cumul.% | Both Sexes | Cumul.% | Male | Cumul.% | Female | Cumul.% |
| Total (000's) | 18,457 | | 8,201 | | 10,256 | | 128,707 | | 61,776 | | 66,930 | |
| Total with earnings (000's) | 12,334 | | 5,846 | | 6,488 | | 89,468 | | 48,228 | | 41,239 | |
| Percent | 100 | | 100 | | 100 | | 100 | | 100 | | 100 | |
| $1 to $2,499 or less | 6.6 | 6.6 | 5.2 | 4.2 | 8.8 | 8.8 | 6.9 | 6.9 | 4.4 | 4.4 | 9.9 | 9.9 |
| $2,500 to $4,999 | 4.7 | 11.3 | 3.4 | 7.6 | 5.9 | 14.7 | 4.1 | 11.0 | 2.5 | 6.9 | 6.1 | 16.0 |
| $5,000 to $7,499 | 6.5 | 17.8 | 6.2 | 13.8 | 6.7 | 21.4 | 4.8 | 15.8 | 3.1 | 10.0 | 6.9 | 22.9 |
| $7,500 to $9,999 | 5.9 | 23.7 | 4.8 | 18.6 | 7.0 | 28.4 | 4.4 | 20.2 | 2.8 | 12.8 | 6.2 | 29.1 |
| $10,000 to $12,499 | 9.1 | 32.8 | 7.6 | 26.2 | 10.4 | 38.8 | 6.2 | 26.4 | 4.3 | 17.1 | 8.5 | 37.6 |
| $12,500 to $14,999 | 6.5 | 39.3 | 5.9 | 32.1 | 7.1 | 45.9 | 4.1 | 30.5 | 2.8 | 19.9 | 5.6 | 43.2 |
| $15,000 to $17,499 | 8.7 | 48.0 | 8.2 | 40.3 | 9.3 | 55.2 | 6.3 | 36.8 | 5.3 | 25.2 | 7.5 | 50.7 |
| $17,500 to $19,999 | 6.1 | 54.1 | 5.9 | 46.2 | 6.3 | 61.5 | 4.6 | 41.4 | 3.8 | 29.0 | 5.5 | 56.2 |
| $20,000 to $22,499 | 7.3 | 61.4 | 7.7 | 53.9 | 6.9 | 68.4 | 6.5 | 47.9 | 6.1 | 35.1 | 6.9 | 63.1 |
| $22,500 to $24,999 | 4.4 | 65.8 | 4.5 | 58.4 | 4.3 | 72.7 | 4.2 | 52.1 | 4.0 | 39.1 | 4.5 | 67.6 |

Table 10A

(continued)

**Total Money Earnings in 1994 of Persons 25 Years Old and Over, by Sex and Race**

**UNITED STATES**

**ALL PERSONS**

| | Black | | | | | | Both | | White, not Hispanic | | | |
|---|---|---|---|---|---|---|---|---|---|---|---|---|
| | Both Sexes | Cumul.% | Male | Cumul.% | Female | Cumul.% | Sexes | Cumul.% | Male | Cumul.% | Female | Cumul.% |
| $25,000 to $29,999 | 9.3 | 75.1 | 10.4 | 68.8 | 8.3 | 81.0 | 9.4 | 61.5 | 9.5 | 48.6 | 9.2 | 76.8 |
| $30,000 to $34,999 | 7.2 | 82.3 | 8.0 | 76.8 | 6.5 | 87.5 | 8.2 | 69.7 | 9.2 | 57.8 | 7.0 | 83.8 |
| $35,000 to $39,999 | 5.1 | 87.4 | 6.2 | 83.0 | 4.1 | 91.6 | 6.5 | 76.2 | 8.0 | 65.8 | 4.8 | 88.6 |
| $40,000 to $44,999 | 3.5 | 90.9 | 4.3 | 87.3 | 2.8 | 94.4 | 5.6 | 81.8 | 7.2 | 73.0 | 3.6 | 92.2 |
| $45,000 to $49,999 | 2.3 | 93.2 | 3.2 | 90.5 | 1.5 | 95.9 | 3.6 | 85.4 | 4.7 | 77.7 | 2.3 | 94.5 |
| $50,000 to $59,999 | 3.2 | 96.4 | 4.6 | 95.1 | 1.9 | 97.8 | 5.4 | 90.8 | 7.7 | 85.4 | 2.6 | 97.1 |
| $60,000 to $74,999 | 1.9 | 98.3 | 2.5 | 97.6 | 1.3 | 99.1 | 4.0 | 94.8 | 6.0 | 91.4 | 1.6 | 98.7 |
| $75,000 and over | 1.6 | 100.0 | 2.4 | 100.0 | 0.9 | 100.0 | 5.3 | 100.0 | 8.5 | 100.0 | 1.5 | 100.0 |
| Median earnings ($'s) | 18,268 | | 21,224 | | 16,110 | | 23,728 | | 30,555 | | 17,294 | |
| Stardard error ($'s) | 299 | | 341 | | 270 | | 148 | | 133 | | 124 | |

| White-Black Ratios Median Earnings | | | | Male-Female Ratios Median Earnings | |
|---|---|---|---|---|---|
| Both Sexes | Male | Female | | Black | hite, Not Hispanic |
| 1.30 | 1.44 | 1.07 | | 1.32 | 1.77 |

39

Table 11

## Total Money Earnings in 1994 of Persons 15 Years Old and Over, by Sex and Race

### YEAR-ROUND, FULL-TIME WORKERS

UNITED STATES

| | Black | | | | | | White, not Hispanic | | | | | |
|---|---|---|---|---|---|---|---|---|---|---|---|---|
| | Both Sexes | Cumul.% | Male | Cumul.% | Female | Cumul.% | Both Sexes | Cumul.% | Male | Cumul.% | Female | Cumul.% |
| Total (000's) | 9,319 | | 4,761 | | 4,558 | | 66,413 | | 40,471 | | 25,942 | |
| Total with earnings (000's) | 9,317 | | 4,761 | | 4,556 | | 66,376 | | 40,455 | | 25,921 | |
| Percent | 100 | | 100 | | 100 | | 100 | | 100 | | 100 | |
| $1 to $2,499 or less | 1.1 | 1.1 | 1.1 | 1.1 | 1.1 | 1.1 | 1.5 | 1.5 | 1.5 | 1.5 | 1.6 | 1.6 |
| $2,500 to $4,999 | 0.9 | 2.0 | 0.8 | 1.9 | 0.9 | 2.0 | 0.7 | 2.2 | 0.5 | 2.0 | 0.9 | 2.5 |
| $5,000 to $7,499 | 2.4 | 4.4 | 2.5 | 4.4 | 2.3 | 4.3 | 1.5 | 3.7 | 1.1 | 3.1 | 2.1 | 4.6 |
| $7,500 to $9,999 | 4.7 | 9.1 | 3.4 | 7.8 | 6.0 | 10.3 | 2.2 | 5.9 | 1.4 | 4.5 | 3.5 | 8.1 |
| $10,000 to $12,499 | 9.3 | 18.4 | 8.2 | 16.0 | 10.5 | 20.8 | 5.3 | 11.2 | 3.9 | 8.4 | 7.7 | 15.8 |
| $12,500 to $14,999 | 7.9 | 26.3 | 7.4 | 23.4 | 8.5 | 29.3 | 4.3 | 15.5 | 3.0 | 11.4 | 6.3 | 22.1 |
| $15,000 to $17,499 | 10.6 | 36.9 | 9.2 | 32.6 | 12.0 | 41.3 | 7.2 | 22.7 | 5.7 | 17.1 | 9.5 | 31.6 |
| $17,500 to $19,999 | 7.6 | 44.5 | 6.4 | 39.0 | 9.0 | 50.3 | 5.5 | 28.2 | 4.2 | 21.3 | 7.5 | 39.1 |
| $20,000 to $22,499 | 8.8 | 53.5 | 8.4 | 47.4 | 9.2 | 59.5 | 7.6 | 35.8 | 6.6 | 27.9 | 9.2 | 48.3 |
| $22,500 to $24,999 | 5.6 | 58.9 | 5.3 | 52.7 | 6.0 | 65.5 | 5.1 | 40.9 | 4.3 | 32.2 | 6.2 | 54.5 |

Table 11

(continued)

## Total Money Earnings in 1994 of Persons 15 Years Old and Over, by Sex and Race

**UNITED STATES**  YEAR-ROUND, FULL-TIME WORKERS

| | Black | | | | | | White, not Hispanic | | | | | |
|---|---|---|---|---|---|---|---|---|---|---|---|---|
| | Both Sexes | Cumul.% | Male | Cumul.% | Female | Cumul.% | Both Sexes | Cumul.% | Male | Cumul.% | Female | Cumul.% |
| $25,000 to $29,999 | 11.2 | 70.1 | 11.6 | 64.3 | 10.7 | 76.2 | 11.6 | 52.5 | 10.6 | 42.8 | 13.1 | 67.6 |
| $30,000 to $34,999 | 8.5 | 78.6 | 8.8 | 73.1 | 8.1 | 84.3 | 9.8 | 62.3 | 10.0 | 52.8 | 9.5 | 77.1 |
| $35,000 to $39,999 | 6.3 | 84.9 | 7.2 | 80.3 | 5.3 | 89.6 | 8.0 | 70.3 | 8.9 | 61.7 | 6.6 | 83.7 |
| $40,000 to $44,999 | 4.3 | 89.2 | 4.9 | 85.2 | 3.5 | 93.1 | 6.9 | 77.2 | 8.1 | 69.8 | 5.2 | 88.9 |
| $45,000 to $49, 999 | 2.8 | 92.0 | 3.7 | 88.9 | 1.9 | 95.0 | 4.5 | 81.7 | 5.3 | 75.1 | 3.2 | 92.1 |
| $50,000 to $59,999 | 3.8 | 95.8 | 5.4 | 94.3 | 2.1 | 97.1 | 6.7 | 88.4 | 8.7 | 83.8 | 3.5 | 95.6 |
| $60,000 to $74,999 | 2.3 | 98.1 | 3.0 | 97.3 | 1.6 | 98.7 | 4.9 | 93.3 | 6.6 | 90.4 | 2.3 | 97.9 |
| $75,000 and over | 1.9 | 100.0 | 2.6 | 100.0 | 1.2 | 100.0 | 6.6 | 100.0 | 9.6 | 100.0 | 2.0 | 100.0 |
| Median earnings ($'s) | 21,557 | | 23,742 | | 19,911 | | 28,539 | | 32,639 | | 23,196 | |
| Stardard error ($'s) | 238 | | 549 | | 329 | | 172 | | 261 | | 188 | |

**White-Black Ratios**
**Median Earnings**

| Both Sexes | Male | Female |
|---|---|---|
| 1.32 | 1.37 | 1.16 |

**Male-Female Ratios**
**Median Earnings**

| Black | White, Not Hispanic |
|---|---|
| 1.19 | 1.41 |

41

## Table 12

## Total Money Earnings in 1994 of Persons 15 Years Old and Over, by Sex and Race

**SOUTH**

**ALL PERSONS**

| | Black | | | | | | White, not Hispanic | | | | | |
|---|---|---|---|---|---|---|---|---|---|---|---|---|
| | Both Sexes | Cumul.% | Male | Cumul.% | Female | Cumul.% | Both Sexes | Cumul.% | Male | Cumul.% | Female | Cumul.% |
| Total (000's) | 13,376 | | 6,087 | | 7,289 | | 50,163 | | 24,124 | | 26,040 | |
| Total with earnings (000's) | 8,604 | | 4,115 | | 4,490 | | 34,396 | | 18,480 | | 15,916 | |
| Percent | 100 | | 100 | | 100 | | 100 | | 100 | | 100 | |
| $1 to $2,499 or less | 12.1 | 12.1 | 10.2 | 10.2 | 13.9 | 13.9 | 10.1 | 10.1 | 7.6 | 7.6 | 13.0 | 13.0 |
| $2,500 to $4,999 | 7.2 | 19.3 | 6.1 | 16.3 | 8.2 | 22.1 | 6.3 | 16.4 | 4.7 | 12.3 | 8.2 | 21.2 |
| $5,000 to $7,499 | 7.5 | 26.8 | 6.6 | 22.9 | 8.2 | 30.3 | 5.9 | 22.3 | 4.2 | 16.5 | 8.0 | 29.2 |
| $7,500 to $9,999 | 7.4 | 34.2 | 6.5 | 29.4 | 8.3 | 38.6 | 5.2 | 27.5 | 3.6 | 20.1 | 7.1 | 36.3 |
| $10,000 to $12,499 | 10.0 | 44.2 | 9.4 | 38.8 | 10.6 | 49.2 | 7.0 | 34.5 | 5.5 | 25.6 | 8.7 | 45.0 |
| $12,500 to $14,999 | 7.2 | 51.4 | 6.6 | 45.4 | 7.7 | 56.9 | 4.5 | 39.0 | 3.4 | 29.0 | 5.8 | 50.8 |
| $15,000 to $17,499 | 9.2 | 60.6 | 8.6 | 54.0 | 9.7 | 66.6 | 6.6 | 45.6 | 5.9 | 34.9 | 7.4 | 58.2 |
| $17,500 to $19,999 | 5.3 | 65.9 | 5.2 | 59.2 | 5.4 | 72.0 | 4.8 | 50.4 | 4.2 | 39.1 | 5.5 | 63.7 |
| $20,000 to $22,499 | 6.3 | 72.2 | 6.1 | 65.3 | 6.4 | 78.4 | 6.1 | 56.5 | 6.2 | 45.3 | 5.9 | 69.6 |
| $22,500 to $24,999 | 3.6 | 75.8 | 3.8 | 69.1 | 3.5 | 81.9 | 3.9 | 60.4 | 3.9 | 49.2 | 4.0 | 73.6 |

Table 12

(continued)

**Total Money Earnings in 1994 of Persons 15 Years Old and Over,
by Sex and Race**

**SOUTH**

**ALL PERSONS**

| | Black | | | | | | Both | | White, not Hispanic | | | |
| --- | --- | --- | --- | --- | --- | --- | --- | --- | --- | --- | --- | --- |
| | Both Sexes | Cumul.% | Male | Cumul.% | Female | Cumul.% | Sexes | Cumul.% | Male | Cumul.% | Female | Cumul.% |
| $25,000 to $29,999 | 6.9 | 82.7 | 8.9 | 78.0 | 5.1 | 87.0 | 8.7 | 69.1 | 9.1 | 58.3 | 8.2 | 81.8 |
| $30,000 to $34,999 | 5.3 | 88.0 | 6.1 | 84.1 | 4.5 | 91.6 | 7.3 | 76.4 | 8.5 | 66.8 | 5.8 | 87.6 |
| $35,000 to $39,999 | 3.6 | 91.6 | 4.6 | 88.7 | 2.8 | 94.4 | 5.4 | 81.8 | 6.5 | 73.3 | 4.1 | 91.7 |
| $40,000 to $44,999 | 2.2 | 93.8 | 2.7 | 91.4 | 1.8 | 96.2 | 4.3 | 86.1 | 5.8 | 79.1 | 2.5 | 94.2 |
| $45,000 to $49,999 | 1.5 | 95.3 | 2.0 | 93.4 | 1.0 | 97.2 | 2.5 | 88.6 | 3.3 | 82.4 | 1.6 | 95.8 |
| $50,000 to $59,999 | 2.2 | 97.5 | 2.9 | 96.3 | 1.4 | 98.6 | 4.2 | 92.8 | 6.0 | 88.4 | 2.1 | 97.9 |
| $60,000 to $74,999 | 1.3 | 98.8 | 1.5 | 97.8 | 1.0 | 99.6 | 3.1 | 95.9 | 4.8 | 93.2 | 1.1 | 99.0 |
| $75,000 and over | 1.1 | 100.0 | 1.9 | 100.0 | 0.4 | 100.0 | 4.1 | 100.0 | 6.8 | 100.0 | 1.0 | 100.0 |
| Median earnings ($'s) | 14,496 | | 16,293 | | 12,764 | | 19,767 | | 25,356 | | 14,686 | |
| Standard error ($'s) | 309 | | 373 | | 381 | | 215 | | 247 | | 263 | |

**White-Black Ratios**
**Median Earnings**

| Both Sexes | Male | Female |
| --- | --- | --- |
| 1.36 | 1.56 | 1.15 |

**Male-Female Ratios**
**Median Earnings**

| Black | White, Not Hispanic |
| --- | --- |
| 1.28 | 1.73 |

Table 12A

## Total Money Earnings in 1994 of Persons 25 Years Old and Over, by Sex and Race

**SOUTH**

| | Black | | | | | | ALL PERSONS | | White, not Hispanic | | | |
| --- | --- | --- | --- | --- | --- | --- | --- | --- | --- | --- | --- | --- |
| | Both Sexes | Cumul % | Male | Cumul % | Female | Cumul % | Both Sexes | Cumul % | Male | Cumul % | Female | Cumul % |
| Total (000's) | 10,279 | | 4,590 | | 5,689 | | 42,320 | | 20,273 | | 22,048 | |
| Total with earnings (000's) | 7,007 | | 3,315 | | 3,692 | | 28,981 | | 15,696 | | 13,285 | |
| Percent | 100 | | 100 | | 100 | | 100 | | 100 | | 100 | |
| $1 to $2,499 or less | 6.3 | 6.3 | 4.3 | 4.3 | 8.2 | 8.2 | 7.0 | 7.0 | 4.6 | 4.6 | 9.9 | 9.9 |
| $2,500 to $4,999 | 5.0 | 11.3 | 3.3 | 7.6 | 6.5 | 14.7 | 4.3 | 11.3 | 2.7 | 7.3 | 6.2 | 16.1 |
| $5,000 to $7,499 | 7.2 | 18.5 | 6.2 | 13.8 | 8.1 | 22.8 | 4.6 | 15.9 | 3.0 | 10.3 | 6.5 | 22.6 |
| $7,500 to $9,999 | 6.9 | 25.4 | 5.6 | 19.4 | 8 | 30.8 | 4.7 | 20.6 | 3.0 | 13.3 | 6.8 | 29.4 |
| $10,000 to $12,499 | 10.4 | 35.8 | 8.9 | 28.4 | 11.7 | 42.5 | 6.5 | 27.1 | 4.6 | 17.9 | 8.7 | 38.1 |
| $12,500 to $14,999 | 7.4 | 43.2 | 6.9 | 35.2 | 7.8 | 50.3 | 4.2 | 31.3 | 2.8 | 20.7 | 5.9 | 44.0 |
| $15,000 to $17,499 | 10.0 | 53.2 | 9.4 | 44.6 | 10.6 | 60.9 | 6.7 | 38.0 | 5.7 | 26.4 | 8.0 | 52.0 |
| $17,500 to $19,999 | 6.1 | 59.3 | 6.1 | 50.7 | 6.1 | 67.0 | 5.0 | 43.0 | 4.1 | 30.5 | 6.1 | 58.1 |
| $20,000 to $22,499 | 7.1 | 66.4 | 7 | 57.7 | 7.2 | 74.2 | 6.6 | 49.6 | 6.6 | 37.1 | 6.5 | 64.6 |
| $22,500 to $24,999 | 4.3 | 70.7 | 4.6 | 62.3 | 4.2 | 78.4 | 4.3 | 53.9 | 4.3 | 41.4 | 4.4 | 69.0 |

Table 12A

**Total Money Earnings in 1994 of Persons 25 Years Old and Over, by Sex and Race**

(continued)

SOUTH

ALL PERSONS

| | Black | | | | | | Both | | White, not Hispanic | | | |
|---|---|---|---|---|---|---|---|---|---|---|---|---|
| | Sexes | Cumul.% | Male | Cumul.% | Female | Cumul.% | Sexes | Cumul.% | Male | Cumul.% | Female | Cumul.% |
| $25,000 to $29,999 | 8.3 | 79.0 | 10.8 | 73.1 | 6.0 | 84.4 | 9.8 | 63.7 | 10.1 | 51.5 | 9.5 | 78.5 |
| $30,000 to $34,999 | 6.5 | 85.5 | 7.5 | 80.6 | 5.6 | 90.0 | 8.4 | 72.1 | 9.8 | 61.3 | 6.9 | 85.4 |
| $35,000 to $39,999 | 4.4 | 89.9 | 5.6 | 86.2 | 3.3 | 93.3 | 6.3 | 78.4 | 7.5 | 68.8 | 4.8 | 90.2 |
| $40,000 to $44,999 | 2.7 | 92.6 | 3.4 | 89.6 | 2.2 | 95.5 | 5.0 | 83.4 | 6.7 | 75.5 | 3.0 | 93.2 |
| $45,000 to $49, 999 | 1.8 | 94.4 | 2.5 | 92.1 | 1.2 | 96.7 | 3.0 | 86.4 | 3.9 | 79.4 | 1.9 | 95.1 |
| $50,000 to $59,999 | 2.6 | 97.0 | 3.6 | 95.7 | 1.8 | 98.5 | 4.9 | 91.3 | 7.0 | 86.4 | 2.4 | 97.5 |
| $60,000 to $74,999 | 1.5 | 98.5 | 1.9 | 97.6 | 1.1 | 99.6 | 3.6 | 94.9 | 5.6 | 92.0 | 1.3 | 98.8 |
| $75,000 and over | 1.3 | 99.8 | 2.4 | 100.0 | 0.4 | 100.0 | 4.9 | 99.8 | 8.0 | 100.0 | 1.2 | 100.0 |
| Median earnings ($'s) | 16,706 | | 19,740 | | 14,885 | | 22,668 | | 28,998 | | 16,859 | |
| Stardard error ($'s) | 245 | | 565 | | 391 | | 243 | | 407 | | 207 | |

| White-Black Ratios Median Earnings | | | | Male-Female Ratios Median Earnings | |
|---|---|---|---|---|---|
| Both S | Male | Female | | Black | hite. Not Hispanic |
| 1.36 | 1.47 | 1.13 | | 1.3 | 1.72 |

45

Table 13

## Total Money Earnings in 1994 of Persons 15 Years Old and Over, by Sex and Race

**SOUTH**　　　　　　　　　　　　　　**YEAR-ROUND, FULL-TIME WORKERS**

| | Black | | | | | | White, not Hispanic | | | | | |
|---|---|---|---|---|---|---|---|---|---|---|---|---|
| | Both Sexes | Cumul.% | Male | Cumul.% | Female | Cumul.% | Both Sexes | Cumul.% | Male | Cumul.% | Female | Cumul.% |
| Total (000's) | 5,395 | | 2,825 | | 2,570 | | 21,973 | | 13,384 | | 8,589 | |
| Total with earnings (000's) | 5,393 | | 2,825 | | 2,569 | | 21,963 | | 13,380 | | 8,583 | |
| Percent | 100 | | 100 | | 100 | | 100 | | 100 | | 100 | |
| $1 to $2,499 or less | 1.4 | 1.4 | 1.6 | 1.6 | 1.1 | 1.1 | 1.5 | 1.5 | 1.6 | 1.6 | 1.3 | 1.3 |
| $2,500 to $4,999 | 0.7 | 2.1 | 0.7 | 2.3 | 0.7 | 1.8 | 0.7 | 2.2 | 0.5 | 2.1 | 0.9 | 2.2 |
| $5,000 to $7,499 | 2.9 | 5.0 | 3.2 | 5.5 | 2.6 | 4.4 | 1.6 | 3.8 | 1.2 | 3.3 | 2.1 | 4.3 |
| $7,500 to $9,999 | 5.7 | 10.7 | 3.7 | 9.2 | 7.8 | 12.2 | 2.7 | 6.5 | 1.8 | 5.1 | 4.3 | 8.6 |
| $10,000 to $12,499 | 11.1 | 21.8 | 9.8 | 19.0 | 12.4 | 24.6 | 5.8 | 12.3 | 4.1 | 9.2 | 8.4 | 17.0 |
| $12,500 to $14,999 | 9.2 | 31.0 | 8.5 | 27.5 | 9.9 | 34.5 | 4.9 | 17.2 | 3.2 | 12.4 | 7.4 | 24.4 |
| $15,000 to $17,499 | 12.1 | 43.1 | 10.9 | 38.4 | 13.4 | 47.9 | 8.0 | 25.2 | 6.3 | 18.7 | 10.6 | 35.0 |
| $17,500 to $19,999 | 7.7 | 50.8 | 6.7 | 45.1 | 8.8 | 56.7 | 6.2 | 31.4 | 4.8 | 23.5 | 8.3 | 43.3 |
| $20,000 to $22,499 | 8.8 | 59.6 | 7.7 | 52.8 | 10.0 | 66.7 | 7.8 | 39.2 | 7.2 | 30.7 | 8.6 | 51.9 |
| $22,500 to $24,999 | 5.5 | 65.1 | 5.4 | 58.2 | 5.7 | 72.4 | 5.2 | 44.4 | 4.6 | 35.3 | 6.2 | 58.1 |

Table 13

**Total Money Earnings in 1994 of Persons 15 Years Old and Over,**
**by Sex and Race**

(continued)

## SOUTH

### YEAR-ROUND FULL-TIME WORKERS

| | Black | | | | | | White, not Hispanic | | | | | |
|---|---|---|---|---|---|---|---|---|---|---|---|---|
| | Both Sexes | Cumul.% | Male | Cumul.% | Female | Cumul.% | Both Sexes | Cumul.% | Male | Cumul.% | Female | Cumul.% |
| $25,000 to $29,999 | 9.9 | 75.0 | 11.5 | 69.7 | 8.1 | 80.5 | 11.8 | 56.2 | 11.0 | 46.3 | 13.1 | 71.2 |
| $30,000 to $34,999 | 7.5 | 82.5 | 8.2 | 77.9 | 6.6 | 87.1 | 10.0 | 66.2 | 10.8 | 57.1 | 8.8 | 80.0 |
| $35,000 to $39,999 | 5.4 | 87.9 | 6.4 | 84.3 | 4.3 | 91.4 | 7.4 | 73.6 | 8.2 | 65.3 | 6.3 | 86.3 |
| $40,000 to $44,999 | 3.3 | 91.2 | 3.8 | 88.1 | 2.7 | 94.1 | 6.2 | 79.8 | 7.6 | 72.9 | 4.0 | 90.3 |
| $45,000 to $49,999 | 2.3 | 93.5 | 2.9 | 91.0 | 1.7 | 95.8 | 3.7 | 83.5 | 4.4 | 77.3 | 2.7 | 93.0 |
| $50,000 to $59,999 | 3.1 | 96.6 | 4.1 | 95.1 | 2.0 | 97.8 | 6.1 | 89.6 | 7.7 | 85.0 | 3.5 | 96.5 |
| $60,000 to $74,999 | 1.8 | 98.4 | 2.2 | 97.3 | 1.4 | 99.2 | 4.4 | 94.0 | 6.1 | 91.1 | 1.8 | 98.3 |
| $75,000 and over | 1.7 | 100.0 | 2.6 | 100.0 | 0.7 | 100.0 | 6.0 | 100.0 | 8.8 | 100.0 | 1.6 | 100.0 |
| Median earnings ($'s) | 19,763 | | 21,548 | | 18,078 | | 26,887 | | 31,159 | | 21,937 | |
| Standard error ($'s) | 354 | | 502 | | 460 | | 172 | | 219 | | 241 | |

**White-Black Ratios**
**Median Earnings**

| Both Sexes | Male | Female |
|---|---|---|
| 1.36 | 1.45 | 1.21 |

**Male-Female Ratios**
**Median Earnings**

| Black | White, Not Hispanic |
|---|---|
| 1.19 | 1.42 |

47

Table 13A

(continued)

## Total Money Earnings in 1994 of Persons 25 Years Old and Over, by Sex and Race

**SOUTH**

**YEAR-ROUND, FULL-TIME WORKERS**

| | Black | | | | | | Both | | White, not Hispanic | | | |
|---|---|---|---|---|---|---|---|---|---|---|---|---|
| | Both Sexes | Cumul.% | Male | Cumul.% | Female | Cumul.% | Both Sexes | Cumul.% | Male | umul.% | Female | Cumul.% |
| $25,000 to $29,999 | 10.5 | 72.6 | 12.5 | 66.8 | 8.4 | 79.0 | 12.3 | 53.2 | 11.4 | 42.8 | 13.6 | 69.3 |
| $30,000 to $34,999 | 8.1 | 80.7 | 9.0 | 75.8 | 7.1 | 86.1 | 10.6 | 63.8 | 11.3 | 54.1 | 9.4 | 78.7 |
| $35,000 to $39,999 | 5.9 | 86.6 | 7.0 | 82.8 | 4.7 | 90.8 | 7.9 | 71.7 | 8.7 | 62.8 | 6.6 | 85.3 |
| $40,000 to $44,999 | 3.6 | 90.2 | 4.2 | 87.0 | 2.9 | 93.7 | 6.6 | 78.3 | 8.1 | 70.9 | 4.3 | 89.6 |
| $45,000 to $49,999 | 2.5 | 92.7 | 3.2 | 90.2 | 1.8 | 95.5 | 4.0 | 82.3 | 4.7 | 75.6 | 2.9 | 92.5 |
| $50,000 to $59,999 | 3.4 | 96.1 | 4.6 | 94.8 | 2.2 | 97.7 | 6.5 | 88.8 | 8.3 | 83.9 | 3.8 | 96.3 |
| $60,000 to $74,999 | 2.0 | 98.1 | 2.4 | 97.2 | 1.5 | 99.2 | 4.8 | 93.6 | 6.6 | 90.5 | 2.0 | 98.3 |
| $75,000 and over | 1.8 | 100.0 | 2.8 | 100.0 | 0.6 | 100.0 | 6.4 | 100.0 | 9.4 | 100.0 | 1.7 | 100.0 |
| Median earnings ($'s) | 20,748 | | 23,116 | | 18,801 | | 28,195 | | 32,247 | | 22,725 | |
| Stardard error ($'s) | 326 | | 692 | | 466 | | 300 | | 219 | | 329 | |

**White-Black Ratios**
**Median Earnings**

| Both Sexes | Male | Female |
|---|---|---|
| 1.36 | 1.40 | 1.21 |

**Male-Female Ratios**
**Median Earnings**

| Black | White, Not Hispanic |
|---|---|
| 1.2 | 1.42 |

48

Table 14

## Total Money Earnings in 1994 of Persons 15 Years Old and Over, by Sex and Race

### ALL PERSONS

NORTH AND WEST

| | Black | | | | | | | | White, not Hispanic | | | |
| --- | --- | --- | --- | --- | --- | --- | --- | --- | --- | --- | --- | --- |
| | Both Sexes | Cumul.% | Male | Cumul.% | Female | Cumul.% | Both Sexes | Cumul.% | Male | Cumul.% | Female | Cumul.% |
| Total (000's) | 10,546 | | 4,738 | | 5,808 | | 103,326 | | 50,114 | | 53,212 | |
| Total with earnings (000's) | 6,501 | | 3,080 | | 3,420 | | 72,884 | | 39,005 | | 33,879 | |
| Percent | 100 | | 100 | | 100 | | 100 | | 100 | | 100 | |
| $1 to $2,499 or less | 12.3 | 12.3 | 8.8 | 8.8 | 15.4 | 15.4 | 10.8 | 10.8 | 8.3 | 8.3 | 13.7 | 13.7 |
| $2,500 to $4,999 | 6.6 | 18.9 | 5.7 | 14.5 | 7.3 | 22.7 | 6.3 | 17.1 | 4.6 | 12.9 | 8.2 | 21.9 |
| $5,000 to $7,499 | 6.4 | 25.3 | 6.7 | 21.2 | 6.1 | 28.8 | 6.1 | 23.2 | 4.5 | 17.4 | 8.0 | 29.9 |
| $7,500 to $9,999 | 5.2 | 30.5 | 4.7 | 25.9 | 5.5 | 34.3 | 4.8 | 28.0 | 3.4 | 20.8 | 6.4 | 36.3 |
| $10,000 to $12,499 | 7.5 | 38.0 | 7.1 | 33.0 | 7.9 | 42.2 | 6.5 | 34.5 | 4.9 | 25.7 | 8.4 | 44.7 |
| $12,500 to $14,999 | 5.3 | 43.3 | 5.1 | 38.1 | 5.4 | 47.6 | 4.2 | 38.7 | 3.3 | 29.0 | 5.3 | 50.0 |
| $15,000 to $17,499 | 6.5 | 49.8 | 5.8 | 43.9 | 7.1 | 54.7 | 6.0 | 44.7 | 5.3 | 34.3 | 6.8 | 56.8 |
| $17,500 to $19,999 | 5.7 | 55.5 | 5.1 | 49.0 | 6.2 | 60.9 | 4.1 | 48.8 | 3.6 | 37.9 | 4.7 | 61.5 |
| $20,000 to $22,499 | 6.7 | 62.2 | 7.8 | 56.8 | 5.7 | 66.6 | 5.9 | 54.7 | 5.5 | 43.4 | 6.3 | 67.8 |
| $22,500 to $24,999 | 4.0 | 66.2 | 4.1 | 60.9 | 3.9 | 70.5 | 3.7 | 58.4 | 3.5 | 46.9 | 4.0 | 71.8 |

49

(continued)

Table 14

## Total Money Earnings in 1994 of Persons 15 Years Old and Over, by Sex and Race

### NORTH AND WEST

### ALL PERSONS

| | Black | | | | | | Both Sexes | | White, not Hispanic | | | |
| | Both Sexes | Cumul.% | Male | Cumul.% | Female | Cumul.% | Both Sexes | Cumul.% | Male | Cumul.% | Female | Cumul.% |
|---|---|---|---|---|---|---|---|---|---|---|---|---|
| $25,000 to $29,999 | 9.1 | 75.3 | 8.4 | 69.3 | 9.7 | 80.2 | 8.2 | 66.6 | 8.3 | 55.2 | 8.0 | 79.8 |
| $30,000 to $34,999 | 6.9 | 82.2 | 7.4 | 76.7 | 6.4 | 86.6 | 6.9 | 73.5 | 7.7 | 62.9 | 6.0 | 85.8 |
| $35,000 to $39,999 | 5.1 | 87.3 | 5.9 | 82.6 | 4.3 | 90.9 | 5.6 | 79.1 | 7.0 | 69.9 | 4.0 | 89.8 |
| $40,000 to $44,999 | 3.8 | 91.1 | 4.6 | 87.2 | 3.1 | 94.0 | 4.9 | 84.0 | 6.3 | 76.2 | 3.3 | 93.1 |
| $45,000 to $49,999 | 2.4 | 93.5 | 3.4 | 90.6 | 1.5 | 95.5 | 3.2 | 87.2 | 4.3 | 80.5 | 2.0 | 95.1 |
| $50,000 to $59,999 | 3.2 | 96.7 | 4.8 | 95.4 | 1.9 | 97.4 | 4.7 | 91.9 | 6.8 | 87.3 | 2.2 | 97.3 |
| $60,000 to $74,999 | 1.9 | 98.6 | 2.7 | 98.1 | 1.2 | 98.6 | 3.4 | 95.3 | 5.2 | 92.5 | 1.4 | 98.7 |
| $75,000 and over | 1.6 | 100.0 | 2.0 | 100.0 | 1.2 | 100.0 | 4.6 | 100.0 | 7.4 | 100.0 | 1.4 | 100.0 |
| Median earnings ($'s) | 17,640 | | 20,319 | | 15,779 | | 20,510 | | 26,475 | | 15,031 | |
| Standard error ($'s) | 406 | | 481 | | 465 | | 114 | | 174 | | 161 | |

| White-Black Ratios Median Earnings | | | |
|---|---|---|---|
| | Both Sexes | Male | Female |
| | 1.16 | 1.30 | 0.95 |

| Male-Female Ratios Median Earnings | |
|---|---|
| Black | White, Not Hispanic |
| 1.29 | 1.76 |

Table 14A

## Total Money Earnings in 1994 of Persons 25 Years Old and Over, by Sex and Race

NORTH AND WEST

ALL PERSONS

| | Black | | | | | | Both | | White, not Hispanic | | | |
|---|---|---|---|---|---|---|---|---|---|---|---|---|
| | Both Sexes | Cumul.% | Male | Cumul.% | Female | Cumul.% | Both Sexes | Cumul.% | Male | Cumul.% | Female | Cumul.% |
| Total (000's) | 8,178 | | 3,610 | | 4,567 | | 86,387 | | 41,504 | | 44,883 | |
| Total with earnings (000's) | 5,327 | | 2,532 | | 2,795 | | 60,486 | | 32,532 | | 27,954 | |
| Percent | 100 | | 100 | | 100 | | 100 | | 100 | | 100 | |
| $1 to $2,499 or less | 7.0 | 7.0 | 4.2 | 4.2 | 9.6 | 9.6 | 6.9 | 6.9 | 4.3 | 4.3 | 9.9 | 9.9 |
| $2,500 to $4,999 | 4.4 | 11.4 | 3.6 | 7.8 | 5.2 | 14.8 | 4.1 | 11.0 | 2.4 | 6.7 | 6.0 | 15.9 |
| $5,000 to $7,499 | 5.6 | 17.0 | 6.3 | 14.1 | 4.9 | 19.7 | 4.9 | 15.9 | 3.1 | 9.8 | 7.0 | 22.9 |
| $7,500 to $9,999 | 4.7 | 21.7 | 3.7 | 17.8 | 5.6 | 25.3 | 4.2 | 20.1 | 2.7 | 12.5 | 5.9 | 28.8 |
| $10,000 to $12,499 | 7.3 | 29.0 | 5.9 | 23.7 | 8.6 | 33.9 | 6.1 | 26.2 | 4.1 | 16.6 | 8.4 | 37.2 |
| $12,500 to $14,999 | 5.4 | 34.4 | 4.6 | 28.3 | 6.1 | 40.0 | 4.0 | 30.2 | 2.8 | 19.4 | 5.4 | 42.6 |
| $15,000 to $17,499 | 7.1 | 41.5 | 6.6 | 34.9 | 7.5 | 47.5 | 6.1 | 36.3 | 5.1 | 24.5 | 7.2 | 49.8 |
| $17,500 to $19,999 | 6.0 | 47.5 | 5.6 | 40.5 | 6.4 | 53.9 | 4.4 | 40.7 | 3.7 | 28.2 | 5.2 | 55.0 |
| $20,000 to $22,499 | 7.6 | 55.1 | 8.7 | 49.2 | 6.6 | 60.5 | 6.4 | 47.1 | 5.8 | 34 | 7.1 | 62.1 |
| $22,500 to $24,999 | 4.4 | 59.5 | 4.4 | 53.6 | 4.5 | 65.0 | 4.2 | 51.3 | 3.9 | 37.9 | 4.6 | 66.7 |

Table 14A

(continued)

**Total Money Earnings In 1994 of Persons 25 Years Old and Over, by Sex and Race**

**NORTH AND WEST**

**ALL PERSONS**

| | Black | | | | | | Both | | White, not Hispanic | | | |
|---|---|---|---|---|---|---|---|---|---|---|---|---|
| | Sexes | Cumul.% | Male | Cumul.% | Female | Cumul.% | Sexes | Cumul.% | Male | Cumul.% | Female | Cumul.% |
| $25,000 to $29,999 | 10.6 | 70.1 | 9.8 | 63.4 | 11.3 | 76.3 | 9.2 | 60.5 | 9.2 | 47.1 | 9.1 | 75.8 |
| $30,000 to $34,999 | 8.1 | 78.2 | 8.6 | 72.0 | 7.7 | 84.0 | 8.1 | 68.6 | 8.9 | 56.0 | 7.1 | 82.9 |
| $35,000 to $39,999 | 6.1 | 84.3 | 6.9 | 78.9 | 5.3 | 89.3 | 6.6 | 75.2 | 8.2 | 64.2 | 4.8 | 87.7 |
| $40,000 to $44,999 | 4.5 | 88.8 | 5.5 | 84.4 | 3.6 | 92.9 | 5.8 | 81.0 | 7.5 | 71.7 | 3.9 | 91.6 |
| $45,000 to $49,999 | 2.9 | 91.7 | 4.1 | 88.5 | 1.9 | 94.8 | 3.9 | 84.9 | 5.1 | 76.8 | 2.5 | 94.1 |
| $50,000 to $59,999 | 3.9 | 95.6 | 5.8 | 94.3 | 2.2 | 97.0 | 5.6 | 90.5 | 8.1 | 84.9 | 2.6 | 96.7 |
| $60,000 to $74,999 | 2.3 | 97.9 | 3.3 | 97.6 | 1.5 | 98.5 | 4.1 | 94.6 | 6.2 | 91.1 | 1.7 | 98.4 |
| $75,000 and over | 1.9 | 99.8 | 2.4 | 100.0 | 1.5 | 100.0 | 5.5 | 100.1 | 8.8 | 99.9 | 1.6 | 100.0 |
| Median earnings ($'s) | 20,814 | | 22,987 | | 8,468 | | 24,255 | | 31,137 | | 17,533 | |
| Standard error ($'s) | 350 | | 785 | | 570 | | 176 | | 160 | | 183 | |

| White-Black Ratios Median Earnings | | | | Male-Female Ratios Median Earnings | |
|---|---|---|---|---|---|
| Both Se | Male | Female | | Black | White, Not Hispanic |
| 1.17 | 1.35 | 0.95 | | 1.24 | 1.78 |

52

Table 15

## Total Money Earnings in 1994 of Persons 15 Years Old and Over, by Sex and Race

**NORTH AND WEST**  —  **YEAR-ROUND, FULL-TIME WORKERS**

| | Black | | | | | | White, not Hispanic | | | | | |
|---|---|---|---|---|---|---|---|---|---|---|---|---|
| | Both Sexes | Cumul.% | Male | Cumul.% | Female | Cumul.% | Both Sexes | Cumul.% | Male | Cumul.% | Female | Cumul.% |
| Total (000's) | 3,924 | | 1,936 | | 1,987 | | 44,440 | | 27,087 | | 17,353 | |
| Total with earnings (000's) | 3,924 | | 1,936 | | 1,987 | | 44,413 | | 27,075 | | 17,338 | |
| Percent | 100 | | 100 | | 100 | | 100 | | 100 | | 100 | |
| $1 to $2,499 or less | 0.8 | 0.8 | 0.5 | 0.5 | 1.2 | 1.2 | 1.5 | 1.5 | 1.4 | 1.4 | 1.7 | 1.7 |
| $2,500 to $4,999 | 1.1 | 1.9 | 1.0 | 1.5 | 1.2 | 2.4 | 0.7 | 2.2 | 0.5 | 1.9 | 1.0 | 2.7 |
| $5,000 to $7,499 | 1.6 | 3.5 | 1.4 | 2.9 | 1.9 | 4.3 | 1.5 | 3.7 | 1.1 | 3.0 | 2.1 | 4.8 |
| $7,500 to $9,999 | 3.4 | 6.9 | 3.0 | 5.9 | 3.8 | 8.1 | 2.0 | 5.7 | 1.2 | 4.2 | 3.1 | 7.9 |
| $10,000 to $12,499 | 6.9 | 13.8 | 5.8 | 11.7 | 7.9 | 16.0 | 5.1 | 10.8 | 3.7 | 7.9 | 7.3 | 15.2 |
| $12,500 to $14,999 | 6.2 | 20.0 | 5.7 | 17.4 | 6.6 | 22.6 | 4.0 | 14.8 | 2.9 | 10.8 | 5.7 | 20.9 |
| $15,000 to $17,499 | 8.5 | 28.5 | 6.7 | 24.1 | 10.2 | 32.8 | 6.7 | 21.5 | 5.3 | 16.1 | 8.9 | 29.8 |
| $17,500 to $19,999 | 7.5 | 36.0 | 5.8 | 29.9 | 9.2 | 42.0 | 5.2 | 26.7 | 3.9 | 20.0 | 7.1 | 36.9 |
| $20,000 to $22,499 | 8.7 | 44.7 | 9.3 | 39.2 | 8.1 | 50.1 | 7.6 | 34.3 | 6.3 | 26.3 | 9.5 | 46.4 |
| $22,500 to $24,999 | 5.8 | 50.5 | 5.3 | 44.5 | 6.3 | 56.4 | 5.0 | 39.3 | 4.2 | 30.5 | 6.3 | 52.7 |

53

Table 15

## Total Money Earnings in 1994 of Persons 15 Years Old and Over, by Sex and Race

### NORTH AND WEST

### YEAR-ROUND FULL-TIME WORKERS

|  | Black | | | | | | White, not Hispanic | | | | | |
|---|---|---|---|---|---|---|---|---|---|---|---|---|
|  | Both Sexes | Cumul.% | Male | Cumul.% | Female | Cumul.% | Both Sexes | Cumul.% | Male | Cumul.% | Female | Cumul.% |
| $25,000 to $29,999 | 13.0 | 63.5 | 11.8 | 56.3 | 14.1 | 70.5 | 11.4 | 50.7 | 10.4 | 40.9 | 13.1 | 65.8 |
| $30,000 to $34,999 | 9.8 | 73.3 | 9.6 | 65.9 | 10.1 | 80.6 | 9.8 | 60.5 | 9.7 | 50.6 | 9.9 | 75.7 |
| $35,000 to $39,999 | 7.5 | 80.8 | 8.4 | 74.3 | 6.6 | 87.2 | 8.2 | 68.7 | 9.2 | 59.8 | 6.7 | 82.4 |
| $40,000 to $44,999 | 5.6 | 86.4 | 6.7 | 81.0 | 4.6 | 91.8 | 7.3 | 76.0 | 8.3 | 68.1 | 5.8 | 88.2 |
| $45,000 to $49,999 | 3.5 | 89.9 | 4.9 | 85.9 | 2.1 | 93.9 | 4.9 | 80.9 | 5.7 | 73.8 | 3.5 | 91.7 |
| $50,000 to $59,999 | 4.7 | 94.6 | 7.3 | 93.2 | 2.2 | 96.1 | 7.0 | 87.9 | 9.2 | 83.0 | 3.5 | 95.2 |
| $60,000 to $74,999 | 3.0 | 97.6 | 4.2 | 97.4 | 1.8 | 97.9 | 5.2 | 93.1 | 6.9 | 89.9 | 2.6 | 97.8 |
| $75,000 and over | 2.3 | 100.0 | 2.7 | 100.0 | 2.0 | 100.0 | 7.0 | 100.0 | 10.0 | 100.0 | 2.3 | 100.0 |
| Median earnings ($'s) | 24,770 | | 26,760 | | 22,471 | | 29,608 | | 34,424 | | 23,921 | |
| Stardard error ($'s) | 488 | | 564 | | 608 | | 205 | | 376 | | 221 | |

| White-Black Ratios Median Earnings | | | | Male-Female Ratios Median Earnings | |
|---|---|---|---|---|---|
| Both Sexes | Male | Female | | Black | White, Not Hispanic |
| 1.19 | 1.29 | 1.06 | | 1.19 | 1.44 |

Table 15A

## Total Money Earnings in 1994 of Persons 25 Years Old and Over, by Sex and Race

NORTH AND WEST

YEAR-ROUND, FULL-TIME WORKERS

| | Black | | | | | | White, not Hispanic | | | | | |
| | Both Sexes | Cumul.% | Male | Cumul.% | Female | Cumul.% | Both Sexes | Cumul.% | Male | Cumul.% | Female | Cumul.% |
|---|---|---|---|---|---|---|---|---|---|---|---|---|
| Total (000's) | 3,613 | | 1,783 | | 1,830 | | 41,135 | | 25,245 | | 15,890 | |
| Total with earnings (000's) | 3,613 | | 1,783 | | 1,830 | | 41,114 | | 25,237 | | 15,877 | |
| Percent | 100 | | 100 | | 100 | | 100 | | 100 | | 100 | |
| $1 to $2,499 or less | 0.8 | 0.8 | 0.5 | 0.5 | 1.1 | 1.1 | 1.5 | 1.5 | 1.4 | 1.4 | 1.7 | 1.7 |
| $2,500 to $4,999 | 0.9 | 1.7 | 0.9 | 1.4 | 0.8 | 1.9 | 0.6 | 2.1 | 0.4 | 1.8 | 0.8 | 2.5 |
| $5,000 to $7,499 | 1.3 | 3.0 | 1.1 | 2.5 | 1.5 | 3.4 | 1.3 | 3.3 | 0.9 | 2.7 | 1.6 | 4.1 |
| $7,500 to $9,999 | 3.1 | 6.1 | 2.3 | 4.8 | 3.8 | 7.2 | 1.6 | 4.9 | 1.0 | 3.7 | 2.5 | 6.6 |
| $10,000 to $12,499 | 5.7 | 11.8 | 3.8 | 8.6 | 7.4 | 14.6 | 4.2 | 9.1 | 2.8 | 6.5 | 6.5 | 13.1 |
| $12,500 to $14,999 | 5.7 | 17.5 | 4.8 | 13.4 | 6.6 | 21.2 | 3.4 | 12.5 | 2.2 | 8.7 | 5.2 | 18.3 |
| $15,000 to $17,499 | 8.3 | 25.8 | 7.0 | 20.4 | 9.5 | 30.7 | 6.1 | 18.6 | 4.6 | 13.3 | 8.4 | 26.7 |
| $17,500 to $19,999 | 7.1 | 32.9 | 5.8 | 26.2 | 8.4 | 39.1 | 5.0 | 23.6 | 3.6 | 16.9 | 7.2 | 33.9 |
| $20,000 to $22,499 | 8.9 | 41.8 | 9.4 | 35.6 | 8.4 | 47.5 | 7.3 | 30.9 | 6.0 | 22.9 | 9.5 | 43.4 |
| $22,500 to $24,999 | 5.8 | 47.6 | 5 | 40.6 | 6.5 | 54 | 5 | 35.9 | 4.2 | 27.1 | 6.4 | 49.8 |

Table 15A

(continued)

## Total Money Earnings in 1994 of Persons 25 Years Old and Over, by Sex and Race

**NORTH AND WEST**

**YEAR-ROUND, FULL-TIME WORKERS**

| | Black | | | | | | Both | | White, not Hispanic | | | |
|---|---|---|---|---|---|---|---|---|---|---|---|---|
| | Sexes | Cumul.% | Male | Cumul.% | Female | Cumul.% | Sexes | Cumul.% | Male | Cumul.% | Female | Cumul.% |
| $25,000 to $29,999 | 13.5 | 61.1 | 12.5 | 53.1 | 14.6 | 68.6 | 11.5 | 47.4 | 10.3 | 37.4 | 13.4 | 63.2 |
| $30,000 to $34,999 | 10.4 | 71.5 | 10.2 | 63.3 | 10.7 | 79.3 | 10.2 | 57.6 | 10.1 | 47.5 | 10.5 | 73.7 |
| $35,000 to $39,999 | 7.9 | 79.4 | 8.7 | 72.0 | 7.2 | 86.5 | 8.8 | 66.4 | 9.7 | 57.2 | 7.3 | 81.0 |
| $40,000 to $44,999 | 5.9 | 85.3 | 7.2 | 79.2 | 4.7 | 91.2 | 7.8 | 74.2 | 8.8 | 66.0 | 6.2 | 87.2 |
| $45,000 to $49,999 | 3.8 | 89.1 | 5.3 | 84.5 | 2.3 | 93.5 | 5.2 | 79.4 | 6.1 | 72.1 | 3.8 | 91.0 |
| $50,000 to $59,999 | 5.1 | 94.2 | 7.9 | 92.4 | 2.4 | 95.9 | 7.5 | 86.9 | 9.8 | 81.9 | 3.8 | 94.8 |
| $60,000 to $74,999 | 3.3 | 97.5 | 4.6 | 97.0 | 2.0 | 97.9 | 5.6 | 92.5 | 7.4 | 89.3 | 2.7 | 97.5 |
| $75,000 and over | 2.5 | 100.0 | 2.9 | 99.9 | 2.1 | 100.0 | 7.5 | 100.0 | 10.7 | 100.0 | 2.4 | 99.9 |
| Median earnings ($'s) | 25,740 | | 28,082 | | 23,479 | | 30,899 | | 35,899 | | 25,053 | |
| Standard error ($'s) | 375 | | 969 | | 697 | | 125 | | 169 | | 189 | |

**White-Black Ratios**
**Median Earnings**

| Both Sexes | Male | Female |
|---|---|---|
| 1.20 | 1.28 | 1.07 |

**Male-Female Ratios**
**Median Earnings**

| Black | White, Not Hispanic |
|---|---|
| 1.20 | 1.43 |

Blacks and whites who acquire additional years of education significantly increase their earnings. For blacks, the earnings difference between a worker without a high school diploma and an employed high school graduate is $4,737, while for whites the difference amounts to $6,441. Between high school graduates and college graduates (including those who have completed more than a bachelor's degree) the difference is even greater, roughly $15,000 for blacks and $16,000 for whites. As would be expected, the earnings gap between those with a bachelor's degree or more and those without a high school diploma is the most pronounced at $19,731 and $22,495 for blacks and whites, respectively.

Black women and white men who are high school graduates receive the greatest earnings premiums for that credential — white male high school graduates earn $8,493 more than white men without a high school diploma, and black women earn $5,155 more, a 58 percent increase in earnings over black women who have not completed high school.

Table 16

**TOTAL MONEY EARNINGS IN 1994 OF PERSONS
25 YEARS AND OVER, BY EDUCATIONAL ATTAINMENT,
RACE, SEX, AND REGION**

**ALL PERSONS (MEDIAN EARNINGS)**

**UNITED STATES**

|  | Not A High School Graduate | High School Graduate | B.A. Degree Or More |
|---|---|---|---|
| **Black** |  |  |  |
| Both Sexes | $11,455 | $16,192 | $31,186 |
| Males | $14,574 | $18,926 | $32,911 |
| Females | $8,938 | $14,093 | $30,346 |
| | | | |
| White, non Hispanic |  |  |  |
| Both Sexes | $13,275 | $19,766 | $35,770 |
| Males | $17,436 | $25,929 | $42,902 |
| Females | $9,239 | $14,128 | $27,488 |

Relative to less educated blacks, more educated blacks earn higher incomes. However, the returns that white males, in particular, receive for additional education are significantly greater than the returns to education for blacks. Consequently, increases in education do little to close the earnings gaps between blacks and whites. The white-to-black median earnings ratio for those with a high school diploma is 1.16 — for every dollar blacks earn, whites earn a $1.16. For males the ratio is a little higher at 1.20. Among high school graduates, the white-to-black ratio actually *increases* to 1.22. Stated differently, blacks without a high school degree earn 86 percent of what whites earn with the same level of education. Black high school graduates earn 82 percent of what white high school graduates earn. Among males, the gap is even wider — for every dollar earned by white males without a high school degree, similarly educated black males earn 84 cents. For every dollar white male high school graduates earn, black male graduates earn 74 cents.

Black male high school graduates earn only $1,490 a year more than white males without a high school diploma. The additional years of schooling acquired by blacks in that case increased earnings to just $124 a month, or $31 a week, or, over the course of a 40-hour work week, just 78 cents per hour. Black males with a bachelor's degree or more earn only $6,982 more annually than white males with only a high school diploma. Similarly, that credential for blacks results in increased earnings of $581 a month, or $145 a week, or, over a 40-hour work week, $3.63 an hour.

Table 17

## TOTAL MONEY EARNINGS IN 1994 OF PERSONS
## 25 YEARS OLD AND OVER, BY EDUCATIONAL ATTAINMENT,
## SEX AND RACE

### YEAR-ROUND, FULL-TIME WORKERS
### MEDIAN EARNINGS

**UNITED STATES**

| | Not a H.S. Graduate | High School Graduate | B.A. Degree or More |
|---|---|---|---|
| **Blacks** | | | |
| Both Sexes | $16,523 | $20,023 | $33,899 |
| Males | $19,941 | $22,028 | $36,072 |
| Females | $13,949 | $17,754 | $31,890 |
| **Whites** | | | |
| Both Sexes | $19,808 | $24,806 | $41,475 |
| Males | $22,466 | $29,321 | $48,591 |
| Females | $14,928 | $20,039 | $33,720 |

## V. Policy Recommendations

We offer four broad categories of policy recommendations to improve economic opportunity and labor market outcomes for black Americans: (1) supply-side policies to enhance the human capital of current and future workers and their ability to achieve more favorable labor market outcomes, (2) demand-side policies to stimulate the creation of employment opportunities, (3) policies which match labor supply and demand, and (4) policies to make work pay.

### A. Supply-Side Policies

### (1) "First Chance" Investments in Education

"First chance" investments in education that begin in early childhood and continue through young adulthood are the most effective means to develop human capital. Public school systems should be reformed so that basic competencies are taught more effectively and mastered by a larger proportion of graduating students. Increased parental involvement, effective professional leadership, safe and secure learning environments, high teacher expectations for all students, and increased resources are essential components of educational reform.

In school districts with disproportionately high drop-out rates or where students are otherwise "at risk," intensive tutoring, remedial education, mentoring, and after-school programs should be developed, supported, and expanded to improve academic performance and reduce drop-out rates. Innovative programmatic models exist. For example, the Quantum Opportunities Program, initially funded by the Ford Foundation, combined adult mentors and tutors, life-skills training, community service, stipends, and financial bonuses toward college or post-secondary training. *It increased the high school graduation rate of participating students from low-income families by 20 percentage points over a randomly selected control group.* (Hahn, 1994)

Innovative school-to-work programs which start in the ninth or tenth grade have also demonstrated that they can successfully reach at-risk students. (Pauly, Kopp, and Haimson, 1994) These programs come in various guises: career academies, occupational-academic clusters, restructured vocational education, tech preps, and youth apprenticeships. The common elements of successful school-to-work programs are the integration of academic and vocational learning, workplace experience, and extra support for students. The number of school-to-work programs should be greatly expanded. Unfortunately, the School-To-Work Opportunities Act passed by Congress two years ago — which has provided $320 million — is now threatened with repeal. Additional resources should be provided for the curriculum planning and student support services required by successful school-to-work programs. Although widespread employer involvement remains a major challenge, the potential payoffs are great: education directly relevant to the world of work, and early, positive connection and exposure to the job market.

It is absolutely essential that teen-agers graduate from high school. Future earnings and economic self-sufficiency are much higher for those who graduate than for those who drop out. For example, high school drop-outs ages 25 to 34 are three times more likely to be on public assistance than high-school graduates who have not gone to college — 17 percent compared with six percent. *Among 25- to 34-year-old black Americans, 36 percent of those who have completed 9 to 11 years of school receive public assistance, compared with 13 percent of those with high school diplomas.* (U.S. Department of Education, 1995)

Finally, the geographic concentration of lower-income blacks continues to impose fiscal constraints on many locally financed public school systems. Consequently, economically disadvantaged black children will face increasingly formidable challenges as they attempt to secure the human capital required for future labor market success. Higher levels of government, mostly notably the states, should intervene to reduce the disparities in financial resources among school districts. (Levy, 1995)

### (2) "Second Chance" Investments in Employment Training

Unfortunately, the results of more than three decades of "second chance" investments in employment training to assist the poor and disadvantaged have been quite disappointing. (Grubb, 1996; Orr et al, 1996) They have generally been low-cost, low-intensity programs of limited duration that have not produced much skill upgrading. Although the programs have typically resulted in modest earnings increases of a few hundred dollars a year — which have tended to decay over time — they have been worthwhile to the extent that the benefits have exceeded the even more modest program expenditures. Furthermore, the observed annual earnings gains have, in large measure, been due to increases in hours worked, rather than increases in the hourly wage rate of the participants' post-program jobs.

The federal government's largest initiative, the Job Training Partnership Act (JTPA), funds a variety of programs for economically disadvantaged adults and out-of-school youths, including classroom training in occupational skills, on-the-job training, job-search assistance, basic education, and work experience in temporary entry-level jobs. A recent evaluation of JTPA programs found program-induced gains for adults of $900 per year in earnings. Every $1.00 invested returned $1.50 in earnings gains to enrollees. The programs were more effective for adult women than men, and were largely ineffective for youths. (Orr et al, 1996)

There are successful program models for adults. For example, the Center for Employment Training (CET) in San Jose, California, has produced above average earnings gains for enrollees. (Orr et al, 1996) CET is a moderately intensive program in which education is integrated into skills training to make it more relevant and less intimidating to those who have previously not succeeded in the classroom. Training is connected to the local labor market through close working relationships with local employers, who are involved in training design, instruction, and the placement of graduates.

It is difficult to find successful employment training program models for out-of-school youths. In our view, the absence of any proven initiatives indicates that this population has significantly different service needs requiring a more intensive, holistic approach focused on building self-esteem, motivation, and responsibility, as well as academic, vocational, and job-seeking skills.

The challenge is to improve the effectiveness of job training programs, not abolish them. The U.S. Department of Labor spends $4.5 billion per year on employment and training programs for the disadvantaged, mostly through the JTPA. It is a rather limited federal commitment. Of the 25 million persons aged 16 to 55 eligible for targeted programs only 700,000 (3 percent) are served each year, excluding the summer jobs program. Funding should be increased with greater emphasis on integrating academic and vocational education and training programs into a continuous system of life-long learning opportunities — community colleges should play a major role. (Grubb, 1996) More resource-intensive and comprehensive demonstration programs for out-of-school youths should be funded to determine cost-effective ways to improve their earnings prospects.
Employment training programs should stress "hard" skills — literary, numeracy, and specific technical expertise — as well as "soft" skills — people skills, demeanor, work attitude, and the ability to interact with customers and co-workers. They should help enrollees develop the code-switching skills needed to bridge the cultural divide that often exists between employers and potential employees. (Holzer, 1996 b, c; Moss and Tilly, 1995 a, b, c) Finally, while efforts should be made to improve the effectiveness of training programs for out-of-school youths and adults, they will undoubtedly be very expensive. A reasonable alternative to devoting large amounts of scarce public resources to "training" these individuals, which may also prove to be more efficient, would be to provide employers with incentives to hire them at prevailing wages and supplement their work efforts through the Earned Income Tax Credit, which is discussed in more detail below. (Blank, 1994; Heckman, 1994; Katz, 1994)

### (3) Health Insurance and Child Care Services

A reformed health insurance system with greater coverage and more flexibility that permits workers to change jobs without sacrificing benefits would improve labor market outcomes. It would also eliminate a significant disincentive for public assistance recipients to enter the labor market — the loss of Medicaid benefits.

There are over 40 separate federal expenditure- and tax-based programs providing some form of child care-related assistance. The most visible program, Head Start, serves forty percent of eligible 4-year-olds and less than 20 percent of eligible 2-year-olds. (U.S. Department of Education, 1995) It should be improved and expanded to provide places for all eligible children. However, the largest program — accounting for over half of all federal spending — is the Child and Dependent Care Tax Credit. Parents with taxable earnings may deduct up to $4,800 from their federal income taxes. Currently, only one-fourth of the benefits accrue to the bottom half of the income distribution — many lower-income households have very limited tax liability. (Robins, 1995) The credit should be made refundable and more progressive by increasing its value for low-income families and gradually phasing out or capping it for those with higher incomes.

### B. Demand-Side Policies

### (1) Tight Labor Markets

*Tight labor markets with relatively low unemployment rates sustained over time are a necessary, but not sufficient, condition for improved employment prospects and earnings trajectories for black Americans.* Macroeconomic monetary and fiscal policies should foster the rapid private-sector job growth needed to drive up the demand for labor. (Blank, 1994; Bound and Freeman, 1992) All other things being equal, employers tend to be less selective when labor markets are tight. They are compelled by economic necessity to hire even those workers who stand at the end of the hiring queue, where black men and women are disproportionately situated. (Holzer, 1994; Moss and Tilly, 1991)

### (2) Direct Job Creation

There is a shortage of available jobs in central cities for unemployed workers with no more than a high school education. (Holzer, 1996 c; Newman and Lennon, 1995) This imbalance will be exacerbated by welfare reform initiatives with mandated work requirements. Even with growth-oriented macroeconomic policies, direct job creation will be required to expand opportunities for workers with limited academic credentials and skills. Subsidized employment in the private sector and public-service employment are two proven strategies that productively employ the least skilled and minimally educated.

Private-sector employment growth could be accelerated through federal wage subsidies paid to private employers for some or all of the net new jobs created over the course of a year. The New Jobs Tax Credit (NJTC), a two-year program enacted as part of the 1977 economic stimulus package, did precisely that by providing a tax credit equal to 50 percent of the first $6,000 in wages paid to new workers that increased a firm's total employment. Because the subsidy accounted for a higher proportion of the wages of less-skilled workers, it provided an incentive for firms to hire that segment of the labor force. An evaluation of the credit showed that it created jobs for low-skilled workers at relatively low cost. (Haveman and Scholz, 1994; Perloff and Wachter, 1979)

Some variant of a NJTC should be enacted to influence firms' incremental hiring decisions. It is less costly to subsidize private-sector employment growth for the less-skilled than to create public-service employment; furthermore, the experience and skill gained in private-sector jobs may be more favorably received by future employers than that gained in public-service employment. Despite its higher cost, public-service employment has the advantage of high-target efficiency — very specific groups of individuals can be assisted — and workers can be deployed to meet specific public infrastructure needs. *Both types of direct job creation should be implemented.*

### *(3) Direct Job Creation in Community Development Corporations and Black-Owned Businesses*

Non-profit community development corporations (CDCs) and black-owned businesses provide additional opportunities, albeit quite modest relative to needs, to create jobs for black Americans — there are 350,000 paid employees of black-owned firms, compared to more than 13 million employed blacks and 1.5 million who are unemployed. (U.S. Bureau of the Census, 1996) CDCs and black-business development should be supported for the economic opportunities and other benefits they offer to black communities. Recent research unequivocally documents that black-owned firms hire black employees at a greater rate than other firms. (Bates, 1994) Nonetheless, the success of black businesses and their ability to provide employment for blacks — whom they overwhelmingly hire even when the firms are not located in black communities — would be enhanced if: (1) policies which attempt to combine community and business development incentives were more flexible regarding where black-owned firms should locate; and (2) more attention was paid to a firm's capital requirements, potential viability, and access to markets with effective demand. (Bates, 1995)

### (4) Antidiscrimination and Affirmative Action Enforcement

For three decades the federal government has pursued — with varying degrees of enthusiasm — a two-part antidiscrimination and affirmative action strategy: (1) beginning with the Civil Rights Act of 1964, legislation has made it illegal for employers to discriminate in the hiring, compensation, and promotion of minorities and women; and (2) executive orders have mandated that federal contractors undertake affirmative actions to hire minorities and women. This strategy was intended to remedy the systematic exclusion of talented individuals based on race and gender — to compensate for opportunities denied. (Hacker, 1996; Patterson, 1995) *During the 1960s and 1970s this strategy raised the relative employment, earnings, and occupational status of minorities and women;* unfortunately, in the following decade, federal enforcement efforts were quite limited. (Leonard, 1990, 1996) Relative to the 1980s, enforcement has increased in recent years.

These programs contributed significantly to the integration of the American workplace and to the growth of the black middle-class; debates continue on the degree to which they have imposed costs on whites and blacks. The courts and public opinion have not been kind to these initiatives in recent years. These realities notwithstanding, there is still a clear need, in our view, for aggressive antidiscrimination and affirmative action enforcement with an emphasis on class-action hiring and promotion cases. (Holzer, 1996 a)

Significant disparities exist in employment and earnings by race and gender, even after controlling for observable differences in individual characteristics and jobs. (Bernstein, 1995; Bound and Freeman, 1992; Juhn, Murphy, and Pierce, 1993) While unobservable skill differentials may account for some of the disparities, discrimination undoubtedly plays a role. Direct evidence of discrimination comes from two sources: (1) labor market audits and (2) interviews with employers. In the audits, pairs of white and black job applicants matched on all relevant characteristics — such as education and work experience — were sent to seek employment offers. The black applicants had a lower probability of receiving an offer. (Fix and Struyk, 1993) *Interviews with employers in a number of metropolitan areas have documented their very negative perceptions of black workers, especially black men.* Black applicants, unlike their white counterparts, are compelled to find ways to signal to potential employers that racial stereotypes do not apply to them. (Holzer, 1996 a, c; Kirschenman, Moss, and Tilly, 1995; Kirschenman and Neckerman, 1991; Moss and Tilly, 1995 a; Neckerman and Kirschenman, 1991)

External pressure must continue to be applied to spur employers to reduce discrimination and take affirmative steps to integrate their workplaces. The words Justice Blackmun wrote over 20 years ago in the *Bakke* decision remain true today, "to get beyond racism, we must first take account of race." (Hacker, 1996)

## C. Matching Supply and Demand

### (1) Making Connections

A legacy of systematic exclusion, discrimination, and residential isolation has severely limited black Americans' access to the informal networks — the social capital — that are so critical to labor market success. If black labor force participants are to have greater success in the labor market, the public sector and non-profit intermediary organizations must assist black job seekers in making connections to opportunities in the mainstream economies of metropolitan areas. This is especially true in central cities. (Wilson, 1987)

The public sector needs to invest the resources required to provide timely, high-quality labor market information to employers and job seekers. The information barrier is one of the key factors perpetuating the reproduction of existing labor force relationships that consistently disadvantage black Americans. For example, local or state government agencies, after consultation with employers and those most familiar with specific entry-level job tasks and requirements, should certify the work skills of young workers. This would appreciably reduce the search costs and "uncertainties" that firms argue they face when they hire young black workers. It also has the potential to reduce the statistical discrimination — the use of group racial characteristics to predict individual productivity — some employers use as a screening device in the hiring process. (Holzer, 1996 b,c; Katz, 1994; Moss and Tilly, 1995 a)

Along with the public-sector, non-profit community development corporations and other locally-based organizations could perform an important job matching function for residents of their communities, using the labor market information, government work-skills certification, local knowledge, and relationships they have developed with employers throughout metropolitan areas. Non-profits could function as labor market intermediaries and clearinghouses for job seekers and potential employers. They could recruit workers, provide job search assistance directly or through referrals, and build bridges to link job seekers to the larger economy. (Harrison, 1995)

Improving connections will also require overcoming transportation barriers between central cities and surrounding suburban areas. Mobility strategies must compensate for truncated public transportation systems and lower rates of automobile ownership among central-city workers. The extension of public transit, particularly bus routes, will undoubtedly be required to access suburban employment sites. With tight labor markets, more flexible types of transportation, such as minibuses, van pools, and ride-sharing arrangements, may be effective ways to increase workers' mobility. Here, too, there is a role for community-based organizations, especially those interested in revenue-generating enterprise development. Local market conditions are likely to dictate that subsidies from the public and private sectors will be required. (Hughes, 1995)

### (2) Residential Mobility

As blacks have remained concentrated in central cities and jobs have decentralized throughout metropolitan areas — especially in manufacturing and retail and wholesale trade — a spatial mismatch has developed. (Holzer, 1991; Holzer and Ihlanfeldt, 1996; Kain, 1992) The central-city supply of black labor has not benefited from the growing suburban labor market demand. Housing discrimination has generated a pattern of residential segregation that has limited blacks' residential choices, and inadequate public transportation and low rates of automobile ownership have constrained adjustments in commuting patterns. *The interaction of race and space has produced a geography of economic opportunity in metropolitan areas that severely compromises the labor-market opportunities of black Americans.* Although there is significant debate on the extent of the spatial mismatch, there is consensus that where the labor supply resides and where jobs are located impacts blacks more than whites.

Aggressive government actions are required to enhance black residential choice and reduce the locational barriers to economic opportunity. Federal, state, and local fair-housing laws should be enforced. New public and publicly assisted housing should be scattered throughout metropolitan areas and meaningful affirmative marketing efforts undertaken. To the extent that they expand and improve the locational choices of blacks, especially those of limited means, greater use should be made of federal rental housing vouchers. (Rosenbaum and Popkin, 1991) Exclusionary suburban land-use practices, such as large-lot zoning and bans on multi-family housing, should be challenged. And, the Community Reinvestment Act and Home Mortgage Disclosure Act should be actively utilized by federal regulators to increase the flow of mortgage funds to black home buyers.

### D. Making Work Pay

### (1) Earned Income Tax Credit

The Earned Income Tax Credit (EITC) was created in 1975 during the Ford administration and has been expanded during the Reagan, Bush, and Clinton administrations. President Reagan described it as "the best anti-poverty, the best pro-family, the best job creation measure to come out of Congress." (Bluestone and Ghilarducci, 1996)

The EITC is a refundable tax credit, conditioned on work effort, available to low-income working parents with children. If the credit due exceeds a worker's tax liability, a refund check for the difference is mailed to the taxpayer. In 1996, an eligible worker will receive a 40 percent wage subsidy on the first $8,900 in earnings (a maximum benefit of over $3,500), which will be gradually phased out by the time earnings reach $28,000. (U.S. General Accounting Office, 1995) This has a significant impact on returns to work; for example, with the credit the hourly wage of a worker with more than one child employed at the current minimum of $4.25 would increase to $5.95. (Burkhauser, Couch, and Glenn, 1995) The EITC has a high target efficiency (a high proportion of benefits go to poor workers with children); a high level of participation (over 80 percent of eligible workers receive the credit); and it increases labor force participation. (Bluestone and Ghilarducci, 1996; Eissa and Liebman, 1996; Scholz, 1994)

*The major expansion of the EITC in 1993 is one of the Clinton administration's most important pieces of social legislation.* It greatly increased the benefits to working parents and, for the first time, extended very limited benefits to poor workers without children.

In dollar terms, the EITC is a relatively expensive program for taxpayers — it costs the federal government 1.7 times as much as Aid to Families with Dependent Children. (Eissa and Liebman, 1996) As Congress has broadened coverage and increased the size of the credit, the cost of the program has risen rapidly to $25 billion this year; it is projected to grow to $30 billion by the year 2000. (U.S. General Accounting Office, 1995) The program is currently under assault by a Congress that is unwilling to confront the costs of assisting a significant proportion of the working poor.

The trend in declining real wages for many of the less-skilled and less-credentialed workers, a disproportionate number of whom are black, is likely to continue. The impacts of this structural economic problem should be cushioned by the periodic expansion of the EITC to working parents, as well as to other poor workers.

## *(2) Minimum Wage*

The EITC and the minimum wage are complementary policies to make work pay for those at the bottom of wage distribution. In May, the House of Representatives voted to increase the minimum wage in two steps from $4.25 to $5.15 per hour, the first increase in six years. On July 9, the Senate followed suit; at the writing of this chapter, a House-Senate conference must convene to reconcile a few remaining differences between the two bills. The real purchasing power of the minimum wage had reached nearly a 40-year low, and the recently approved increase will not make up for the inflation of the 1980s. (Greenstein, 1996) Nevertheless, it will raise the annual earnings of a full-time minimum wage worker from $8,500 to $10,300, and will help address the growth in wage inequality, especially among women. (Mishel, Bernstein, and Rosell, 1995)

While the focus of the recent Congressional debate was, as always, on the potential negative employment effects of an increase in the minimum wage, the weight of recent evidence indicates that the effects of a moderate increase could be positive or negative but, undoubtedly, will be very small. (Card and Krueger, 1995) What is unambiguous, however, is that 40 percent of minimum wage employees are the sole wage earner in their households, two-thirds of the teenagers earning minimum wages reside in households with below-average incomes, nearly 60 percent of minimum wage workers are women, and a disproportionate number, 15 percent, are black. The increase in the minimum wage will directly increase the earnings of more than 12 million workers, including nearly two million black Americans. (Mishel, Bernstein, and Rosell, 1995) Assuming the House-Senate conferees agree on a minimum wage bill in the coming weeks, it will be only the second increase approved in the past 15 years. In the future, the minimum wage should be increased on a far more regular basis.

## CONCLUSION
Although the federal budget deficit and lack of political consensus constrain action, we believe that these policies should be implemented to improve economic opportunity and labor market outcomes for blacks. Implementing them will also improve the economic circumstances of millions of other American workers. The needs are clear. Addressing them as we have suggested is a matter of national priorities and political will.

# REFERENCES

Addison, John T., Douglas A. Fox, and Christopher J. Ruhm. 1995. "Trade Displacement in Manufacturing": Monthly Labor Review, No. 4, April, pp. 58-67.

American Federation of Labor and Congress of Industrial Organizations, Department of Economic Research. 1996. "America Needs A Raise": Washington, D.C.: AFL-CIO.

Badgett, Lee, and Rhonda M. Williams. 1994. "The Changing Contours of Discrimination: Race, Gender, and Structure Economic Change" in M. Bernstein and D. Adler eds. Understanding American Economic Decline, Cambridge: Cambridge University Press.

Baker, Dean, and Lawrence Mischel. 1995. "Profits Up, Wages Down: Worker Losses Yield Big Gains For Business": Briefing Paper. Washington, D.C.: Economic Policy Institute.

Bates, Timothy. 1994. "Utilization of Minority Employees in Small Business: A Comparison of Nonminority and Black-Owned Urban Enterprises". Review of Black Political Economy 23: 113-21.

Bates, Timothy. 1995. "Why Do Minority Business Development Programs Generate So Little Minority Business Development?" Economic Development Quarterly 9: 3-14.

Bergmann, Barbara R. 1996. In Defense of Affirmative Action. New York: Basic Books.

Bernstein, Jared. 1995. "Where's the Payoff? The Gap Between Black Academic Progress and Economic Gains. Washington, D.C.": Economic Policy Institute.

Blank, Rebecca M. 1990. "Are Part-Time Jobs Bad Jobs?" In G. Burtless ed. A Future of Lousy Jobs: The Changing Structure of U.S. Wages, Washington, D.C.: Brookings Institution.

Blank, Rebecca M. 1994. "The Employment Strategy: Public Policies to Increase Work and Earnings." In Sheldon H. Danziger, Gary D. Sandefur, and Daniel H. Weinberg, eds. Confronting Poverty: Prescriptions for Change. Cambridge: Harvard University Press.

Blau, Francine, and Andrea H. Beller. 1992. "Black-White Earnings Over the

1970's and 1980's: Gender Differences in Trends." Review of Economics and Statistics. May.

Bluestone, Barry, and Teresa Ghilarducci. 1996. "Rewarding Work: Feasible Antipoverty Policy." The American Prospect, no. 26, pp. 40-46.

Bound, John, and Richard B. Freeman. 1992. "What Went Wrong? The Erosion of the Relative Earnings and Employment Among Young Black Men in the 1980s." Quarterly Journal of Economics 107: 201-32.

Burkhauser, Richard V. Kenneth A. Couch, and Andrew J. Glenn. 1995. "Public Policies for the Working Poor: The Earned Income Tax Credit versus Minimum Wage Legislation." Discussion Paper 1074-95. Madison: Institute for Research on Poverty.

Burstein, Paul, ed. 1994. Equal Employment Opportunity: Labor Market Discrimination and Public Policy. New York: Walter De Gruyter.

Burtless, Gary, ed. 1990. A Future of Lousy Jobs: The Changing Structure of U.S. Wages, Washington, D.C.: Brookings Institution.

Card, David, and Alan B. Krueger. 1995. Myth and Measurement: The New Economics of the Minimum Wage. Princeton: Princeton University Press.

Carnoy, Martin. 1994. Faded Dreams: The Politics and Economics of Race in America. Cambridge: Cambridge University Press.

Danziger, Sheldon, and Peter Gottschalk, ed. 1993. Uneven Tides: Rising Inequality in America, New York: Russell Sage Foundation.

Dzialo, Mary. 1993. "Labor Markets on Atlantic and Pacific Coasts Hit Hard in Early 1990s." Monthly Labor Review No.2, February.

Eissa, Nada, and Jeffrey B. Liebman. 1996. "Labor Supply Response to the Earned Income Tax Credit." Quarterly Journal of Economics 111: 605-37.

Fix, Michael, and Raymond J. Struyk, eds. 1993. Clear and Convincing Evidence: Measurement of Discrimination in America. Washington, D.C.: Urban Institute Press.

Frazis, Harley J., Diane Herz, and Michael W. Horrigan. 1995. "Employer-Provided Training: Results from a New Survey," Monthly Labor Review No. 5, May.

pps. 3-17.

Fullerton, Howard N., Jr. 1993. "Another Look At the Labor Force." Monthly Labor Review, No. 11, November.

Gardner, Jennifer M. 1994. "The 1990-91 Recessions: How Bad Was the Labor Market?" Monthly Labor Review, No. 6, June. pps. 3-11.

Gardner, Jennifer M. 1995. "Worker Displacement: A Decade of Change." Monthly Labor Review, No. 4, April. pps. 45-57.

Gittleman, Maury, and Mary Joyce. 1995. "Earnings Mobility in the United States, 1967-91": Monthly Labor Review, No. 9, September. pps.3-13.

Greenstein, Robert. 1996. "Raising Families with a Full-Time Worker Out of Poverty: The Role of an Increase in the Minimum Wage." Washington, D.C.: Center on Budget and Policy Priorities.

Grubb, W. Norton. 1996. Learning to Work: The Case for Reintegrating Job Training and Education. New York: Russell Sage Foundation.

Hacker, Andrew. 1996. "Goodbye to Affirmative Action?" New York Review of Books, 11 July, pp. 21-29.

Hacker, Andrew. 1995. Two Nations: Black and White, Separate, Hostile, Unequal, New York: Ballatine Books.

Hahn, Andrew. 1994. "Evaluation of the Quantum Opportunities Program (QUOP): Did the Program Work?" Waltham: Brandeis University.

Hammonds, Keith H., Wendy Zellner, and Richard Melcher. 1996. "Writing and New Social Contract": Cover Story, Business Week, 11 March. pps. 60-61.

Harrison, Bennett. 1995. "Building Bridges: Community Development Corporations and the World of Employment Training." New York: Ford Foundation.

Haveman, Robert H., and John Karl Scholz. 1994. "The Clinton Welfare Reform Plan: Will It End Poverty As We Know It?" Discussion Paper 1037-94. Madison: Institute for Research on Poverty.

Hecker, Daniel E. 1995. "Earnings of College Graduates," 1993. Monthly Labor Review, No. 12, December. pp. 3-17.

Hecker, Daniel E. 1995. "Further Analyses of the Labor Market for College Graduates": Monthly Labor Review, No. 2, February. pp. 39-41.

Hecker, Daniel E. 1992. "Reconciling Conflicting Data On Jobs for College Graduates," Monthly Labor Review, No. 12, December.

Heckman, James J. 1994. Commentary: Active Labor Market Policies to Expand Employment and Opportunity. In Reducing Unemployment: Current Issues and Policy Options. Symposium sponsored by the Federal Revenue Bank of Kansas City, Missouri, pp. 291-311.

Holzer, Harry J. 1994. "Black Employment Problems: New Evidence, Old Questions." Journal of Policy Analysis and Management 13: 699-732.

Holzer, Harry J. 1996 (a). "Employer Hiring Decisions and Antidiscrimination Policy. Discussion Paper 1085-96. Madison: Institute for Research on Poverty.

Holzer, Harry J. 1996 (b). "Employer Skill Needs and Labor Market Outcomes by Race and Gender." Discussion Paper 1087-96. Madison: Institute for Research on Poverty.

Holzer, Harry J. 1991. " The Spatial Mismatch Hypothesis: What Has the Evidence Shown?" Urban Studies 25: 105-22.

Holzer, Harry J. 1996 (c). What Employers Want: Job Prospects for Less-Educated Workers. New York: Russell Sage Foundation.

Holzer, Harry J., and Keith R. Ihlanfeldt. 1996. "Spatial Factors and the Employment of Blacks at the Firm Level." Discussion Paper 1086-96. Madison: Institute for Research on Poverty.

Hughes, Mark Alan. 1995. "A Mobility Strategy for Improving Opportunity." Housing Policy Debate 6: 271-97.

Ilg, Randy E. 1992 "Long-Term Unemployment In Recent Recessions." Monthly Labor Review, No.6, June. pps.12-13.

Jacobsen, Joyce P., and Laurence M. Levin. 1995. "Effects of Intermittent Labor Force Attachment of Women's Earnings." Monthly Labor Review, No. 9, September. pp.14-19.

Jeffries, John M., and Randall E. Brock. 1996. <u>Barriers to Employment and Entre-</u>
<u>preneurship in Battle Creek, Michigan: A Report to The Kellogg Foundation</u>. Co-
lumbia University.

Jeffries, John M. 1996. <u>Expanding the Supply of Family Day Care in Upper Man-</u>
<u>hattan: Issues, Considerations, and Recommendations</u>. Columbia University:
Empowerment Zone Monitoring and Assistance Project.

Juhn, Chinhui, Kevin M. Murphy, and Brooks Pierce. 1993. "Wage Inequality and
the Rise in Returns to Skill." <u>Journal of Political Economy</u> 101: 410-42.

Kain, John F. 1992. "The Spatial Mismatch Hypothesis: Three Decades Later."
<u>Housing Policy Debate</u> 3: 371-460.

Karoly, Lynn. 1993. "The Trend in Inequality Among Families: Individuals, and
Workers in the United States" in S. Danziger and P. Gottschalk, eds. <u>Uneven Tides:</u>
<u>Rising Inequality in America</u>. New York: Russell Sage Foundation.

Katz, Lawrence F. 1994: "Active Labor Market Policies to Expand Employment
and Opportunity." In <u>Reducing Unemployment: Current Issues and Policy Op-</u>
<u>tions</u>. Symposium sponsored by the Federal Reserve Bank of Kansas City, Mis-
souri, pp. 239-90.

Katz, Lawrence F., and Kevin M. Murphy. 1992. "Changed in Relative Wages,
1963-87: Supply and Demand Factors." <u>The Quarterly Journal of Economics</u>. February.

King, Mary C. 1992. "Occupational Segregation by Race and Sex, 1940-88."
<u>Monthly Labor Review</u>, No. 4, April.

Kirschenman, Joleen, Philip Moss, and Chris Tilly. 1995. "Employer Screening
Methods and Racial Exclusion: Evidence from New In-Depth Interviews with
Employers." Working Paper. New York: Russell Sage Foundation.

Kirschenman, Joleen, and Kathryn M. Neckeman. 1991. "We'd Love to Hire Them,
But ...": The Meaning of Race for Employers. In Christopher Jencks and Paul E.
Peterson, eds. <u>The Urban Underclass</u>, Washington, D.C.: Brookings Institution.

Leonard, Jonathan S. 1990. "The Impact of Affirmative Action Regulation and
Equal Employment Law on Black Employment." <u>Journal of Economic Perspec-</u>
<u>tives</u> 4: 47-63.

Leonard, Jonathan S. 1996. "Wage Disparities and Affirmative Action in the 1980's." American Economic Review Papers and Proceedings 86: 285-89.

Levy, Frank, 1995. "The Future Path and Consequences of the U.S. Earnings Gap." Federal Reserve Bank of New York Economic Policy Review 1: 35-41.

Levy, Frank, and Richard J. Murnane. 1992. "U.S. Earnings Levels and Earnings Inequality: A Review of Recent Trends and Proposed Explanations." Journal of Economic Literature.

Mandel, Michael J. 1996. "Is All That Angst Misplaced?" Business Week, 11 March, pp. 52-56.

McNamee, Mike, and Pul Magnussen. 1996. "Let's Get Growing," Cover Story, Business Week, 11 March, pp. 90-98.

Mishell, Lawrence, and Jared Bernstein. 1992. The Declining Wages for High School and College Graduates. Washington, D.C.: Economic Policy Institute.

Mishell, Lawrence, and Jared Bernstein. 1994. The State of Working America 1994-95. Armonk, New York: M.E. Sharpe.

Mishel, Lawrence, Jared Bernstein, and Edith Rosell. 1995. "Who Wins With A Higher Minimum Wage." Briefing Paper. Washington, D.C.: Economic Policy Institute.

Moss, Philip, and Chris Tilly. 1995 (a). "Raised Hurdles for Black Men: Evidence from Interviews with Employers." Working Paper. New York: Russell Sage Foundation.

Moss, Philip, and Chris Tilly. 1995 (b). "Skills and Race in Hiring: Quantitative Findings from Face-to-Face Interviews." Eastern Economic Journal 21: 357-74.

Moss, Philip, and Chris Tilly. 1995 (c). "Soft" Skills and Race: An Investigation of Black Men's Employment Problems. Working Paper 80. New York: Russell Sage Foundation.

Moss, Philip, and Chris Tilly. 1991. "Why Black Men Are Doing Worse in the Labor Market: A Review of Supply-Side and Demand-Side Explanations." New York: Social Science Research Council.

Neckerman, Kathryn M., and Joleen Kirschenman. 1991. "Hiring Strategies, Racial Bias, and Inner-City Workers." Social Problems 38: 433-47.

Newman, Katharine, and Chauncy Lennon. 1995. "The Job Ghetto." The American Prospect, no. 22, pp. 66-67.

O'Neill, June, and Solomon Polachek. 1993. "Why the Gender Gap in Wages Narrowed in the 1980s." Journal of Labor Economics.

Orr, Larry L., et al. 1996. Does Training for the Disadvantaged Work? Evidence from the National JTPA Study. Washington, D.C.: Urban Institute Press.

Patterson, Orlando. 1995. "Affirmative Action, On the Merit System." New York Times, 7 August, p. A13.

Pauly, Edward, Hilary Kopp, and Joshua Haimson. 1994. "Home-Grown Lessons: Innovative Programs Linking Work and High School." New York: Manpower Demonstration Research Corporation.

Pennar, Karen, Susan B. Garland, and Elizabeth Roberts. 1996. Economic Anxiety. Business Week. 11 March, pp. 50-52.

Perloff, Jeffrey M., and Michael L. Wachter. 1979. "The New Jobs Tax Credit: An Evaluation of the 1977-78 Wage Subsidy Program." American Economic Review 69: 173-79.

Plunkert, Lois M., and Howard V. Hayghe. 1995. "Strong Employment Gains Continue in 1994." Monthly Labor Review, No. 2. February. pps. 3-17.

Roberts, Stephen V., Dorian Friedman, Debra Schwartz, and Jonathan Sapers. 1996. Workers Taking It On the Chin. U.S. News and World Report, 22 January, pp. 44-46.

Robins, Philip K. 1995. "Child Care Policy and Research: An Economist's Perspective." In David M. Blau, ed. The Economics of Child Care. New York: Russell Sage Foundation.

Rosenbaum, James, and Susan Popkin. 1991. "Employment and Earnings of Low-Income Blacks Who Move to Middle-Class Suburbs." In Christopher Jencks and Paul E. Peterson, eds. The Urban Underclass. Washington, D.C.: Brookings Institution.

Ryscavage, Paul. 1995. "A Surge In Growing Income Inequality." Monthly Labor Review, No. 8, August. pp. 51-61.

Saunders, Lisa. 1995. "Relative Earnings of Black Men to White Men By Region, Industry." Monthly Labor Review, No. 4, April. pp. 68-72.

Schafer, Tod and Jeff Faux, eds. 1996. Reclaiming Property: A Blueprint for Progressive Economic Reform. Armonk, New York: M.E. Sharpe.

Scholz, John Karl. 1994. "The Earned Income Tax Credit: Participation, Compliance, and Antipoverty Effectiveness": National Tax Journal 47: 63-87.

Singleton, Christopher J.. 1993. "Industry Employment and the 1990-91 Recession": Monthly Labor Review, No.7, July. pp. 15-25.

Tomaskovic-Devy, Donald. 1993. Gender and Racial Inequality at Work: The Sources and Consequences of Job Segregation. Ithaca: Industrial Labor Relations Press.

Tyler, John, Richard J. Murnane, and Frank Levy. 1995. "Are More College Graduates Really Taking 'High School' Jobs?" Monthly Labor Review, No. 12, December. pps.18-28.

U.S. Bureau of the Census. 1996. 1992 Economic Census: Survey of Minority-Owned Business Enterprises - Black. Washington, D.C.: Government Printing Office.

U.S. Department of Education, National Center for Education Statistics. 1995. The Condition of Education, 1995. Washington, D.C.: Government Printing Office.

U.S. General Accounting Office. 1995. Earned Income Credit: Targeting to the Working Poor. Washington, D.C: Government Printing Office.

Warner, Joan. 1996. Clinging to the Safety Net. Business Week, 11 March, p.62.

Wiatrowski, William J. 1995. Who Really Has Access to Employer-Provided Health Insurance Monthly Labor Review, No. 6, June. pp. 36-44.

Wilson, William Julius. 1987. The Truly Disadvantaged. Chicago: University of Chicago Press.

# BIOGRAPHICAL SKETCHES

John M. Jeffries is director of the Neighborhood Economic Development, Public Safety and Justice program at the Vera Institute of Justice in New York City. He has been Dean of the Graduate School of Management and Urban Policy at the New School for Social Research and a Visiting Associate professor of Urban Planning and Associate Director of the Empowerment Zone Monitoring Project at Columbia University.

Richard L. Schaffer is Visiting Professor of Urban Planning and Director of the Empowerment Zone Monitoring and Assistance Project at Columbia University, and former Chairman of the New York City Planning Commission. He has served as Dean of the Graduate School of Management and Urban Policy at the New School for Social Research, Chairman of the Division of Urban Planning and Historic Preservation and Vice Dean of the Graduate School of Architecture and Planning at Columbia University, and Vice President of the Bedford-Stuyvesant Restoration Corporation.

# CRIME AND JUSTICE IN BLACK AMERICA

by
Christopher E. Stone

# ABSTRACT

Black Americans face a paradox when it comes to crime and justice. Black Americans suffer disproportionately from most crime, yet when blacks and whites join forces to fight crime, the injustices felt in black communities at the hands of the criminal justice system are often either ignored or discounted by the larger population.

Escaping this paradox requires candor about the scope of the crime problem in black America. There is good news here, as serious crime is falling in most major cities; but the levels of black victimization and black crime are still high. This chapter documents the extent of crime and explores possible reasons for the recent declines within black communities.

Escaping the paradox also requires clarity about the injustices in the present system. At an individual level, the perceived prevalence by blacks of injustices within the criminal justice system has lead to mistrust and has compromised black America's confidence in the system's capacity to protect and mete out justice. At the level of policy, criminal justice is becoming much more harsh. There is evidence which strongly suggests that this is politically possible only because the policies, even when applied in a color-blind fashion, will apply principally to black Americans.

Understanding the scope of the twin problems of crime and injustice allows us to identify and support programs and policies that attempt to address both.

# INTRODUCTION

There is too much crime and too little justice in the lives of black Americans today. But while the problem of crime is widely shared in the United States, the problem of injustice is not. As a result, doing something constructive about the twin problems of crime and injustice is politically complicated. Government agencies and officials across the United States enthusiastically attack the crime problem in ways that often either ignore or aggravate the problems of injustice with which black Americans are especially concerned. Quests for justice—for a government that acts fairly, equitably, and respectfully— although acknowledged, are frequently discounted when black Americans join forces with white Americans to fight crime. It is a paradox that black Americans, who suffer from crime disproportionately, have mixed feelings, at best, regarding its support of and confidence: in the criminal justice system as it operates today. The only way out of this paradox is to address the problems of crime and injustice simultaneously: changing the nature of the courts, criminal punishments and law enforcement agencies and their agents while honestly acknowledging the scope of the crime problem and working for peace in black America. It is difficult work, but possible; indeed, it is already happening.

This chapter examines the crime problem, injustice, and finally suggests strategies aimed at remaking the criminal justice system in ways that give us a way out of this paradox. To move forward, we need honesty and plain talk about the problems themselves.

People are hurt by crime; they are scared and angry. Public officials, criminal justice experts, and the captains of America's new penal industries appeal to this pain, fear, and anger. Some even exploit the population's anxiety for their own economic and/or political gain. At the risk of oversimplyfying, these appeals might be tolerable if they also solved the crime problem. Unfortunately, the appeals are often followed by policies which have no significant impact on the crime problem. Despite astronomical expenditures of public money for criminal justice (about $2 billion dollars annually for New York City alone), victims of crime remain uncompensated, young and old grow more fearful, and public anger only intensifies as the number of prisons multiplies. In the meantime, to those sincerely striving on modest budgets to lift the sieges of their own neighborhoods, the causes of both crime and injustice seem distant and unyielding.

Fortunately, there are glimmers of hope and signs of progress today that can begin to allay the fear and despair that these issues so easily evoke. The level of reported, violent crime is falling quickly in many cities, lowering the chances of victimization among black as well as other urban dwellers. And the growing popularity of community policing has created opportunities for some criminal justice agencies and officials to improve their services and accountability to black Americans. Police chiefs and politicians claim the credit for the drop in crime as soon as they release the numbers; but they are not the only people who are contributing to a more peaceful society. Indeed, the public agencies are probably less significant than the individuals and local organizations throughout America's diverse urban communities who have been working for peace at least as hard. These peace workers aim to do more than end the drug wars, the gang wars, and the gun wars: they aim to expand safety in their communities, to build mutual respect within an increasingly diverse black America, and to build systems of mutual support with the agencies of government that should embody justice.

If we are to build on the gains of the last year or two, we must document, celebrate, and extend the contributions of these communities and their leading citizens to the drop in crime and perhaps even to an expansion of justice.

# CRIME

*Victimization*

The burden of crime is widely shared across the color line. Black and white people across the United States are victims of crime, are afraid of being victimized, and pay the price of crime in endless installments. So it is good news for all that, in the United States as a whole, criminal victimizations are slowly declining. The best evidence for this comes from the National Crime Victimization Survey, conducted annually by the Census Bureau for the U.S. Justice Department. According to these surveys, the national rate of criminal victimization rose through the 1970s, peaked in the early '80s, and has been coming down ever since.

But the United States is not one whole, and the crimes that cause suffering are different from one neighborhood to the next. When documenting crime in general, government agencies and the media pay most attention to "index crimes." There are four violent index crimes: (1) murder and non-negligent manslaughter; (2) rape, (3) robbery, and (4) aggravated assault (meaning an assault with a weapon or causing an injury requiring medical treatment). There are three property index crimes: (1) burglary (entering premises to commit a crime, usually theft), (2) personal theft or larceny, and (3) theft of a motor vehicle.

Most of the index crimes that people report are property crimes, and these are the crimes that have been steadily declining across the United States for the past 10 to 15 years. In cities, people report property crimes in all kinds of neighborhoods, but the highest rates of theft are found in neighborhoods with lots of business activity and with middle-and high-income residents. Households with annual incomes of more than $50,000 have a theft rate 50 percent higher than households earning less than $7,500 annually. For burglary, the relationship is reversed, with low-income households reporting a rate almost twice that for high-income households. Black households experience all property crimes at rates greater than white households, but the difference here is not as great as that between the rates for Hispanic versus non-Hispanic households, high-income versus low-income, or urban versus suburban or rural.

Violent crimes, while less frequent, attract more attention. Nationally, these declined only briefly in the early '80s, increased from 1986 to 1992, and levelled off in 1993 and '94. In the nine American cities with more than 1 million people, however, violent crimes reported to the police declined 8 percent in 1994, and the preliminary figures for 1995 suggest that this decline is continuing.

Again, the risk of violent victimization is different for different people. Black and white women are victims of rape or sexual assault at about the same rates, with women in households earning less than $15,000 annually showing rates three times greater than those in higher income households, according to the National Crime Victimization Survey. For other violent crimes—homicides, robberies, and assaults causing severe injuries—young, urban, black males in low-income households experience the highest rates of victimization. It is in these crime categories that the recent reductions are most pronounced.

Consider the risk of being shot, killed, or robbed in New York City. In the first six months of 1995, there were 1,608 gunshot victims citywide, 961 of whom were black. In contrast, during the same six month period a year earlier, there had been 2,274 gunshot victims, 1,329 of whom were black. And the numbers had been even higher in previous years. Homicides also dipped dramatically after 1992, as did robberies after 1991. (See Figures 1 and 2).

What all this means is that there is still a lot of crime in urban America. But it also means that the risk seems to be coming down: that black Americans in most big cities are less likely to be robbed, shot, or murdered today than a few years ago. These figures also suggest that black Americans are committing less crime.

## Figure 1
## Homicides in New York City by Quarter, 1990-1995

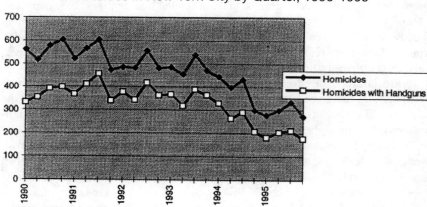

Source: New York City Police Department, Crime Analysis and Program Planning Section

## Black Crime

This last point—that black Americans are committing less crime—has received almost no attention in the national press. When violent crime was rising in many American cities in the late 1980s, press accounts were full of stories about the moral depredation of black Americans. But now, as the media report crime falling, they focus on the work of police and the numbers of people in prisons rather than on the changes within black America.

To understand the fall in black crime, we have to understand where it is falling from. At the start of the 20th century, W.E.B. DuBois was alarmed by the high rate of crime among black Americans, attributing it to the high rate of poverty and to the degradation and social dislocation caused by slavery. In the second half of the century, as crime generally increased, the high rate of black crime appears to have increased as well. The data used to derive black and white crime rates have always been subject to criticism because most of the data come from arrest reports which reflect policing strategies and prejudices as well as crime; but recent research has shown that the proportion of black arrestees on robbery and burglary charges, for example, is very close to the proportion of black offenders reported by the victims of these crimes in the National Crime Victimization Survey, which does not depend on police data. For the most serious crimes, the rates of arrest appear to be good indicators of rates of offending.

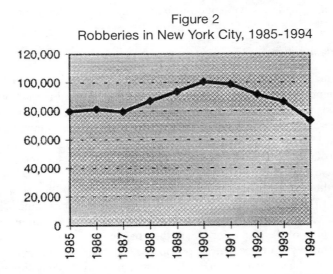

### Figure 2
### Robberies in New York City, 1985-1994

Source: New York State Division of Criminal Justice Services, 1994 *Crime and Justice Annual Report* (Albany, New York: 1995) p.23.

Judging by arrest rates recorded over the last 50 years, black crime rates have remained substantially higher than white crime rates in all the major crime categories, including theft, burglary, aggravated assault, robbery, rape, and murder. But at least since the 1960s, the *fluctuations* in the black and white arrest rates for some crimes, notably theft, burglary, and robbery have been almost identical: the black and white rates for each have risen and fallen together over these years, suggesting that the factors that lead to rising or falling rates of these crimes are affecting both black and white Americans. Black and white rates of homicide, in contrast, have moved separately. After years of relative stability, both the black and white murder rates began to climb in 1963, the black rate faster than the white. Then, from 1970 to 1982, the black rate held steady or fell while the white rate continued to climb. From 1982 to 1985, both rates fell, but in 1986 the black rate began to climb steeply while the white rate held steady. It is this recent surge in the black murder rate alone, lasting from 1986 to 1992, that focused energy in black communities across the United States on the scourge of violence and the deaths it brought to so many young men.

Many people have associated the rise in deadly violence within black America with the proliferation of guns. Indeed, in 1987, 59 percent of homicides were committed with guns, but by 1993 it was 70 percent. And since 1993, in cities such as Chicago, Los Angeles, and New York where homicides are now down dramatically, there are parallel reductions in other firearm offenses. To address the reduction in black crime, we should therefore ask, Why in the last few years black Americans are engaging in less violent crime and using guns less frequently?

### Prisons and Communities

One explanation worth rejecting at the start is that black crime is falling because of the imprisonment of so many black Americans. Today there are over 1 million sentenced prisoners in state institutions and several hundred thousand more in federal prisons and local jails—many just awaiting trial. These numbers have tripled in the last 15 years. And while the numbers going into prison have grown, so has the length of imprisonment for violence: Since 1975, the average time served per violent crime tripled.

Some pundits, like William Bennett, the former Secretary of Education and Director of Drug Policy, have suggested that this growth in imprisonment is a major reason that crime is down. "Most prisoners are violent or repeat offenders," he insists, regardless of the crime for which they happen to be convicted most recently. So the more you incapacitate in prison, the less crime on the streets.

But crime rates have not responded to the growth in prisons as this argument predicts. As we have already seen, while the number of people in prison was steadily soaring in the late '70s and throughout the '80s, the rate of violent crime dipped then soared as well, apparently impervious to the increased incarceration of offenders.  There is nothing about the growth in the number of prisoners since 1992 that would explain why the growth in violent crime stopped and began to reverse after 15 years of prison expansion.

Indeed, the recent reduction in violent crime may be occurring despite the burdens that these increases in incarceration are placing on urban, low-income communities.  These are the neighborhoods to which prisoners return when released from jail or prison, and one overlooked result of the growth of the jail and prison population in the United States is that more people each year are returning to their neighborhoods having done time. Because their time in jail or prison has often made it harder for them to live and work peacefully in their communities, these ex-offenders often become repeat offenders.  In fact, the larger the prison population has grown the higher the recidivism rate of those released has climbed.  In New York, for example, more than half of those released now return to prison within five years. (See Figure 3).

People living in these neighborhoods know all this.  During the community meetings organized to plan Harlem's application for federal Empowerment Zone funds, for example, residents repeatedly surprised the experts in the priority they gave to jobs and training for those coming home from Rikers Island, the city's enormous jail compound.  More than 20,000 men will return to New York City this year from state prisons, and many times that will return from shorter periods of time in the city jails.  While some may have been chastened by the experience, most will have learned lessons and behavior that will make it harder than ever for them to avoid further conflict with their neighbors and the police.

In the face of these realities, the last year or two of twenty years of growth in the prison population of the United States is insufficient to explain the recent reversal of violent crime rates.  The answer is more likely to lie in black communities.

## Peacemaking

In the early 1990s, with violent crime among urban black Americans at its apex, Geoffrey Canada and his colleagues at the Rheedlen Center in Harlem organized the Countee Cullen Community Center in a Central Harlem school as part New York City's Beacon School program.  They picked an elementary school that had more than its share of problems: people selling drugs on its two corners and junkies sitting on an old couch right outside. The housing project and neighborhood surrounding it had the highest number of children living in temporary housing in Harlem, and the week before the center opened a young man was shot and killed next to the school entrance.

Canada describes the Beacon School program and Rheedlen's version of it as a "community development strategy." The community center makes use of the school building from 3:00 p.m. into the night, providing a range of services and activities for kids and families.  But more than that, Rheedlen's center became the hub of a host of community organizing activities. As Canada explains:

## Figure 3
## Persons Released from New York State Prisons and Percent Returned to Prison within Five Years, 1970-1994

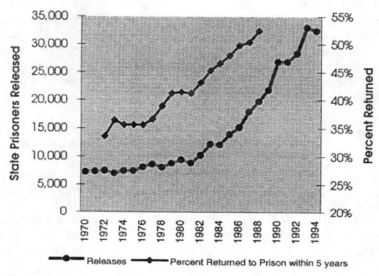

New York State Department of Correctional Services

"We knew that the truth of the matter was that most people in the neighborhood were good people, not involved with crime, drugs, or anything else illegal. They just happened to be poor, and often scared. It was the fear that had run them inside.... We knew we had to get them back outside and talking with one another."

Over the next few years, the Countee Cullen staff built a program activities for adults—including education, aerobics, and African dance—late night services and sports for adolescents, and the availability of trained social workers for families that needed intensive counseling. But beyond the walls of the school, the staff organized a block association, they sponsored several performances by a theatre company right on the block, they created a play street for neighborhood children, and they helped the center's Teen Youth Council fight to have cigarette and alcohol advertising outside replaced by an advertisement for the United Negro College Fund.

Today, crime and violence are down in that neighborhood, and the drugs and violence are gone from the street corners around the school. There are fewer killings, there are fewer guns. Why? Is it the Beacon School? Is it the Mayor's and Police Commissioner's new police strategies? These same questions could be posed in neighborhoods across urban America where black crime has begun to decline.

The answer, of course, is neither and both. Neither the Beacon School program nor the strategies of the police are sufficient to explain the drop in violent crime: the same strategies and programs are not producing the same effect everywhere, and crime is falling in other places where these particular programs are not in place. In the late 1980s, moreover, people in one neighborhood or another were trying very similar policing and community development strategies without bringing down the crime rate. But both of these forces together may represent something new and very powerful: not just a good police strategy or a good neighborhood program, but a determined focus on reducing crime and violence in black communities that unites the efforts of local police, local activists, and local residents. In Harlem and in dozens of other urban black communities, the last three years have seen a far-reaching, but not necessarily formally "organized," mobilization against violence that has included religious leaders, gang leaders, schools, parents, and businesses in addition to the police and other government agencies. That each program or strategy within this broader mobilization is only a partial solution, that none on its own can actually solve the problem of crime should not distract us from the contribution that each makes.

In this corner of Harlem, it may be the combination of Rheedlen's local leadership, government support through the Beacon School program, and the police department, together with dozens of unrecognized active residents that made the difference. In another neighborhood, a different combination may be equally effective. The point is that the government programs and police strategies provide a framework within which people in a community can work together to make a difference. Without good people—organizers, local police, adults, and children from the community—no pre-packaged strategy is worth much. Without supportive government policies and programs providing a framework, the most creative people cannot sustain these kinds of efforts. The remarkable thing about the last few years and the falling rates of crime in these neighborhoods is that both government agencies and community institutions, while in many instances distrustful of one another, seem to be working toward the same ends and reinforcing each other's efforts. It is only a beginning—there is still far too much crime and fear—but it is a promising beginning worth noting and exploring its potential for use in other communities.

# CRIMINAL JUSTICE FOR AN INCLUSIVE SOCIETY

## Injustice

If the experience of criminal victimization binds Americans together, the experience of injustice tends to divide blacks from whites. Injustice comes in the form of mistreatment by police, prosecutors, public defenders, judges, probation officers, prison guards, and parole boards. It comes in the form of laws and policies that damage the families and communities of black Americans. And these days, it increasingly comes under the banner of fighting crime. Again we see the paradox: these are the institutions that are widely expected to solve the problems of crime, yet the people who need them most have learned, justifiably, to mistrust them.

The pervasiveness of injustice in ordinary encounters between black Americans and the justice system was brought home to me when colleagues and I at the Vera Institute established the Neighborhood Defender Service of Harlem in 1990. The office—a new kind of public defender— under contract with the city and state governments provides free legal representation to Harlem residents accused of crimes; but unlike a traditional public defender that gets its work from court assignments, the Neighborhood Defender Office gets its cases when Harlem residents call for help. The call usually comes from a relative or a close friend of someone who has just been arrested.

A surprising number of calls are about routine encounters between residents and police that go wrong. One of the early calls came from a man who had been awakened in the middle of the night by someone leaning on his apartment's downstairs doorbell. It was the police, trying to get into the building by ringing buzzers at random. When he came downstairs and realized that they had no business with him, he told them off and found himself arrested. He was released without charges the next day.

Another man, walking with his granddaughter in a park adjacent to Harlem, was stopped by police who, based only on the man's presence in a park near a homeless shelter, thought he might have kidnapped the girl. He, too, was briefly arrested and, in his case, separated from his young granddaughter.

A young man, on his way to pay his tuition at the city university was stopped and arrested because of his proximity to a drug market: his cash was confiscated. It was months before the police and prosecutors agreed to return his money to him.

On the scale of human rights abuses around the world, these qualify only as petty harassment; but it is not their severity that makes them significant, it is their pervasiveness. Such stories, and worse, are generated every day and circulate through the community, forming the general background within which Harlem residents understand the criminal justice system. There are versions of these stories circulating in virtually every black family in the United States. In stark contrast, they are largely unknown in white families.

The reaction of city officials when the Neighborhood Defender Service brings lawsuits on behalf of the victims of these injustices is also telling. In the case of the man awakened in the middle of the night, for example, the city attorney defending the police department was baffled by the lawsuit. The attorney was willing to concede almost immediately that the police had violated this man's constitutional rights, but could not understand that any harm had been done. "Where are the damages?" the attorney asked, suggesting that this was a frivolous suit.

The damage, of course, is evident throughout black America. Law abiding black Americans who do not have the money or status to insulate themselves from these kinds of encounters, fear the police and the prospect of wrongful arrest. While most of this fear has been concentrated among young black men, it is increasingly present among young black women as well. Even among those whose good fortune has allowed them to live and work in neighborhoods where such harassment is uncommon, there is a healthy distrust of police encounters and a constant attention to things like dress and behavior in public that might provide some degree of protection.

If these stories were the only evidence of injustice and the mounting distrust between the victims of crime in black America and the criminal justice system, the solution might be straightforward: better training, supervision, and institutional discipline to remove the offensive behavior from within the system. Although these strategies are worthwhile, the accounts of injustice are so prevalent that they are also easily interprered as evidence that the society as a whole places little value on justice in black America. Unfortunately, that perception is further reinforced by evidence of more systemic bias.

## Bias in the System

In 1990, the Sentencing Project attracted national attention by reporting that one-in-four black men in their twenties throughout the United States was either incarcerated or on probation or parole. In 1995, the same group reported that the proportion had grown to one-in-three. While no one disputes these statistics, some see them as evidence that young black men are committing a lot of crime, while others see them as a sign that our criminal justice system is becoming merely a system of policing and imprisoning black America.

Both are right. As we have seen, young black men are indeed committing a lot of crime, but the criminal justice system that deals with that crime reeks of economic and racial bias. And while it is almost impossible to separate the effects of these twin biases, the experience of those administering the system provides ample evidence of the racial component.

Just as it was important to understand the component parts of the crime problem, it is necessary to understand the components of the justice system. The police are the most visible part. They are present in record numbers throughout urban America, and are expected to do everything from solving murders to directing traffic. While much of their attention is devoted to serious crime, most of the arrests made by police are for minor offenses where their discretion is far greater. In 1993, for example, police officers throughout the United States made more than 14 million arrests, but only about 750,000 of these were for violent index crimes, and about 2.1 million were for index property crimes. In the same year, the police made 1.5 million arrests for drunk driving, 1.1 million for drug offenses, 1.1 million for minor assaults, about 725,000 each for disorderly conduct and public drunkenness, and more than 300,000 for vandalism.

Prosecutors take over the cases after arrest, deciding whether or not to press charges and what sentence to insist upon in plea negotiations. More than 90 percent of criminal convictions are obtained as a result of guilty pleas. Here, too, the discretion of prosecutors is greater for the less serious offenses.

While judges have limited power to dismiss charges, their principal role is in sentencing. In the past, judges discretion was quite broad. Currently, that discretion is now constrained by plea bargains, by mandatory sentencing statutes, and by sentencing guidelines. The impact of these constraints on individual sentences varies widely from one state to the next and for different offenses.

Within each of these parts of the justice system, it is useful to distinguish two kinds of racial bias, both present to some degree. One is overt discrimination: people or institutions treating similarly situated black and white people differently. The second is covert discrimination: the willingness to craft and implement harsh policies because of the knowledge that, even if applied in a color-blind fashion, they will apply principally to black Americans.

Overt discrimination plays on the availability of discretion. Police, prosecutors, and judges exercise varying amounts of discretion in the system, and bias can be introduced at any stage. As Judge Theodore McKee—recently appointed to the U.S. Court of Appeals for the Third Circuit, and formerly a state court trial judge in Philadelphia—has explained with regard to this kind of bias among judges:

"I think it is very easy for that very subtle, subliminal racism to creep in, and when the defendant comes into court you just disregard him and dehumanize him. That subliminal racism—and it is subliminal—that kind of racism is there when the judge thinks of a black defendant as part of the stereotype of this dangerous mass out there waiting to take over our schools and our streets and break into our homes.... Bias [also] creeps into the system at less obvious levels, at the level where an individual's discretion determines who gets arrested, who gets prosecuted, how the guilty are sentenced, and who gets these mandatories."

This is the kind of bias that was revealed in a recent study of jail and prison sentences in New York State. The research compared sentences of white and black defendants convicted of felony charges throughout New York State between 1990 and 1992, and it found that when the crime and the defendant's prior record were the same, black defendants were sentenced to jail and prison more frequently than white defendants. To make the point most starkly, the report from New York State's Division of Criminal Justice Services explained that its results showed that between 1990 and 1992 approximately 578 black offenders had been sentenced to prison in New York who would not have been sentenced to prison had they been white, and 8,174 black offenders had been sentenced to jail who would not have been sentenced to jail had they been white.

Critics of the criminal justice system see the rising numbers and proportion of black Americans in prison as resulting, in part, from this kind of overt bias.

While the number of people in state and federal prisons has topped 1 million, rising from only about 100,000 seventy years ago, the proportion of black people among those entering prison each year has grown from 21 percent in 1926, to more than 55 percent today. The bias that drives these numbers, critics like Jerome Miller claim, does not just appear at the sentencing hearing, but is built up as well through the accumulation of arrests and minor sentences to which black Americans are subject from a young age for conduct that would not lead to an arrest of a white adolescent.

Judge McKee knows that this kind of overt racism occurs with black judges, like himself, as well as with white judges.

If I'm walking down a street in Center City Philadelphia at two in the morning, and I hear some footsteps behind me, and I turn around, and there is a couple of young white dudes behind me, I am probably not going to get very uptight. I'm probably not going to have the same reaction if I turn around and there is the proverbial black urban youth behind me.

Yet Judge McKee believes that this kind of overt racism is less of a problem with black officials. "I think it still happens with black judges," he says, "but I hope it doesn't happen to the same degree." If he is right, this kind of bias should be diminishing, at least in the federal courts, for Judge McKee was one of a record number of black judges appointed to the bench by President Clinton in the first half of his term. In most urban police departments, as well, the number of black officers is rising, and we can hope that their growing presence will change the behavior of their fellow officers as well.

Covert bias is more problematic. Over the last 30 years, politicians in legislatures and executive mansions across the country have been raising maximum, minimum, and mandatory prison sentences at the same time that black people have become the majority of people receiving those sentences. And where politicians hold back, voters have enacted new sentencing laws through ballot initiatives despite evidence that the laws will bankrupt their states. Drug crimes have given this kind of bias an easy opportunity in recent years, as drug arrests have become increasingly concentrated in black America. (See Figure 4). In the face of these kinds of arrest numbers, increasing penalties for drug offenses will have the predictable effect of increasing the punishment of black Americans in particular, even if the penalties are imposed on offenders in a neutral manner.

It would be one thing if those harsher penalties had been shown to deter or prevent crime; but no such evidence is offered. Instead, the harsher sentences reflect a chilling eagerness to exclude offenders for life from civil society, even in early adolescence, despite its enormous financial cost. Would these same policies be pursued if the people being incarcerated were overwhelmingly white? No one knows. But the question haunts black politicians and officials in federal and state governments across the country, even as they support the latest bills to increase prison sentences, to increase the power of the police, and to raise the level of pain inflicted within our society's penal system.

*Community Policing and Inclusive Justice*

The white police officer who resides in the suburbs and comes to work to patrol an inner city black neighborhood—disconnected from the community, maintaining control through intimidation rather than respect—is a familiar image that could describe the plight of the entire criminal justice system from the police through prosecution and the courts, to prison, probation, and parole. While part of the solution is to integrate the police departments and the other agencies making discretionary decisions, another part is to change the way they all, black and white, are really expected to do their job.

All Americans are taught that justice consists of fairness and equality, but black Americans generally know the importance of a third element as well: respect. The criminal law and its justice system can try to command obedience through intimidation; but to be worthy of the name, justice needs to command respect as well, and it can only do so by showing respect for those whose allegiance it seeks.

This is the ambitious promise of community policing. To skeptical police departments, community policing is sold as a way to get more information from a community in order to pursue the same job: arresting the bad guys. But to skeptical communities, the officer on the beat, talking with residents and trying to solve local problems, is sold as a new service: a respectful, helpful, even deferential approach to police work. Despite the fact that the federal government has enshrined the term in legislation and is funding community policing across the country, what it means in practice varies from one community to the next.

Figure 4
Arrest Rates for Drug Offenses (per 100,000 population), by Age and Race, 1965-1992

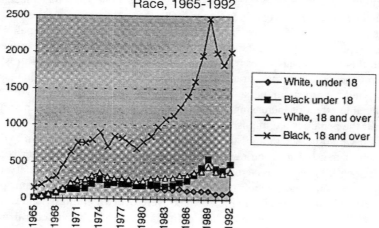

Source: U.S. Department of Justice, Office of Justice Programs, Bureau of Justice Statistics, Sourcebook of Criminal Justice Statics, 1994 (Washington, D.C.: 1995) p.413.

92

In Chicago, where some of the most thorough research on community policing is now under way, it means engaging local residents in councils to set priorities for police work and establish long-term plans; it means deploying officers on small beats to handle problems they encounter that can lead to crime, with less distraction from 911 calls; and it means developing tools within the police department in addition to arrest for coping with the crime problems in communities. It is not easy, and many problems experienced in Chicago are repeating themselves in cities elsewhere: police-resident councils are not often good at crafting long-range goals or the plans to reach them; police commanders are often skeptical that this new approach can improve their relations with residents; and freeing officers from the need to respond to 911 calls and take on other assignments is bureaucratically complicated at best.

That the enthusiasm for community policing is spreading to prosecutors, public defenders, the judiciary, and penal administrators is not evidence of its demonstrated success. It is evidence that it has struck a chord in people outside the criminal justice system that until now has only been struck by tougher prison sentences. So prosecutors in Washington, D.C., are now walking around black neighborhoods, trying to help residents arrange the removal of abandoned cars; judges and prosecutors in Brooklyn, New York, are trying to open a community court in the Red Hook public housing development that will provide services requested by local residents as it dispenses justice. If community policing remains only vaguely understood, community prosecution and community courts are still only slogans in search of definition. But that they are generating interest and activity at all is important.

The falling crime rate in urban America has probably not been caused by community policing, but it has given community policing some time to develop: a rare privilege for any politically popular initiative. In the time available, local organizers and residents need to make common cause with community police initiatives.

Community policing aspires to a respectful, inclusive system of justice. That is why it is popular, and that is why we must make it succeed, whatever its early difficulties. But it is not the only example.

Hundreds of small efforts are under way across urban America to punish offenders for crimes while demonstrating a determination to include them within their communities. Community service programs, for example, are beginning to be taken more seriously as punishments in their own right. But inclusive justice does not have to operate as an alternative to prison sentences: it can follow prison sentences.

Among the largest and most ambitious of programs of this kind is New York City's Center for Employment Opportunities, which provides job training and paid, transitional employment to young men and women returning to New York City from prison. What makes CEO particularly interesting is that it does not handpick its participants; it provides paid work to all of its participants at minimum wage as soon as they are released from prison, and it uses this paid work experience to help the ex-offenders find permanent, better-paid employment.

As CEO illustrates, inclusive justice need not be lenient, for these ex-offenders have been through some of the toughest prisons in New York State. But the message at the end is clear: you are returning to live with your neighbors, to work, and to participate in our society. It is the opposite of the message sent by the increasingly severe three-strikes-and-you're-out laws which preach exclusion and raise the fear that bias is covertly at play.

For now we cannot fully escape the paradox with which we began: black Americans suffer from crime and injustice, yet the efforts to stop crime seem to fuel injustice. What the Rheedlen Center, the Neighborhood Defender Service, and the Center for Employment Opportunities, and community policing all illustrate, however, is that government-community partnerships can be crafted that avoid this paradox by working on problems of crime and injustice simultaneously. There are examples of such efforts in virtually every city in America.

## BIOGRAPHICAL SKETCH

Christopher E. Stone is director of the Vera Institute of Justice, where he created New York's Center for Alternative Sentencing and Employment Services, Inc. (1989), and the Neighborhood Defender Service of Harlem (1990). Before joining Vera, he served as a public defender in Washington, D.C. He is a graduate of Harvard College, The Institute of Criminology at Cambridge University, and Yale Law School.

# THE HEALTH OF AFRICAN AMERICANS:

## PROGRESS TOWARD *HEALTHY PEOPLE 2000*

**June Jackson Christmas, M.D.**

# ABSTRACT

Data suggest that national goals for *Healthy People 2000* will not be reached by African-Americans. Major disparities persist between the health status of Blacks and other groups in spite of policy initiatives to improve health care for poor people. While lack of insurance and limited access are contributory, leading causes of death and disability among blacks also reflect "the new morbidity" of behavioral disorders. If access improves through insurance, primary care, and culturally competent services, these changes alone will not ensure better health unless attention is given also to alleviating poverty and discrimination, increasing education, and encouraging healthy behaviors. Using health promotion and disease prevention objectives of *Healthy People 2000*, the review presents comparative data on selected indicators throughout the life cycle. It closes by discussing implications of current policies for improved health status.

*Healthy People 2000*, a seminal report issued in 1990 by the U.S. Department of Health and Human Services, resulted from a policy decision to develop a national strategy to improve the nation's health by addressing the prevention of major chronic illnesses, injuries, and infectious diseases (USDHHS, 1990). Task forces of health professionals, policy makers, advocates, and consumers worked together to produce a set of measurable targets to be achieved by the year 2000. It was reviewed and updated as *Healthy People 2000 Review 1994* (USDHHS, 1995). In spite of limited progress since the first report, the data in each dramatically reiterate findings in the earlier report of the Secretary of Health and Human Services (USDHHS, 1985).

The Secretary's Task Force on Black and Minority Health studied excess deaths in the Afro-American population, defined as "... the difference between the number of deaths actually observed and the number of deaths that would have occurred in that group if it experienced the same death rates for each age and sex as the White population". Analysis of mortality data from 1979 to 1981 found that 42.3 percent of the deaths of all Afro-Americans dying before the age of 70 could be called excess. Four out of five were due to cancer, cardiovascular disease and stroke, chemical dependency, diabetes, homicides and accidents, and infant mortality.

In 1993, as it has since the beginning of the century, life expectancy at birth for blacks (69.3 years) lagged behind that of the total population (75.5 years) and that of whites (76.3 years). The gap is widening. Although white life expectancy rose in the '80s, black life expectancy actually declined from a high of 69.5 years in 1984 to 69.3 in 1993. The disparity is more dramatic for black men, whose life expectancy is 8.3 years less than that of their white counterparts (National Center for Health Statistics, 1995).

Since blacks began at a lower level on many indicators, gaps persist. Within the total population, there are disparities on most indicators between the health of people of African ancestry (12 percent of the population) and the population as a whole, as well as in comparison to Euro-Americans. Although blacks are represented in all socioeconomic strata, one-third live in poverty, a rate three times that of whites. Even when socioeconomic status is eliminated as a variable, the health status of African Americans compares poorly with that of others.

## BACKGROUND

Race is a social rather than a biological construct. It relates more to self-identification and social identity than to genetics. In some instances, there is greater variety within racial groups than between them. Still, the federal government uses the terms *White, Black, Asian* or *Pacific Islander* and *American Indian* or *Alaskan Native*, considered as races, plus *Hispanic* (of any race), for ethnicity. To consider race as a single variable related to health outcomes is an oversimplfication. Krieger *et al.* (1993), in an extensive article, consider possible interrelationships among racism, sexism, and social class as a fruitful direction for exploring the poorly understood racial/ethnic differences in diseases. *African Americans* are heterogeneous in many ways — origin, ethnicity, socio-economic status, residence, and degree and type of interaction with the wider society. Heterogeneity adds to complex interactions among biological, social and psychological factors in health and illness.

Nevertheless, some generalizations can be made about the health of *black Americans*. Interrelated problems of the delivery system affect blacks disproportionately (Blendon, 1989; Lieu, 1992). Poverty, lack of culturally competent providers, and ineffective health education approaches are compounding factors (Byrd, 1992). While lack of health insurance and limited access to services are contributory, leading causes of death and disability among *blacks* (such as hypertension, heart disease, homicide, lung cancer, cirrhosis, AIDS, and drug addiction) also reflect "the new morbidity" of behavioral disorders. In part they are influenced by choices people make about nutrition, exercise, sexual behavior, legal and illicit drugs, and medical advice, as well as by individual and cultural definitions of health and illness. If access were to increase through insurance, primary care, and culturally sensitive services, such changes alone would not ensure better health unless attention were also given to alleviating poverty and racism, increasing opportunities, and encouraging healthy behaviors (Christmas, 1983).

A developmental view of the health of *black Americans* is useful. Infants suffer from the effects of pregnancy-related problems and diseases contracted *in utero*. Young children are more likely to have certain malignancies, be victims of accidents (the leading cause of death), or require hospitalization for conditions worsened by deteriorated housing and environmental pollutants, such as asthma, that respond to ambulatory care. Adolescents experience problems resulting from risk-taking behaviors, such as early pregnancy, substance abuse, sexually transmitted diseases, and vehicular and firearm accidents. The leading causes of adult deaths are influenced in part by individual behaviors as well as by access to quality services. Older people try to maintain functioning and cope with disability as well as disease.

Using the health promotion and disease prevention objectives of *Healthy People 2000*, this review presents

- Year 2000 objectives targeted to blacks and, where set, objectives for the total population;

- Comparative data of blacks, whites, and total population on selected indicators through the life cycle;

- Discussion of major health problems throughout life and of exemplary initiatives;

- Brief consideration of the implications of trends in health policy.

# Birth and Infancy

Access to medical care, nutrition, education, income, housing, genetics, and healthy maternal behaviors all contribute to but cannot guarantee a healthy start in life. Effects of the prenatal period and early life are long-lasting. Infant mortality, low birth weight, prenatal care and maternal mortality are four critical measures of this period; in each *African Americans* as a group are in need of improvement.

## INFANT MORTALITY

Infant mortality is the death of infants under age 1. The infant mortality rate is defined as the number of deaths to infants under one year of age per 1,000 live births. It is an indicator used widely to assess health and monitor the effectiveness of public and personal health care. While genetic factors play a role, social factors are critical. Infant mortality is particularly responsive to interventions such as early prenatal care, good maternal nutrition to prevent low birth weight, and adequate infant nutrition. Yet this is one indicator in which in 1993 the U.S. was surpassed by 22 major industrialized nations. If *African Americans* were considered as a separate population group in the world, they would rank 40th. They have the highest rates of infant deaths nationally.

**Objective for Total Population:** Reduce the infant mortality rate to no more **than 7 per 1,000 live births. (1987 Baseline: 10.1 per 1,000 live births)**

**Targeted Population Objective:** Reduce the infant mortality rate among blacks to no more than 11 per 1,000 live births. (1987 Baseline: 17.9 per 1,000 live births)

Although infant mortality rates decreased from 1980 to 1992 in all groups, the rate of decline was less for black infants (24 percent) than for white (36 percent) with an overall decline for all groups of 33 percent (NCHS, 1995). Much of the decline was due to neonatal intensive-care technology that, at great financial costs, saved premature, low birth-weight infants rather than due to increased access to early prenatal care and primary care, both less costly.

## Table 1

### INFANT MORTALITY RATE

| | 1987 | 1991 | 1992 | Year 2000 Target |
|---|---|---|---|---|
| **Infant Deaths** | | | | |
| Total | 10.1 | 8.9 | 8.5 | 7 |
| White | 8.5 | 7.3 | 6.9 | N/A |
| Black | 17.5 | 17.6 | 16.8 | 11 |

*Note: Infant mortality rate is defined as infant deaths under one year per 1,000 live births.*

Source: National Center for Health Statistics, *Vital Statistics of the United States*

In 1992 the black infant mortality rate (16.8) was more than twice as high as the rate for white infants (6.9) and almost the same as white infant mortality 22 years earlier (17.8) (Table 1). The rate of infant deaths for all races was 8.5 per 1,000 live births. The leading causes of death are congenital anomalies, sudden infant death syndrome, disorders due to short gestation and low birth weight, and respiratory distress. For black infants the difference is that AIDS is a leading cause of death. Sudden infant death syndrome (SIDS) is the major killer after the first month of life. Other causes of infant death more prevalent in blacks than in the total population are respiratory distress syndrome, infections, and injuries.

Poverty plays a major role in infant mortality. In the neonatal period (birth to >28 days), poverty plays a role in causes of death, such as low birth weight, congenital anomalies, and influences of the prenatal, childbirth, and newborn periods. In the postneonatal period (28 days to one year), factors related to poverty include poor nutrition, substandard housing, injuries, and lack of access to good health care for infections and other disorders. A recent study by the Centers for Disease Control and Prevention (1995) found infant mortality rates in 1988 to be 60 percent higher for women living below the poverty line than for women above it. The gap due to poverty was stronger for the neonatal period; babies of poor women were twice as likely to die during that period. The study concluded that poverty had as large an effect as other factors such as the mother's marital status, age and education; cigarette smoking during pregnancy; time of first prenatal visit; and race.

## LOW BIRTHWEIGHT

Another health indicator is the number and rate of low birth-weight births per 100 live births. Low birth weight is defined as below 2,500 grams (5 pounds 8 ounces). It is the greatest single damaging factor to infant health. A major factor in both infant mortality and low birth weight is exposure of infants *in utero* to drugs, such as alcohol, nicotine, heroin, cocaine, and methadone. Low socioeconomic status and environmental toxins are risk factors. Low birth weight and prematurity are more likely with very young or old mothers, with those who poor, malnourished, poorly educated, with late or no prenatal care. Although black mothers are disproportionately among the poor and of low-educational status, for reasons not understood, black women at all economic levels have a higher risk of delivering low birth weight infants and having other problematic outcomes (Collins and David, 1990).

**Objective for Total Population:** Reduce low birth weight to an incidence of no more than 5 percent of live births. (1987 Baseline: 6.9 percent)

**Targeted Population Objective:** Reduce low birth weight in blacks to an incidence of no more than 9 percent. (1987 Baseline: 12.7 percent)

Table 2 shows that low birthweight in blacks increased slightly from a rate of 12.7 in 1987 to 13.6 in 1991 and 13.3 in 1992. The continuing crack cocaine epidemic may have contributed to the move away from the Year 2000 goal of no more than 9 percent. The rate for the total population remained almost constant, 6.9 in 1987 and 7.1 in 1991 and in 1992.

Low birth weight contributes to disability for those whom neonatal technology saves. With higher rates of poor health, subnormal growth, and developmental problems, many such children require care that takes an emotional and physical toll on families and exacts high financial costs of society. The National Association for Perinatal Addiction Research and Education has estimated that 375,000 infants are born each year to mothers who abuse drugs (Watson, 1995). Drug-exposed infants are four times more likely to be born at low birth weight and three times more likely to die in the first year of life than non-exposed infants.

Table 2

## LOW BIRTH WEIGHT

|  | 1987 | 1991 | 1992 | Year 2000 Target |
|---|---|---|---|---|
| Percent of Births at Low Birth weight |  |  |  |  |
| Total | 6.9 | 7.1 | 7.1 | 5 |
| White | 5.7 | 5.8 | 5.8 | N/A |
| Black | 12.7 | 13.6 | 13.3 | 9 |

*Note: The prevalence of low birth weight is measured by the percentage of live born infants weighing under 2,500 grams at birth (5 lb., 8 oz.).*

Source: National Center for Health Statistics, *Vital Statistics of the United States.*

### PRENATAL CARE

Prenatal care, from the beginning of pregnancy through labor and delivery, contributes to a positive outcome. Such a healthy start can help offset the risk factors of extreme youth and poverty. Infants born to mothers who have late or inadequate prenatal care are at greater risk of low birth weight, being stillborn, or death in the first year. The increasing rate of early entry into prenatal care that occurred between 1970 and 1980 has slowed.

**Objective for Total Population:** Increase to at least 90 percent the proportion of all pregnant women who receive first trimester prenatal care. (1987 Baseline: 76 percent of live births)

**Targeted Population Objective:** Increase to at least 90 percent the proportion of pregnant black women who receive first trimester prenatal care. (1987 Baseline: 61.1% of live births)

Table 3 indicates that there was a slight increase in the percentage of black women receiving first trimester care from 61.9% in 1991 to 63.9% in 1992. The 1992 rate for white women is 80.8%. The change does not bode well for black women reaching the 90% goal.

Table 3

## PERCENTAGE OF BIRTHS TO WOMEN RECEIVING
## EARLY PRENATAL CARE

| | 1991 | 1992 | Year 2000 Target |
|---|---|---|---|
| Percent of Births to Women Receiving Early Prenatal Care | | | |
| Total | 76.2 | 77.7 | 90 |
| White | 79.5 | 80.8 | 90 |
| Black | 61.9 | 63.9 | 90 |

*Note: Early prenatal care is care begun in the first trimester of pregnancy.*
Source: Source: National Center for Health Statistics, *Vital Statistics of the United States*

Initiatives targeted at communities with high rates of low birth weight help offset some risks of poverty and extreme youth. Healthy Start programs use community workers and prenatal networks to reach young women with parenting classes, educational, health and social services and links to other programs. A major CDC study in Central Harlem, *Harlem Birth Right*, looks at women in their natural social context to learn what social conditions influence pregnancy outcomes and health in general (Mullings, 1995).

## MATERNAL MORTALITY

The maternal mortality rate is calculated as the rate per 100,000 live births from deliveries and complications of pregnancy, childbirth, and the puerperium. It is an indicator in which a marked disparity between blacks and whites leads to an objective targeted to blacks.

**Targeted Population Objective:** Reduce the maternal mortality rate among blacks to no more than 5 per 100,000 live births. (1987 Baseline: 14.2 per 100,000 live births)

As shown in Table 4, in 1970 black women were more than four times as likely as white women to die from complications of pregnancy or childbirth. By the baseline year of 1987, the rates for both had decreased, and the risks of maternal death for black women were nearly three times those of white women. However, by 1992, black women, with a rate of 20.8 deaths per 100,000 live births, were again four times as likely to die as white women (a rate of 5.0) and had nearly three times the death rate of the total population (7.8).

Table 4

## MATERNAL MORTALITY RATE

| | 1970 | 1987 | 1991 | 1992 | Year 2000 Target |
|---|---|---|---|---|---|
| Maternal Deaths | | | | | |
| Total | 21.5 | 6.6 | 7.9 | 7.8 | N/A |
| White | 14.4 | 5.1 | 5.8 | 5 | N/A |
| Black | 59.8 | 14.2 | 18.3 | 20.8 | 5 |

*Note: Maternal mortality rate is measured as deaths per 100,000 live births from deliveries and complications of pregnancy, childbirth, and the puerperium.*

Source: National Center for Health Statistics, *Vital Statistics of the United States*

Many factors contribute to maternal deaths: late or no prenatal care, lack of access to quality medical care, fewer annual visits to physicians, and complications from conditions prevalent in black women, including diabetes, hypertension, and obesity. A black woman is more likely to die of hypertension, stroke, cirrhosis of the liver, AIDS, or cancer than is a white woman. She is more likely to assess herself as being in fair or poor physical health and mental health, more likely to lose days of work due to illness or disability, and less likely to take advantage of preventive care. Initiatives targeted at women's health, not just their maternal health, and to the culture-specific aspects of the health of black girls and women may address their healthy development and decrease maternal deaths.

## Childhood

Childhood is a critical period for physical, intellectual, and psychological development, for social learning of human relationships within and beyond the family, and for establishing patterns of acquiring knowledge and skills. It is a time in which children are exposed to the world, with family support and protection. For all children, accidents are a leading cause of death. But there are other threats for children trapped in poverty, with young, uneducated, unemployed parents, for children who lack immunization against communicable diseases, and for those who are exposed to dilapidated housing in a neglected community. The health of many black children is affected by such conditions. Even in genetic conditions such as sickle cell disease social factors operate. As new family forms develop, their strengths and the difficulties they face need to be understood in order for health status to improve and services to be used.

## SICKLE CELL DISEASE

Sickle cell disease is a group of inherited disorders in which red blood cells change to sickle shaped crescents that block blood vessels. In the United States most of the people with sickle cell disease and trait are of African ancestry. The disease affects over 50,000 persons nationally. About one in 375 *African American* children has the disease. Yet, research funding does not reflect this extent. About 8 percent of the *African American* population carries the sickle cell trait. They are asymptomatic; the trait does not become the disease. Screening and counseling are critical, since the disease and the trait are transmitted genetically.

Sickle cell anemia, the most common form of the disease, leads to easy tiring. Children with sickle cell disease require routine childhood immunizations, ongoing antibiotics, and specific immunizations to prevent life-threatening infections by *H. influenzae,* hepatitis B, and pneumococcus. Besides chronic symptoms of anemia and joint swelling, frequent acute episodic crises of severe pain and stroke occur. The disease causes lifelong disability. Frequent school absences and clinic appointments are a stressful burden for families that may have other economic difficulties, or that may find it hard to continue to give medicine when a child seems well. Support groups, clinical services, education, and research are all critical.

## IMMUNIZATION

Immunity to disease is the ability of an individual to resist infection; it may be conferred by artificial immunization or through previous natural infection. Nine childhood diseases are preventable with proper immunization: diphtheria, pertussis, tetanus, measles, mumps, rubella, poliomyelitis, *Haemophilus influenzae type B*, and hepatitis B.

**Objective for Total Population:** Increase to at least 90 percent the proportion of all children who have completed their basic immunization series by age 2 — measles, mumps, rubella, polio, diphtheria, pertussis, and tetanus (1989 Baseline estimated 70-80 percent).

Currently, the national rate among preschool children is below 75 percent; in inner cities and rural areas the rate is lower. Because school entrance requires immunization, young children are at greatest risk. In the past decade, inadequate levels of immunization led to measles epidemics in young children and college students in many states. In 1990 and 1991 New York faced the largest epidemic in 10 years (NYCDOH, 1994). Blacks and Latinos in poor neighborhoods were over-represented, with 47 percent of confirmed cases in Hispanic and 29 percent in Black children. For children under 5 34 percent were Hispanic and 19 percent were black. Measles complications in the young include ear infections, pneumonia, encephalitis, and death.

Immunization is a proven cost-effective public-health preventive. Yet, federal and state cutbacks have weakened the infrastructure of local health departments; the policy of "less government" politicized the debate on immunization while children remain in need.

## LEAD POISONING

A major health problem affecting urban children is lead poisoning; it is completely preventable. The greatest risk is for children living in old, deteriorating housing, as many poor black families do. Although lead toxicity can affect people of all ages and damage all organs, the developing nervous system and digestive system in young children are more vulnerable. Children with low levels of lead may be asymptomatic or have mild symptoms; more elevated levels can produce intellectual retardation and stunted growth, impaired hearing, and behavioral disorders. Coma, convulsions, and death can occur.

**Targeted Population Objective:** Reduce the prevalence of blood lead levels exceeding 15 ug/dL and 25 ug/dL among inner city low-income black children to no more than 75,000 and zero, respectively. (1984 Baseline: An estimated 234,900 had levels exceeding 15ug/dL and 36,700 had levels exceeding 25 uv/dL)

Although all states do not collect racial data for lead levels and although there are differences in screening methods, there is agreement that blacks and other children of color are over-represented among families living in housing with peeling lead-based paint. Besides education and removal activities of local health departments, there are other initiatives promoted by health activists who oppose environmental racism. They advocate for prevention as well as lead abatement after the fact. For example, they push for job training (particularly in abatement procedures), literacy training, and education, so that residents of local communities can work with program officials to provide a safer environment for their children and be empowered in the process. Despite limited data, lead poisoning remains a problem for black children with implications for their physical, intellectual, and social development.

## AIDS AND TUBERCULOSIS

Most mothers with *AIDS/HIV* who gave birth to infants exposed to the virus *in utero* became at risk by being injecting drug users or having sex with persons infected with HIV. *HIV/AIDS* has devastated black communities and continues to do so. A percentage of children born HIV positive will develop AIDS.

**Targeted Population Objective:** Confine the prevalence of HIV infection (per 100,000 women giving birth to live-born infants) to 100. (1989 Baseline: 150).

Although not specifically noted, this objective relates to black women. Most infants born with HIV/AIDS are born to *African American* and Hispanic women. Nationally (through June 1995), of the 6,611 cumulative pediatric AIDS cases in all ethnicities, slightly more than half (3,758), were in black children and adolescents. New York City has the most pediatric cases. Of its cumulative cases, 55 percent are black, 37 percent Latino and 8 percent white (NYSDOH, 1994). The impact of HIV on the mortality of *African American* children is marked. In 1990, of all 358 pediatric (under 13) deaths nationally, 217 were of black children.

Among the social consequences of maternal AIDS are the large numbers of children orphaned by AIDS and now raised by grandmothers or other relatives or placed in foster care. Over 80 percent of these children in New York City are offspring of women of color (Michaels and Levine, 1993). New cases continue to be identified. Nationally black children comprised 573 of the 977 cases reported from July 1994 through June 1995.

Today, there is a resurgence of tuberculosis, particularly drug-resistant strains, often occuring with AIDS. Blacks represent most of the pediatric and adolescent tuberculosis cases.

## CHILD ABUSE AND NEGLECT

**Objective for Total Population:** Reduce to less than 25.2 per 1,000 children the rising incidence of maltreatment of children younger than age 18. (1986 Baseline: 25.2 per 1,000)

Child abuse and neglect occur in all classes and races. Abuse occurs when a parent or other person legally responsible for the care of a child intentionally causes or places the child at substantial risk of death, disfigurement, or impairment of physical or mental health. Neglect or maltreatment occurs when a child under 18 is in danger because a parent or legally responsible adult has failed to provide food, shelter, clothing, education, or medical care (NYSDOH, 1994). Most abused children are male; most sexually abused children and adolescents are girls. Risk factors include poverty, isolation, and unemployment; prematurity; serious disability or chronic illness in the child; a family history of being abused; parental immaturity, alcoholism and lack of knowledge of childhood development. Others suggest that standards of corporal discipline in black families provide tolerance for parental abuse.

Mandatory reporting of suspected abuse and neglect to a Central Register does not always occur. Because many poor black families tend to be known to public agencies, they may be more readily reported. Data are not reliable or consistent from state to state; they reflect reported cases rather than incidence. With these caveats, however, the Children's Defense Fund analysis of state reports for 1991 showed 2,695,010 children reported abused or neglected (1995). Of these, black children were 27.9 percent, Latinos 10,0 percent, white 58.2 percent, and others 3.9 percent. No matter how inadequate the data, child welfare and health workers consider abuse and neglect a major risk to the physical and mental health and well-being of black children and youth. Programs that help young parents gain parenting skills, learn reasonable expectations of child development, and change behaviors have a greater likelihood of success when there is also access to child care, counseling, education, and work.

# Adolescence and Young Adulthood

Beginning in puberty and continuing into the early twenties, adolescence is a transition from childhood to adulthood. The tasks of adolescence include developing psycho-sexual identity, resolving the conflict between dependence and independence, building a value system, and preparing for work. It is a period in which learning can flourish and healthy behaviors can be established. Black youth share attributes common to all adolescents. But for many, institutionalized racism, personal life experiences, and the socioeconomic context make transition to healthy adulthood riskier than that of the average, non-poor majority adolescent.

Black youth are at risk of the "new morbidity": health problems with social and behavioral origins. Innovative culturally sensitive multidisciplinary programs use the coping skills of black youth in programs of peer support, leadership development, conflict resolution, and problem-solving. Centers such as The Door, El Puente, and The Valley in New York City include varying elements of education, job preparedness, and health and social services, to address the realities of their daily lives. Yet, separation of behavioral health from other health, elimination of physical education in public schools, and cutbacks in school-based health clinics undermine such holistic efforts to develop healthy behaviors and positive values.

## TOBACCO, ALCOHOL AND OTHER DRUGS

Use of mind-altering chemicals and addiction among youth continue to increase. Most young people smoke and experiment with chemicals before reaching 18. Half of the deaths of adolescents from drowning, fires, suicide, and homicide are alcohol- or drug-related.

**Targeted Population Objective:** Reduce cigarette smoking to a prevalence of no more than 18 percent among blacks aged 20 and older. (1987 Baseline: 34%)

**Targeted Population Objective:** Reduce cirrhosis deaths among black men to no more than 12 per 100,000 black men. (1987 Baseline: 22)

Drug use patterns begun in adolescence frequently continue into adulthood. Alcohol continues to be the most popular drug, though less among blacks. Cigarette use has increased among black adolescents. An Institute for Health Policy survey shows that 5 percent of black youth smoke, compared to 13 percent Hispanic and 21 percent white (IHP, 1993). Thirty-three percent of white youth use alcohol, compared to 32 percent Hispanic and 12 percent black. Use of illegal drugs has increased. Over 90 percent of all high school seniors have tried marijuana. Thirty-one percent of teen-agers and young adults have tried marijuana, of whom one third are regular users. Cocaine use is rising as is the less expensive but more deadly crack cocaine.

Health education has led to a decrease in smoking in pregnancy and in the number of children exposed to tobacco smoke at home. Peer and multiservice programs address drug and tobacco use by black youth. However, for young black adults with coexisting alcohol and drug dependencies, policies supporting separate streams of funding reinforce fragmentation of services. High black male joblessness eliminates work-based programs as a source of help. Self-help groups such as Narcotics Anonymous, Alateen, and Alcoholics Anonymous are now included in clinical programs. More successful drug treatment programs take a holistic approach, including aspects of black culture, and include education and work as goals.

## ADOLESCENT PREGNANCY

Most adolescents are sexually active, yet many risk pregnancy and sexually transmitted diseases, despite having factual information. Being an adolescent parent presents problems for the young people and their offspring. Most teenage parents do not complete school; they have difficulty finding work and child care, as well as raising children alone or with limited support. A teen mother is at greater risk of repeated pregnancies while still an adolescent, and is more likely to have a second pregnancy within 18 months (Duenhoelter *et al.*, 1975).

**Objective for Total Population:** Reduce pregnancies among girls aged 17 and younger to no more than 50 per 1,000 adolescents. (1985 Baseline: 71.1 pregnancies per 1,000 girls 15-17)

**Targeted Population Objective:** Reduce pregnancies among black adolescent girls aged 15 through 19 to no more than 120 per 1,000 black adolescents. (1985 Baseline: 186 per 1,000 non-white adolescents)

Table 5 shows a target for non-white females (75 percent of whom are black) still more than twice that for whites. In 1992 births to adolescents (10-17) were higher among black girls (10.3 percent) than among the total population (4.9 percent) and among the white population (3.9 percent). The high black teen-age pregnancy rate, attributed to earlier initiation of sexual intercourse and low usage of contraception, may also involve cultural, psychological, and socioeconomic factors.

Table 5
### ADOLESCENT PREGNANCIES

|  | 1985 | 1989 | 1990 | Year 2000 Target |
|---|---|---|---|---|
| **All females 15-17 years** | 71.1 | 74.7 | 74.3 | 50 |
| **Non-white females 15-19 years** | 169 | 181 | 177 | 120 |

*Note: Over 75 percent of the nonwhite females 15-19 are black. For black adolescent girls, baseline data are unavailable for those aged 15 through 17. The target is based on data for girls 15 through 19. If more complete data become available, a 35 percent reduction from baseline figures should be used as the target.*

108

Source: National Vital Statistics, CDC.

For young girls, school completion programs help them attend to their own emotional health as young women (not only as mothers) and increase employability. Agencies such as Advocates for Youth use life skills training, Rites of Passage, and peer leadership, with youth of both sexes. Other programs build responsibility in black males and enhance their ability to be legally self-supporting through physical challenges and entrepreneurship. Health promotion can be an effective model for helping adolescents make wise choices (Bayne-Smith, 1994).

## HIV/AIDS

Black youth, 15 perent of the teen-age population, account for 38 percent of all AIDS cases among teens (NYCDOH, 1995). Although the number remains relatively small, it is increasing. The fact that nearly one in five cases of AIDS occurs among people between 20 and 29 suggests that many contracted the disease in adolescence (Brooks-Gunn and Furstenberg, 1990). Data on substance abuse, incidence of sexually transmitted diseases, and contraceptive use indicate that the incidence of HIV will rise dramatically in the next few years (DiClemente, 1990).

Year 2000 objectives include age-appropriate education curricula from grades 4 through 12 as part of quality school health education. Factual knowledge of HIV transmission does not alone stop risky behavior. Approaches that are broader than sex education or anti-drug slogans can assist choice and lessen risk-taking. Programs also must address the distrust many black parents have about AIDS education programs that provide condom availability.

## VIOLENCE

As Table 6 shows, homicide is the leading cause of death of young black men between 15 and 34. From 1987 to 1992, the age-adjusted death rate for black males rose from being 10.7 times that of the total population to 13 times that of the total population in 1991 where it remained in 1992. The homicide rate of black men from 25 to 34 is seven times that of whites. Black youth are victims of homicide at a rate six times that of white youth.

Table 6

## AGE-ADJUSTED DEATH RATES FOR HOMICIDE

|  | 1987 | 1991 | 1992 | Year 2000 Target |
|---|---|---|---|---|
| **Total Population** | 8.5 | 10.8 | 10.3 | 7.2 |
| **Black Males 15-34 years** | 90.5 | 140.8 | 134.2 | 72.4 |
| **Black females 15-34 years** | 20.0 | 24.1 | 22.7 | 16.0 |

Source: National Center for Health Statistics, Vital Statistics of the United States.

**Targeted Population Objective:** Reduce homicides among black men aged 15 through 34 to no more than 72.4 per 100,000 black men. (1987 Baseline: 90.5 per 100,000)

**Targeted Population Objective:** Reduce homicides among black women aged 15 through 34 to no more than 16.0 per 100,000 black women. (1987 Baseline: 20.0 per 100,000)

Violence is increasing among youth, as victims and perpetrators. Between 1987 and 1991 the number of juveniles arrested for murder increased 85 percent. Over half the juveniles killed in 1994 were between 15 and 17; 30 percent were under 6. The extent to which teenagers are themselves victimized by violent crimes is cited in a report of the Office of Juvenile Justice and Delinquency Prevention of the Department of Justice (1996). While there was a 1 percent increase in total murders between 1980 and 1994, there was a 47 percent increase in the number of juveniles murdered. The report noted an increase of 2.5 times in the number of juvenile offenders involved in multiple offender homcides. Black males between 15 and 24 experience violent crime more than any other group. Blacks are also disproportionately killed by legal intervention, generally by police. Easy access makes a gun a weapon of choice for black youth who chose to carry a weapon; this speaks to the need for better gun control.

Since over 80 percent of teen homicide victims are killed during an argument by someone they know, some mental health programs include violence de-escalation techniques and conflict resolution in work with schools, gangs, and community groups. Parents who have lost children to violence and youths who have been victims or perpetrators are effective educators.

Major research by Earls (1994) explores questions about the causes of violence and the relationship between risks and outcomes. He cites risk factors related to neighborhood (high male unemployment, extreme poverty, and social disorganization), school (lack of authority, weapon carrying, and absenteeism), peer networks (delinquency, access to weapons), family (criminality, lack of parental supervision, discord, and parental rejection and abuse), as well as individual psychological problems (school underachievement, low reading skills, poor impulse control) and health problems (head injury history, drug abuse). Stark (1990) sees professional failure to respond to violence as a significant health services problem. Although causation is not definite, violence prevention should be included in youth, health and family life education.

## Adulthood

Today the leading causes of death for blacks are heart disease, cancer, cardiovascular disease/stroke, injuries, homicide, pneumonia/influenza, diabetes, perinatal conditions, chronic obstructive pulmonary diseases, and HIV infection (National Center for Health Statistics, 1994). Heart disease, cancer, stroke, and injuries are leading causes of adult deaths in both blacks and whites. The high homicide rate in black youth raises this cause to fifth in all black deaths. Suicide, the fifth cause of deaths for adult whites, is not among the 10 leading causes of deaths for blacks. Generally, except for suicide and for motor vehicle deaths in youths, most rates are higher for blacks. In a comparison study, the mortality rate among blacks for 12 major causes of death combined was 4.5 times that of whites (Schwartz *et al.*, 1990).

The dramatic effect of AIDS on the mortality of blacks from adolescence through adulthood is illustrated in Table 7. Yet, there are other health status indicators that show the racial disparities in the rate of diseases with a major impact on morbidity and mortality.

Table 8 shows marked racial differences in selected 1992 health status indicators for 1992 by race. The death rate per 100,000 total population was 504.5 deaths. The death rate of 767.5 per 100,000 blacks was 1.6 times that of whites, with a rate of 477.5. For many adult disorders changes in personal behavior, lifestyles, and exposure to risks can have a positive effect.

# Table 7

## ACQUIRED IMMUNODEFICIENCY SYNDROME (AIDS) DEATHS, BY SELECTED CHARACTERISTICS: 1982-1994

| | Number | | % Distribution | |
|---|---|---|---|---|
| | 1982-1994 | 1994 | 1982-1994 | 1994 |
| Characteristic | 258,658 | 31,212 | 100 | 100 |
| **Age in Years** | | | | |
| 13-19 | 850 | 112 | 0.4 | 0.3 |
| 20-29 | 44,770 | 4,868 | 15.6 | 17.3 |
| 30-39 | 117,759 | 14,334 | 45.9 | 45.5 |
| 40-49 | 64,639 | 8,396 | 26.9 | 25.0 |
| 50-59 | 21,415 | 2,550 | 8.2 | 8.3 |
| 60 and over | 9,225 | 952 | 3.1 | 3.6 |
| **Sex** | | | | |
| Male | 229,450 | 26,660 | 85.4 | 88.7 |
| Female | 29,619 | 4,620 | 14.8 | 11.5 |
| **Race/Ethnicity** | | | | |
| White | 37,602 | 14,929 | 47.8 | 53.2 |
| Black | 82,556 | 11,453 | 36.7 | 31.9 |
| Hispanic | 36,244 | 4,488 | 14.4 | 14 |
| Indian | 534 | 97 | 0.3 | 0.2 |
| Asian | 1,750 | 280 | 0.9 | 0.7 |

Note: Data are shown by year of death and are subject to substantial retrospecitve changes.  Based on reporting by State health departments.

Source: US Centers for Disease Control, Surveillance Report, Annual.

# Table 8

## RATES OF SELECTED HEALTH STATUS INDICATORS
## PER 100,000 POPULATION, BY RACE, USA, 1992

RACE

| INDICATOR | Total | White | Black |
|---|---|---|---|
| 1. Total deaths | 504.5 | 477.5 | 767.5 |
| 2. Suicides | 11.1 | 11.8 | 6.9 |
| 3. Homicides | 10.5 | 6.1 | 39.4 |
| 4. Lung cancer deaths | 39.3 | 38.8 | 48.8 |
| 5. Female breast cancer deaths | 21.9 | 21.7 | 27.0 |
| 6. Cardiovascular deaths | 180.4 | 172.8 | 265.3 |
| Deaths—heart disease | 144.3 | 139.2 | 205.4 |
| Deaths—stroke | 26.2 | 24.2 | 45.0 |
| 7. Reported incidence of AIDS | 31.2 | 17.9 | 104.2 |
| 8. Reported incidence of tuberculosis | 9.8 | 3.6 | 29.1 |

Notes: 2. Suicides and homicides are age adjusted to the 1940 standard population.

7. AIDS incidence is reported from 1993 data and is by date of diagnosis, adjusted for delays in    reporting; not adjusted for underreporting.

Sources: 1-6, 9 National Vital Statistics, CDC.

7 AIDS Surveillance System, CDC, NCID.

8 Tuberculosis Morbidity Data, CDC.

Advocates have reduced rates of cigarette smoking, increased hypertension control, and promoted condom use and safe sex. Regulations led to product labeling, nicotine warnings, safer cars, seat belts, and reduced speed limits (although the last was raised in the antiregulatory mood). There has been public concern about drinking and driving. TV antidrug messages are common, although billboards still promote alcohol to youth as an enhancer of social success.

However, black targets for diabetes, stroke, AIDS, tuberculosis, cirrhosis, heart disease and other disorders are distant. Nutrition, exercise, adherence to advice to control diabetes and hypertension, use of alcohol, cigarettes and illicit drugs, and use of seat belts are to some degree under individual control. Limited budgets, inferior nutritious fresh food in local stores, and cultural factors make a balanced diet of low priority. The lure of fast foods, ingrained patterns, and lack of time and opportunity for exercise in a safe place make it more difficult to reduce the rate of overweight in black women from 48 percent in 1992 to the goal of 30 percent by 2000. Other risks such as exposure to workplace hazards and environmental hazards such as toxic waste sites cannot be easily reduced without legislative mandates. While culturally appropriate and age appropriate health-promotion messages are essential, they are not sufficient. Stresses, of urban living exact a psychological toll on many, while others, in all social classes, mobilize individual and family strengths and the supports of church and social networks (Williams, 1992). Even those persons in black communities who cope successfully may not actively follow health-promoting regimens and may instead place themselves at risk when relatively well and, when ill, worsen their ill condition.

How people define health and illness, their attitudes toward risk taking, and their decisions to act proactively need study, along with differences and similarities among various groups within communities of African descent, immigrant- and native born. More needs to be learned about how the coping strategies of black adults operate in health and in illness. However, such needed explorations into individual and family risk reduction and health promotion do not diminish the need for clinical preventive services, for increased access to curative and rehabilitative care, and for societal changes to support health, broadly defined.

## CARDIOVASCULAR DISEASE AND STROKE

*African Americans* have not only higher rates of cardiovascular disease than other groups (for reasons not fully understood), but also a higher mortality from heart disease, hypertension, and stroke. Death rates among black men and women under 75 are higher than for whites at every income level. Diet and exercise can improve cardiac health.

**Targeted Population Objective:** Reduce coronary heart disease deaths among blacks to no more than 115 per 100,000 blacks. (1987 Age-adjusted Baseline: 163 per 100,000)

**Targeted Population Objective:** Reduce stroke deaths among blacks to no more than 27 per 100,000. (1987 Age-adjusted Baseline: 51.2 per 100,000)

Targeted Population Objective: Increase to at least 80 percent the proportion of black hypertensive men aged 18 through 34 who are taking action to help control their blood pressure. (1987 Baseline: 63 percent of aware black hypertensive men aged 18 through 34)

Blacks have the greatest excess of deaths from hypertension over whites for both males and females; the excess risk of death from hypertension occurs at all ages. Blacks between 30 and 49 have a 10-fold excess risk over whites (Sung *et al.*, 1992). Black men have the highest rate of stroke in the nation; their death rate from stroke is twice as high as that of white men and much higher than that of black women.

With heart attacks, blacks are less likely to have a witnessed episode of cardiac arrest, to receive bystander-initiated cardiopulmonary resuscitation, and to be brought to a hospital (Becker, 1993). When admitted, they are half as likely to survive. Factors that may operate in cardiovascular disease include access to care, the type, quality, and aggressiveness of medical care; and behavioral risk factors that place them at a disadvantage (Sorlie *et al.*, 1991). Obesity, failure to be screened or, if screened, failure to follow a regimen of attention to the silent disease of hypertension- and physiological response to external stressors may be at work. Certain of these are responsive to prevention, nutrition, stress management, and exercise. Others are dependent on access to quality care, including a primary care provider.

## CANCER

Several cancers prevalent in blacks are amenable to screening (breast and prostate) and to changes in behavior (lung and liver). Early detection can prolong life. Early treatment can improve the quality of life and its length.

### Breast Cancer

**Targeted Population Objective:** Increase to at least 80 percent the proportion of black women aged 40 and older who have ever received a clinical breast examination and a mammogram, and to at least 60 percent those aged 50 and older who have received them within the preceding one to two years. (1987 Baselines: 28 percent of 40 up, 19 percent of 50 up)

Breast cancer is amenable to screening, including breast self-examination and periodic mammograms. Yet only a small percentage of black women examine their breasts regularly and have mammograms; this suggests the need for improved health promotion (Brown, 1994). Black women with breast cancer are younger and poorer than white women. Mortality from breast cancer may relate to education and social class. Better educated and more financially secure women have more regular medical care and do BSE more regularly.

Breast cancer, the leading cause of cancer mortality for black women, is a disease for which they seek treatment later, have less treatment, and have a more rapid course. Evidence suggests a greater predictive risk in a first-degree relative, with similar risks for both races (Amos, 1991). High-fat consumption may be a risk factor.

Breast cancer is not spoken about openly by black women. They are only now joining or forming support groups such as SHARE or joining the YWCA's Encore program of group discussions and exercise, to aid in recovery. An innovative program funded by the National Cancer Institute, Save Our Sisters (SOS), designed to educate rural black women between 50 and 74, promote prevention, and improve access to medical services (Swanson, 1993a), had equivocal results in terms of improving screening.

## LUNG CANCER
Targeted Population Objective: Reduce cigarette smoking to a prevalence of no more than 18 percent among blacks aged 20 and older. (1987 Baseline: 34 percent)

The connection between smoking and lung cancer has been made. Black men also have occupational exposure; significant associations are seen between lung cancer and length of employment as automobile mechanics, painting machine operators, furnace operators, garbage collectors, and farm workers (Swanson, 1993b). Black men also smoke mentholated cigarettes more than white men do and have an increased risk of lung cancer from them (Sidney, 1995).

Adolescents who smoke generally continue as adults. Besides cancer, chronic pulmonary obstructive disease is a major health problem for blacks. Education may be a stronger factor than race; poorly educated young female smokers in public housing are heavier smokers, have weaker motivation to quit, and hold more health beliefs against quitting (Manfredi, 1992). The fact that black males who have never smoked are twice as likely to develop lung cancer as white males never-smokers (Iwamoto, 1995) suggests a role for other environmental pollutants.

In the black middle class, smoking is still fairly common, even among health workers. Proven smoking cessation programs may need to be modified to attract blacks of all classes.

## CANCER OF THE PROSTATE
Although there is no specific target for prostate cancer, the objective of increasing to at least 50 percent the proportion of blacks who have received all of the screening and immunization appropriate for their age level is relevant. Black men are twice as likely to be diagnosed with non-localized prostate cancer. They may also receive different treatments for localized cancer; the black-white stage difference may be due to modifiable social and medical factors (Liu, 1995). They experience higher mortality. They are less likely to have digital rectal examinations and undergo the prostatic-specific antigen (PSA) blood test.

Churches have been used to reach black men with educational and screening programs. One, using black men who had been diagnosed and treated for prostate cancer as role models of desired behaviors, found that, after completing the program, participants had significantly improved knowledge and self-efficacy scores related to prostate cancer screening (Boehm, 1995). Another found participants more willing to undergo digital rectal examination (Gelfand *et al.*, 1995). Such approaches may help men accept both types of sceening.

## AIDS AND TUBERCULOSIS

**Targeted Population Objective:** Confine the annual incidence of diagnosed AIDS cases among blacks to no more than 37,000 cases. (1989 Baseline: estimated 14,000-15,000)

**Targeted Population Objective:** Reduce tuberculosis among blacks to an incidence of no more than 10 cases per 100,000 blacks. (1988 Baseline: 28.3 per 100,000)

In areas in this nation where AIDS is endemic, its disproportionate incidence among *African Americans* of all ages leads to a disproportionate effect on the infected and the affected. The means of acquisition vary. Intravenous drug use and homosexual or bisexual contact predominate among black men; intravenous drug use and heterosexual contact are the means of contact among black women. Among *African Americans*, certain groups, such as the incarcerated, are a large proportion of the infected. Black women are an increasing proportion of persons acquiring AIDS heterosexually. These trends suggest the need for preventive approaches that take into account a multiplicity of factors, such as age, gender, race/ethnicity, level of education, and social factors as well as knowledge, attitudes, and beliefs.

These and other variables are among those considered in an extensive strategy development project developed by HEALTHWATCH Information and Promotion Service for HIV prevention and risk reduction among *African Americans* in New York State (1995). This study identified several groups requiring targeted attention. They include: adolescents, gay and bisexual men and adolescents, heterosexual men, lesbians, prison inmates (current and former), substance abusers, and women of childbearing age. The findings and recommended strategies relate to knowledge, attitudes, and beliefs; high-risk behavior; the influence of institutionalized racism and poverty; access to and use of AIDS counseling and testing; and the role of the black church and others in leadership. It proposes fruitful directions for research as well as culturally sensitive services.

With the AIDS epidemic, drug-resistant tuberculosis has increased in blacks and others in cities, particularly in shelters, among drug users, and in young black adults. The tuberculosis rate per 100,000 is 9.8; the rate in New York City is 44.2. These cases represent 12.8 percent of the cases nationally. There are combinations of medications that, given over a period of months, can treat the disease. Directly observed therapy, providing food or transportation, and home visits are part of an effective comprehensive public health approach.

Prevention and health promotion still require resources; they do not obviate the need for curative and rehabilitative care. Poverty, poor education, and a restrictive labor market contribute to a situation made more complex by the deteriorated housing, uncontrolled drug trafficking, and cutbacks in health services and entitlements that affect many inner cities.

## DIABETES

Diabetes is a disorder that is susceptible of easy detection; it responds to control with varying degrees of success, depending upon its type and age of onset. Control requires ongoing attention to diet, medication, and lifestyle. Untreated, it can lead to complications in many organs. Continuing medical supervision is needed to prevent the extemes of diabetic coma, or insulin shock, and of death. End-stage renal disease, vision problems, circulatory, and neurological complications exact a high toll of disability (Moritz, 1994).

**Targeted Population Objective:** Reduce diabetes among blacks to a prevalence of no more than 32 per 1,000. (1987 Baseline: 36 per 1000)

**Targeted Population Objective:** Reduce diabetes-related deaths among blacks to no more than 58 per 100,000. (1986 Baseline: 65 per 100,000)

**Targeted Population Objective:** Reduce lower extremity amputations due to diabetes among blacks to no more than 6.1 per 1,000 with diabetes. (1984-1987 Baseline: 10.2) Persons with diabetes are at greater risk of numerous health problems including heart attacks and stroke. The prevalence of diabetes is higher in blacks than in whites, particularly among women. Four risk factors more common in blacks than whites deserve attention. They are physical inactivity, obesity, hypertension, and cigarette smoking (Weaver *et al.*, 1993).

Obesity and hypertension are risk factors strongly affecting black women; they are twice as likely as white women to be overweight. A study by the National Heart, Lung, and Blood Institute Growth and Health Study showed that racial differences in obesity and hypertension are present by the age of 9 and 10 (1992). For both male and female diabetics, this is a risky combination. Hypertension is often silent; when identified, it requires continuing compliance by the patient even when he or she feels well. There are temptations to "go off" the diet prescribed for the diabetic or to assume that the medication will compensate.

Complications of diabetes particularly affect the elderly who often have other diseases causing disability. Black diabetics have a high rate of amputations of lower limbs (10.2 per 1,000 blacks with diabetes). Functional limitations in amputees are severely increased. Early medical attention, awareness of signs of impaired circulation, and exercise are often absent.

The risk of end-stage renal disease (kidney failure requiring dialysis) is increased in persons with both hypertension and diabetes. Control of high blood pressure can slow the progression of such kidney disease (Goldschmid *et al.*, 1995).

This is a situation in which early and consistent intervention by the individual, family support, and primary care may prevent the need for more expensive and complex medical interventions such as dialysis and transplants, to which blacks may or may not have access.

While routine urine and blood testing are likely to detect diabetes, the treatment regimen of insulin or oral medications requires daily patient participation. There is effective treatment: insulin by patient-administered injection, blood glucose (sugar) lowering oral medication, or insulin pumps. For many women cultural tolerance for obesity and for fatty foods and those high in simple carbohydrates makes modifying diet and exercising difficult (Melnyk, 1994). Education in churches, peer support and culture-specific materials from the American Diabetes Associaton and the American Dietetic Association help black diabetics overcome reluctance to inject themselves, take daily medicines, and monitor themselves, and, instead, help them adopt healthful food habits. Effective control can prevent complications and reduce disability and deaths.

## Older Years

Americans as a group are living longer. Although their life span is shorter as a group, if they reach 65, black people may have another decade of life. Black men have an average expectation of 13.5 years, as opposed to white men, with 15.5. Black women of this age have an expectation of 17.4 years, as opposed to white women, with 19.3. By 70, the life expectancy of black women (14.3 years) surpasses that of the total population and is close to that of white women.

However, it is not only the length of life but its quality that is important. For elderly people, maintaining functional independence, handling the activities of daily living, and coping with disability and chronic disorders are critical. For older *African Americans* the likelihood of limited financial resources is an added burden eased only in part by Medicare and Medicaid. The term "years of healthy life" (also referred to as quality-adjusted life years) is a summary measure that combines mortality (quantity of life) and morbidity and disability (quality of life) into a single measure.

**Targeted Population Objective:** Increase years of healthy life among blacks to at least 60 years. (1980 Baseline: An estimated 56 years)

Health problems plaguing *African Americans* in adulthood continue to limit functioning and cause pain and distress in later years. These include diabetes and its complications (Moritz *et al.*, 1994); arthritis, heart disease, hypertension, stroke, cancer, and chronic obstructive pulmonary disease (Bernard, 1993); dementia (Gorelick *et al.*, 1994); and depression (Christmas, 1996). Major causes of death are cardiac and lung disease, cancer, and stroke.

Even in the aging, adopting healthy behaviors, such as giving up smoking, exercising, and maintaining social contacts, can enhance life and functioning. The needs of older people can be met in multi-service centers, church and senior centers that provide nutritional counseling and food prograns, as well as links to health and social services. Intergenerational programs linking older people with young have proven beneficial to both. Older blacks use social networks as a health-care resource, for care-taking, home health care, and material aid (Petchers and Milligan, 1987). Social support, coping skills, and services are all needed.

## Trends in Health Policy: Implications for Health

Trends in health policy, initiated partly by the need to curb escalating costs of health care and partly by a mood of conservatism, may make it harder for *African Americans* to achieve the Year 2000 targets. The change from public responsibility to corporate privatization, hospital mergers, and megasystem networks; block grants to states, a level of government historically inattentive to black Americans; a diminished role for the federal government; managed care as a force for cost-containment and for transforming delivery systems; plans for punitive welfare reform and low priority on full employment; elimination of entitlements; and emphasis on a biological as opposed to a biopsychosocial model at a time when the "new morbidity" is increasing — all these may prove damaging to people who are poor, to those with behaviorally influenced disorders, and to those whose health needs are made more costly by complicating social problems. All these descriptors apply to *African Americans* as a population group in need of improved access to quality health care.

Managed care is a system of cost control in which health insurance plans feature provider risk sharing and active plan involvement in health-care decisions. In managed care, payments may be made in advance for a specified set of services. If they are provided at or below the agreed-upon cost, the health provider/plan gains. If they cost more, as they well may with poor black people, the plan loses. There is an incentive to limit services. People may be disenrolled if their needs are too costly and be sent to an underfunded, shrunken public system.

Many managed-care enrollees are in organized delivery systems such as Health Maintenance Organizations. HMOs provide comprehensive care, prevention, ambulatory and inpatient care, with a primary care physician coordinating care. In a medical model, they often provide minimal social services, prevention and outreach. In the past they enrolled healthier families and avoided the inner city. HMOs have been criticized as restricting appropriate hospitalization and refusing to include minority professionals and essential community providers. It is unlikely that managed care, in any form, will be more effective than fee-for-service in providing culturally appropriate, effective care or more willing than elitist medical centers to grant staff and faculty appointments to *African American* physicians (Christmas, 1995). Further, the policy of cutting back on the number of medical graduates and decreasing the ratio of specialists to primary care doctors does not address the gross underrepresentation of blacks as both specialists and primary- care physicians. *African American* communities may continue to be underserved or be served briefly as plans seek a new source of profit.

While health care should be accessible, available, and appropriate, without financial or cultural barriers, quality health services alone cannot guarantee good health. There has to be both an individual and a societal responsibility for health. For the health status of *African Americans* to approach the objectives of the Year 2000, health policy must address both access and quality, within a context that provides the social and economic support that ensures equity and enables health, and within a rational health-care system.

The author acknowledges the assistance of Kenya Crumel, Emilio Dorcely, and Jackson Sekhobo in the collection of data.

# REFERENCES

Amos, C.I. 1991. "Familiality of Breast Cancer and Socioeconomic Status in Blacks." Cancer Research 51: 1793-1797.

Bayne-Smith, M.A. 1994. "Teen Incentives Program: evaluation of a health promotion model for adolescent pregnancy prevention." *Journal of Health Education 25: 24-29.*

Becker, L.B., B.H. Han, P.M. Meyer, F.A. Wright, K.V. Rhodes, D.W. Smith and J.'Barrett. 1993. "Racial differences in the incidence of cardiac arrest and subsequent survival." *New England Journal of Medicine* 329: 600-606.

Bernard, M.A. 1993. "The health status of African-American elderly." *Journal of the National Medical Association* 85: 521-528.

Blendon, R.J., L.H. Aiken, H.E. Freeman, and C.R. Corey. 1989. "Access to medical care for Black and White Americans: a matter of continuing concern." *Journal of the American Medical Association* 261: 278-281.

Boehm, S., P. Coleman-Burns, E.A.Schlenk, M.M. Funnell, J. Parzuchowski, and I.J. Powell. 1995. "Prostate cancer in African American men: increasing knowledge and self-efficacy." *Journal of Community Health Nursing* 12: 161-169.

Brooks-Gunn, J. and F. Furstenberg. 1990. "Coming of age in the era of AIDS: puberty, sexuality and contraception." *Milbank Quarterly* 68: 59-84.

Brown, L.W. 1994. "Culturally sensitive breast cancer screening programs for older black women." *Nurse Practitioner* 19: 21, 25-26.

Byrd, W. and L.A. Clayton. 1992. "An American health dilemma: a history of Blacks in the health system." *Journal of the National Medical Association* 84: 189-200.

Centers for Disease Control and Prevention. National Center for Health Statistics. 1995 *Infant mortality — United States*, 1988. Hyattsville, Maryland: U.S. Department of Health and Human Services.

Children's Defense Fund. 1994. *The State of America's Children 1994*. Washington, D.C.

Christmas, J.J. 1995. "Health Policy and the Health of Americans of African

Descent" in *Facing Triple Jeopardy*. New York: Urban Issues Group.

Christmas, J.J. 1992. "Municipal efforts." *Bulletin of the New York Academy of Medicine*. 68: 64-73, 1992.

Christmas, J.J. 1983. "Sexism and Racism in Health Policy". In *Genes and Gender: IV — the Second X and Women's Health*, M. Fooden, ed. New York: Guardian Press, 205-215.

Christmas, J.J. "Socio-cultural aspects of late life depression." *Proceedings of Out of the Shadows*, a conference of the Hebrew Home for the Aged and the NewYork Academy of Medicine. In press.

Collins, J.W. and R.J. David. 1990. "The differential effects of traditional risk factors in infant birthweights among blacks and whites in Chicago." *American Journal of Public Health* 27: 457-466.

DiClemente, R.J. 1992. "Epidemiology of AIDS, HIV prevalence, and HIV incidence among adolescents." *Journal of School Health* 62: 325-330.

Duenhoelter, J.H., J.M. Jimenez, and G. Bauman. 1975. "Pregnancy performances of patients under fifteen years of age." *Obstestrics & Gynecology* 46: 49-52.

Earls, F.J. 1994. "Violence and today's youth." *The Future of Children* 4: 4-23.

Goldschmid, M.G., W.S. Domin, D.C., D.L. Gallina, and L.S. Phillips. 1995. "Diabetes in urban African-Americans. II. High prevalence of microalbuminuria and nephropathy in African-Americans with diabetes." *Diabetes Care* 18: 955-961.

Gorelick, P.B., S. Freels, Y. Harris, T. Dollear, M. Billingsley, and N. Brown. 1994. "Epidemiology of vascular and Alzheimer's dementia among African Americans in Chicago, IL: baseline frequency and comparison of risk factors." *Neurology* 44: 1391-1396.

Gelfand, D.E., J. Parzuchowski, M. Cort, and I. Powell. 1995. "Digital rectal examinations and prostate cancer screening: attitudes of African American men."

HEALTHWATCH Information and Promotion Servce. 1995. "AIDS and African-Americans: It's time for action!"

Institute for Health Policy. 1993. "Substance Abuse: The Nation's Number One Health Problem."

Iwamoto, K.C. 1995. "The epidemiology of lung cancer in metropolitan Detroit: racial differences in men." *Dissertation Abstracts* 55:4805.

Krieger, N., D.L. Rowley, A.A. Herman, B.Avery and M.T. Phillips. 1993. "Racism, sexism, and social slass: implications for studies of health, disease, and well-being." *Journal of Preventive Medicine* 9 (supp 2): 82-122.

Lieu, T.A., P.W. Newacheck and M.A. McManus. 1993. "Race, ethnicity, and access to ambulatory care among U.S. adolescents." *American Journal of Public Health* 83: 960-965.

Liu, W. 1995. "Race differences in stage at diagnosis of prostate cancer." *Dissertation Abstracts* 56: 1365.

Manfredi, C., L. Lacey, B. Warnecke and M. Buis. 1992. "Smoking-related behavior, beliefs, and social environment of young black women in subsidized public housing in Chicago." *American Journal of Public Health* 82: 267-272.

Melnyk, M.G. and E. Weinstein. 1994. "Preventing obesity in black women by targeting adolescents: a literature review." *Journal of the American DieteticAssociation.* 94: 536-540.

Michaels, D. and C. Levine. 1993. "The Youngest Survivors: Estimates of the Number of Motherless Youth Orphaned by AIDS in New York City." In *A Death in the Family: Orphans of the HIV Epidemic*. New York: United Hospital Fund of New York.

Moritz, D.J., A.M. Ostfeld, D. Blazer, D. Curb, J.O. Taylor and R.B. Wallace. 1994. "The health burden of diabetes for the elderly in four communities." *Public Health Reports* 109: 782-790.

Mullings, L.P., J. Mitchell and D. McLean. 1995. "Harlem Birth Right". Personal communication.

National Heart, Lung, and Blood Institute. 1992. "Obesity and cardiovascular risk factors in black and white girls: the NHLBI Growth and Health Study." *American Journal of Public Health* 82: 1613-1620.

New York City Department of Health. Summary *Vital Statistics*. 1991-1994.

New York State Department of Health. Vital Statistics. 1991 - 1994.

Petchers, M.K. and S.E. Milligan. 1987. "Social networks and social support among Black elderly: a health care resource." *Social Work in Health Care* 12: 103-117.

Schwartz, E., V.Y. Kofie, M. Rivo, and R.V. Tuckson. 1985. "Black/white comparisons of deaths preventable by medical intervention: United States and the District of Columbia 1980-1986." *International Journal of Epidemiology* 19:1990.

Sorlie, P., E. Rogot, R. Anderson, N.J. Johnson and E. Backlund. 1992. "Black-white mortality differences by family income." Lancet 340: 346-50.

Stark, E. 1990. "Rethinking homicide: violence, race, and the politics of gender." *International Journal of Health Services* 20: 3-26.

*Substance Abuse Funding News*. "Survey Documents Steady Rise in Drug Use by Teens." December, 1995.

Swanson, G.M. 1993a. "Breast cancer among black and white women in the 1980s: changing patterns in the United States by race, age, and extent of disease." *Cancer* 72: 788-797.

Swanson, G.M. 1993b. "Diversity in the association between occupation and lung cancer among black and white men." *Cancer Epidemiology, Biomarkers & Prevention* 2: 313-320.

Sung, J.F., S.A. Harris-Hooker, G. Schmid, E. Ford, B. Simmons and J.W. Reed. 1992. "Racial differences in mortality from cardiovascular disease in Atlanta, 1979-1985." *Journal of the National Medical Association* 84: 259-263.

U.S. Department of Health and Human Services. 1985. "Health status of minorities and low income groups." Washington, D.C.: *Government Printing Office*.

U.S. Department of Justice. Office of Juvenile Justice and Delinquency Prevention. 1996. "Juvenile Offenders and Victims: 1996 Update on Violence." Washington, D.C.: U.S. Government Printing Office.

Watson, R.R., ed. 1995. *Substance Abuse during Pregnancy and Childhood*. New Jersey: Humana Press.

Weaver, A.Y., R.C. Brownson, J.C. Wilkerson, P.O. Akinbola, and J. Jackson-Thompson. 1993. "Racial differences in the prevalence of cardiovasculat factors among persons with diabetes." *Missouri Medicine* 90: 751-754.

Williams, D.R. and C. Collins. 1995. "US socioeconomic and racial differences in health: patterns and explanations." *Annual Review of Sociology* 21: 349-356.

## DATA SOURCES:
U.S. National Center for Health Statistics, *Vital Statistics of the United States*, Annual and Monthly Vital Statistics Reports.

For Objectives and Baseline Data:

U.S. Department of Health and Human Services. 1991. *Healthy People 2000: National Health Promotion and Disease Prevention Objectives.* Washington, D.C.: U.S. Government Printing Office.

U.S. Department of Health and Human Services. 1995. *Healthy People 2000 Review.* Washington, D.C.: U.S. Government Printing Office.


## BIOGRAPHICAL SKETCH
June Jackson Christmas, M.D., Executive Director of the Urban Issues Group, is Professor Emeritus of Behavioral Science, City University of New York Medical School, and Clinical Professor of Psychiatry at Columbia University College of Physicians and Surgeons. Past President of the American Public Health Association, she served from 1972 to 1980 as New York City Commissioner of Mental Health, Mental Retardation and Alcoholism Services. She has published extensively on health and mental-health policy and services.

# DEVELOPING OUR YOUTH: WHAT WORKS

**Karen Fulbright- Anderson, Ph.D.**

# ABSTRACT

Changes in family structure and the economy have increased the challenges to youth of making a successful transition to adulthood. The burden of poverty magnifies this challenge.

The traditional public policy response to youth concerns has been problem focused, remediative, and categorical, operated in an uncoordinated fashion by several different agencies. With few exceptions, residential Job Corps being the most notable example, this approach has been shown to be largely ineffective. This approach has been changing somewhat over the past few years, as intergovernmental agencies have been formed to coordinate activities and services, and the government has introduced new programs like YouthBuild, which have a distinctly developmental focus. However, we still have a long way to go.

There is a research base on youth needs and resilient behavior that provides a prescriptive framework for effective youth programming. And, there is a growing body of evidence from the evaluation field that when programs incorporate the principles espoused by research and theory on youth needs and resiliency, they are able to produce positive outcomes for youth from our most troubled communities. The reach of these programs is limited.

We lack the infrastructure but not the knowledge to apply effective youth programming strategies on a wide scale and into the communities where it is needed the most. There is growing consensus among youth serving and youth oriented organizations that this infrastructure must be based on our knowledge about youth needs and effective programming and have sufficient financial resources to support it.

*They are the children of the shadows: the impoverished youth who live in the tumbledown neighborhoods of the American inner city; the children of often desperate and broken families, where meals are sometimes cereal three times a day; the young people who daily face the lures of drugs, sex, fast money and guns; the unnoticed youths who operate in a maddening universe where things always seem to go wrong....Numbers and trends tell only so much behind them are the young people themselves, their voices, their lives.*

**The New York Times**

Young people between the ages of 14 and 24 represent one out of six Americans. While most young people are managing the transition from the classroom to the workplace successfully, unacceptable numbers are growing up without sufficient support, guidance, and resources to help them become responsible adults.

Conditions for young people have worsened considerably over the past two decades. Increasing numbers of young people are growing up in single parent families, in poverty, and are exposed to violence. At the same time, emotional and behavioral problems among young people have increased. Suicide rates among adolescents have been increasing and in recent years claimed the lives of roughly 10,000 young people annually. Homicide rates soared 77 percent between 1985 and 1990, making it the leading cause of death among young *African-American* males and the second leading cause of death for young white males.

It has been estimated that between 20 percent to 50 percent of youth are engaged in, or at risk of engaging in, behaviors which endanger their future well-being. Some of these behaviors, such as violence, are quite visible while others, such as dropping out of school, are more subtle. Nonetheless, poor outcomes among these young people exact a high cost to society in terms of human and financial resources, and undermine the future stability of this country.

What follows is a profile of the youth population; a description of this country's approach to addressing youth concerns; highlights of key findings from research and theory about what youth need to successfully transition to adulthood and from evaluations of effective programs; future challenges; and recommendations for strategies to meet these challenges.

## DEMOGRAPHIC PROFILE

In 1990, there were 40 million young people between the ages of 14 and 24, comprising 16 percent of the total population. Almost half of these young people, 48 percent, lived in suburban areas, while the remainder, 29 percent, lived in central cities, and in non-metropolitan communities, 23 percent. The absolute numbers of young people are projected to increase over the next several years to 47 million by 2010. Members of minority groups are projected to experience the greatest growth rates relative to their white counterparts throughout this time period.

Most young people, 76 percent, live with both parents. However, it is projected that half of all children will live in a single-parent home before they reach 18 years of age and will spend an average of six years in a single-parent family. *African-American* children are less likely than their white and Hispanic counterparts to live in a two-parent household. In 1992, only 43 percent of *African-American* children lived with both parents.

**Educational Attainment**

Most young people between the ages of 14 and 17, or 96 percent, were enrolled school in 1991. The overwhelming majority of all young adults, 82 percent, had earned a high school diploma or a Graduate Equivalency Diploma (GED); however, significant racial differences existd. Only a slim majority of Hispanics, 54 percent, had earned a diploma or a GED. The academic achievements of *African-American* youth, at 76 percent, was more similar to their white counterparts, whose rate was 82 percent.

The dropout rate for young people between the ages of 16 and 24 was 12.5 percent nationally in 1991; however, dropout rates as high as 50 percent have been reported in one quarter of all urban schools. A number of explanations have been advanced to explain youth dropout rates. High school dropouts cite several reasons for leaving school, including "school was not the place" for them, difficulty in school, poor grades, wanting to seek employment, or marriage or pregnancy. Researchers report that young people also leave school because of peer pressure, alienation, and because of the low expectations about the achievement of some students that is conveyed by the curricula and teachers.

**Employment and Earnings**

Unemployment rates among young people between the ages of 16 and 24 show fairly strong racial differences, with black youth rates slightly higher than twice the rate of white youth. In 1992, *African-American* youths between the ages of 16 and 19 had an unemployment rate of 41 percent compared to their white counterparts whose rate was 17 percent; the rate for Hispanic youth was 30 percent. Although the unemployment rates for older youth are about half that of the younger age cohort, the same racial pattern exists. The unemployment rate in 1992 for *African-American* youth between the ages of 20 and 24 was 22 percent as compared to rates of 9 percent for whites and 15 percent for Hispanics. These figures, however, understate the size of the problem. Actual joblessness rates, which include those who do not have a job, regardless of whether or not they are looking for a one, are roughly two to three times the official unemployment rates.

As one might expect, educational attainment, employment, and earnings are positively correlated. High school graduates are more likely to be employed than those who have dropped out of school. In 1989, approximately 52 percent of non-high school graduates were employed, as compared to 76 percent of high school graduates; 89 percent of those who have completed some college, and 90 percent of those who are college graduates. It bears noting that despite the relationship between education and labor market activity, a fair number of those who have completed high school also experience unemployment.

Regarding earnings, the gap between the more educated and less educated worker is substantial. Those who have college degrees earned $15.21 per hour in 1991, or 57 percent more per hour than high school graduates. Workers who are high school graduates earn $9.71 per hour, 23 percent more per hour than those who have not completed a high school education.

A number of reasons related to supply and demand factors have been advanced to explain youth unemployment rates. For example, on the demand side, it has been documented that youth employment rates are highly sensitive to local and aggregate employment conditions. For every 1 percent increase in unemployment in the general population, the overall youth unemployment rate rises by 1.7 percent, with the rate for *African-American* youth rising by 3.5 percent.

Shifts in the structure of the economy, with the decline in manufacturing concomitant with increases in the service sector, have been particularly problematic for *African-Americans*. Jobs held by *African-Americans* in manufacturing declined from 46 percent of all employed *African-Americans* in 1974 to 26 percent in 1984. This pattern has continued through the 1990s, and *African-American* high school dropouts have been especially hit hard by this decline.

Discrimination is another demand side factor that affects employment rates for *African-American* youths. In a study of Chicago area employers, researchers found that employers believed that *African-Americans* were inappropriate hires for customer service positions because they lacked the requisite basic skills and work experiences. Accordingly, these employers conducted their recruitment efforts through sources that would reach potential applicants who were white. In another study which used matched pairs of comparable *African-Americans* and whites simulating a job search, whites received 50 percent more job offers than their *African-American* counterparts.

On the supply side, parents' employment status, school achievement, and performance on skill tests have been cited as factors in explaining youth employment. For example, one of the strongest predictors of unemployment for those under age 20 is growing up in a low-income family. In addition, it has been estimated that 30 percent of young adults lack the basic skills necessary to carry out unfamiliar tasks. Although standardized test scores have improved for *African-American* youth, they still remain lower than those of whites, which is likely to contribute to differences in earnings and employment rates between these two groups.

## The New Morbidities

There are a number of young people who are engaged in problem behaviors which have been demonstrated to have a direct effect on their future economic

131

outcomes. It has been estimated that between 20 percent to 50 percent of all 10- and 17- year-olds are engaged in risky behavior such as delinquent and criminal acts; school failure; substance abuse; and unprotected sexual activity. There is evidence that these behaviors are strong predictors of negative outcomes in the labor force. For example, engagement in risk behaviors predicts women's receipt of welfare and men's unemployment. Drug use and criminal behavior, in particular, have been found to decrease a young person's schooling and men's employment.

A number of factors have been attributed to these problem behaviors, most of which are related to the economic stress of poverty. For example, Wilson found that the combined impact of high unemployment rates of young *African-American* males; high rates of poverty and welfare dependence; increased concentration of poverty among urban poor *African-Americans* and female heads of households; weak social institutions; limited job opportunities; and few male and employed role models contributed to a chronic set of problems affecting youth development. Parental child-rearing practices which are characterized by insufficient nurturance and inconsistent disciplinary practices have also been found to be direct and indirect causes of depression, loneliness, delinquency, and drug use among youth. These types of parental practices are believed to occur most frequently among families that are under economic stress.

## The Burden of Poverty

*"For Freddie, poverty was not only a dearth of material comforts and opportunities; even more crippling, he wrestled with a poverty of hope."*
– *The New York Times*

Poverty, unfortunately, is a way of life for significant numbers of young people. Approximately 18 percent of all youths between the ages of 16 and 24 were categorized as poor in 1992. Poverty rates for *African-American* and Hispanic youth, at 33 percent and 31 percent, respectively, are more than twice that for white youth. Although *African-American* and Hispanic youth are more likely than their white counterparts to be poor, in absolute numbers there were more white youth below the poverty level than poor African-American and Hispanic youth combined. Males between the ages of 16 and 19 had slightly higher poverty rates than those 22 to 24 years of age, while the reverse was true for females.

The proportion of poor youth who live in central cities and suburban communities is almost a mirror image of the geographic distribution of all youth. Most poor youth, 44 percent, live in central cities, as compared to 31 percent in suburban and 25 percent in non-metropolitan communities. Concentrated poverty, that is communities in which at least 40 percent of all residents have poverty-level incomes, increased substantially during the 1970s. By 1980, almost half of all poor people living in concentrated poverty lived in the 10 largest metropolitan areas, principally in large cities in the Northeast and Midwest. These trends continued throughout the 1980s and by the end of the decade the poverty rate had increased in the 23 of the 30 largest cities.

Low-income, urban youth, particularly racial minorities, face many challenges to their successful development. These challenges are social, educational, health-related, and economic in nature, and are interconnected in a variety of ways.

## CONSEQUENCES OF GROWING UP IN HIGH-POVERTY COMMUNITIES

There is evidence that although many refer to "high risk" youth, perhaps a more realistic assessment is that their environments are high risk. Low-income youth are more likely than others to grow up in environments which do not provide the opportunities, resources, guidance, and support that facilitate healthy development.

### Social Support

Low-income youth often lack stable family lives. In 1992, fifty-nine percent of all poor children lived in single female-headed families. African-American children were roughly twice as likely to live in a single female-headed family as compared to their white and Hispanic counterparts. Single parent families experience poverty rates that are seven to eight times higher than that of two-parent families. The economic stresses on these families make it difficult for them to provide the support their children need to develop successfully. Poor adults have more mental health problems than those with higher incomes and single parents, particularly females, are similarly vulnerable to psychological distress such as anxiety and depression.

Low-income youth grow up in communities that do not typically provide them access to strong social networks of working professionals. A study of 17 to 24 year-olds in high-poverty communities in Boston found that among those interviewed, 50 percent did not know anyone employed in professional activities such as business, accounting, engineering, science, or law. All of these young people knew someone in jail or in trouble with the police. While community-based youth programs have historically and continue to be sources of support for young people, many existing programs do not reach youth who live in low-income communities or provide a consistent level of support.

### Employment Opportunities

*"Economically is it tougher? Maybe because there are less factory jobs. There might be more opportunities in professions. . . then I have it harder, because racism is rising again."*

— Bernardo Vasquez, 17, *The New York Times*

Youth growing up in high-poverty communities also face especially limited employment opportunities. Job growth has occurred largely in suburban communities, which are not easily accessible to inner-city residents. The good jobs that are geographically accessible to low-income youth more often than not require familial contacts, references and have higher skill requirements than youth tend to possess. In addition, discrimination against *African-Americans*, particularly males, persists as a barrier for inner-city youth. Researchers have found that employers expressed strong prejudice against inner-city *African-American* men and screened out job candidates based on class characteristics, particularly those identified as having "ghetto" speech and dress patterns.

Finally, low-income youth generally have little guidance and few resources to help them prepare for adulthood in positive and healthy ways. Many feel that society does not hold a place for them, and they have little confidence in themselves for their futures. The study of 17- and 24-year-olds in high poverty Boston communities also found that 50 percent of these young people believed there was not support in their neighborhoods for people who try to achieve through school and work.

On every indicator of current and future well-being, young people who grow up in high-risk environments characterized by poverty are considerably worse off than their more economically advantaged peers. Research has shown that youth who grow up in high-poverty communities are more likely than their more advantaged counterparts to drop out of school, have higher unemployment rates, become parents at an early age, be exposed to violent crimes, and be victimized. This is true regardless of race and ethnic background.

## YOUTH SERVICES

*"The government's perspective is the short term. You have a bad situation and you provide short-term intervention, getting someone out of alienation into the mainstream in a way that is basically obedient. But you need a community in which people can grow up, that has values and aspirations and support systems. Instead we have communities in which institutions are not working, and so the people who survive are the exceptions. It is not that a few people have deficits and therefore they can't make it and they need productive programs. It is that most of the people are not getting what they need from their community. Therefore we need to rebuild communities in which people can grow up in a healthy context."*

*– Dorothy Stoneman, Executive Director, YouthBuild U.S.A.*

At the same time that there is evidence that too many young people in this country are experiencing problems which are multiple and interconnected, there is agreement that many of the major institutions in which young people are growing up have fallen short of providing the guidance and support youth need to develop in healthy ways. Publicly funded services and programs, especially those targeted

134

to young people from high-risk environments, tend to be short-term, remediative, categorical, and narrowly focused around single problems.

Schools in our poorest communities have fewer material and financial resources than more advantaged areas. These schools often use practices such as tracking, grade retention, and convey low expectations about student capabilities, which exacerbate existing academic and social behavior problems.

In addition, schools have paid little attention to the 50 percent of young people who do not continue on to college. It has been estimated that the federal government invests from between one-seventh to less than one-half as much for the education and training of each non-college bound youth as it does for each young person who attends college.

Unlike other industrialized nations, the United States has no system to facilitate young's people transition to the workplace. Rather, there are separate institutions which operate programs that are largely unconnected to each other and to the workplace. Vocational education programs have typically lacked a conceptual underpinning and seldom accrue long-term benefits for graduates. There is some evidence that these programs decrease drop out rates, but have little effect on academic achievement or motivation to pursue further education.

To date, federal programs focused on youth unemployment problems have been overwhelmingly unsuccessful in producing positive outcomes for youth and, in many instances, produced negative outcomes. Most federal youth employment programs have been short-term and focused on the most immediate causes of youth employment, such as lack of job experience. Evaluations of past federal programs designed to fix youth unemployment reported that when there were positive earnings' impacts, they lasted only while youth were enrolled in the programs. There was no evidence of positive earnings impacts in the longer term. On the contrary, the impacts were either negative or nonexistent. Impact evaluations of more recent federal Job Training Partnership Act (JTPA) programs drew similar conclusions about the longer term earnings impact.

These findings contrast sharply with data from an impact evaluation of one of the most successful federal youth employment and training programs and from other countries. The residential Job Corps offers intensive, long-term job training, and remedial education as well as support services such as counseling, health care, and job placement assistance. Eighty-five percent of Job Corps participants are high school dropouts, yet, evaluators found that those who maintained consistent participation in the residential Job Corps program showed the most favorable employment outcomes. These young people experienced an increase in employment of over three weeks per year and an increase in earnings of approximately $655 per year. They had a fivefold increase in the probability of earning a high school diploma or its equivalent, better health and a reduction in the receipt of financial welfare and unemployment insurance assistance. Evidence from other countries indicates that the greatest success is found in programs that not only prepare youth for employment, but also include and explicit youth development focus as a goal.

The failure of programs to improve outcomes for youth has contributed to a belief that nothing works with youth, especially those from high-risk environments. In response many have advocated shifting attention to young children who are viewed as being more easily affected by interventions. However, there is evidence from research on youth needs and resilient behavior, and from evaluations of effective youth programs that indicates that the flaw may lie in the failed programs' theories of change, not in the youth whose problems the programs attempted to fix. The underlying theory of change of these programs is that youth problems can be fixed by focusing on the immediate causes of youth problems with short-term, relatively low-intensity, single-problem focused programs. There is a growing body of evidence which suggests that a radically different approach is needed to affect change. The theory of change suggested by this evidence is that in order to yield positive outcomes for youth, we must continuously promote positive behavior by helping youth meet their developmental needs in healthy ways.

**Research Findings**

Research and theory about youth tell us that all young people have a core set of basic human needs. To make a successful transition to adulthood, youth must meet these needs in healthy way so that they can develop appropriate attitudes, behaviors, and competencies in such areas as education, personal relationships, health, work, and family. These needs have been summarized as including: achieving a sense of safety and structure in one's life; the mastery of skills viewed as important by others; having close relationships with others; feeling that one belongs to or has membership in a community; feeling valued and having a sense of self-worth; and experiencing independence and control in one's life.

The process of meeting needs is universal. It occurs regardless of ones status, race or gender. The gang member and the honor-roll student are both engaged in the same process; however, they have or perceive different avenues, opportunities, and resources available to them, and make different choices. That gangs are youth development programs, albeit with a negative twist, is well recognized. Carl Taylor's insightful book on the gang culture in Detroit demonstrates with clarity how a young person who joins a gang automatically has an opportunity to meet each one of the needs referred to above. Taylor described how the gangs are highly structured, modeling the best of corporate America. Those in the gangs shared with him the ways in which their fellow gang members protected, accepted, and valued them. They described the skills they learned as a result of their involvement with the gang, and their feelings of independence. And they spoke of the sense of community that they found in their gang membership.

The needs young people have are not unlike those of adults. Adults who have the resources, select housing that has security systems, or other features that increase their feelings of safety. We go to college and graduate to get skills and credentials that increase our value. We join professional organizations, social clubs, and churches to give us a sense of belonging and membership. We marry, stay in touch with friends and family so that we can maintain close relationships with others. And we involve ourselves in work and activities that contribute to our feelings of self-worth.

Unlike adults, who have more direct control over their lives, young people are dependent upon adults to create environments that provide opportunities that enable them to meet their basic needs in positive and healthy ways. Unfortunately, for far too many young people, adults have failed to provide such environments.

There is an emerging body of research about the personal, social, and environmental factors that are associated with positive and resilient behavior among youth. These factors include sustained and nurturing relationships with caring, supportive adults; social competence, such as empathy and caring; problem solving skills; autonomy; a sense of purpose and future; and communities and schools that provide caring and supportive peers and adults, and after-school activities such as sports and music, have high expectations, clear norms, and opportunities for participation.

There is growing evidence that organizations that have a youth development focus contribute to positive, resilient behavior among youth who live in high-risk environments. Several researchers have documented and analyzed how youth development programs provide opportunities for young people to meet their basic needs in healthy ways. Staffs of these programs make sure that participants feel cared for, loved and respected so that they can form close relationships with others. They provide opportunities for young people to develop skills that are valued by others such as musical or artistic ability, reading comprehension, writing, verbal presentation, or housing construction. They give youth a chance to demonstrate their competence through, for example, competitions, contests, peer tutoring, and community-service projects so that young people feel that they have something to contribute and feel good about themselves. They make sure that the program setting is emotionally and physically safe for participants, and activities are structured. Activities are structured, and young people have opportunities to make decisions about program aspects that affect them.

A brief review of three recently evaluated programs that were found to yield positive outcomes for their participants reveals that each one incorporated a youth development approach into the program design and activities. The findings from the first two programs described below are based on impact evaluations.

## The Quantum Opportunities Program (QOP)

QOP is a five-site demonstration project starting in ninth grade and continuing through the high school years. The programs were organized around education activities such as participation in computer-assisted instruction, peer tutoring, homework assistance; service activities such as community service projects, helping with public events, and regular jobs; and development activities such as curricula focused on life/family skills, college and job planning. With one exception, the programs were operated by local Opportunities Industrial Centers (OIC) of America, which was required to deliver program services to a group of 25 very disadvantaged youth, provide monetary incentives for staff and participants, and stick with the same youth for the duration of the project—substitutions were not allowed.

After the first year of the program, the program evaluators did not detect evidence that the experimental group was doing any better than the control group; on the contrary, they found that in several areas, the experimental group was doing worse. After two years, the evaluators found that the experimental groups' academic and functional skills were greater than those of the control group. The differences were even greater, and statistically significant, by the time most of the youth were leaving high school. The evaluators also found that, several months after the time when the youth were expected to have completed high school, they maintained higher performance in academic and functional skill levels, there were statistically significant differences between the experimental and control groups on the following dimensions:

QOP members were less likely than their non-program counterparts to have children, and more likely to:

- graduate from high school;
- attend post-secondary schools;
- have received an honor or award in the past year;
- be involved in community service;
- be hopeful about the future; and
- consider their life a success

It is important to note that the evaluators found large differences in the QOP effect in the four sites. The site that created a group identity among QOP members had a reliable menu of program offerings, and provided stable, consistent relationships between QOP youth, and program staff had consistently higher attendance, strong group morale, and stronger outcomes for its participants. Notably, even the sites that were not able to consistently perform at the same level as the stronger site were able to have a positive effect on the participants. The feature which appears to have contributed to such an effect is staff who demonstrated caring and concern about the participants by calling or visiting them weekly throughout the entire high school period. The program evaluators concluded that year-round and sustained connection with caring adults contributes to positive outcomes for youth.

## *Big Brothers/Big Sisters*

Big Brothers/Big Sisters (BB/BS) is a highly structured program that pairs unrelated adult volunteers with youth from single-parent households. Both the volunteer and youth agree to meet two to four times each month for at least one year, with a typical meeting lasting four hours. BB/BS uses a stringent screening process to identify applicants who do not pose a safety risk and who are likely to honor the time commitment and form positive relationships with the youth. BB/BS agencies provide an orientation for volunteers to explain the program require-ments and rules, and recommend extensive training on the developmental stages of youth, communication and limit-setting skills, tips on relationship-building, and recommendations on the best way to interact with a Little Brother or Little Sister. The pairs are supervised by BB/BS case worker through monthly telephone con-tact with the volunteer and with the parent and/or youth during the first year of the match. After the first year, the case worker reduces contact to once per quarter. The caseworkers support the match by providing guidance when problems arise in the relationship.

Evaluators of the Big Brothers/Big Sisters program found that program par-ticipants were less likely to engage in negative behaviors relative to the control group on a number of dimensions. Specifically, participants were less likely than the control group to hit someone or initiate drug or alcohol use during the study. An even stronger effect was found for minority little brothers and sisters.

The little brothers and sisters were also found to have:

• Skipped fewer days of school and fewer classes than their non-program coun-    terparts, reported feeling more competent about doing schoolwork and showed modest gains in their grade point averages. Gains were strongest among little sisters, particularly minority little sisters.

• Better quality of relationships with parents, due primarily to a higher level of trust in the parent. These effects were strongest for white little brothers.

• Made improvements in peer relationships. This effect was strongest for minority little brothers.

It is important to note that the program did not have an explicit focus on reducing specific behaviors. As such, neither the program staff, nor the big broth-ers or big sisters provided counseling about substance abuse or other problem be-haviors. Instead, as the evaluators note, the big brothers and sisters met a basic human need for having caring, supportive relationships.

## Youth Build

YouthBuild is designed to provide training in construction skills and improve the academic and leadership skills of young people between the ages of 16 and 24 who come from economically disadvantaged backgrounds. The young people spend one year rehabilitating abandoned buildings to provide affordable permanent housing for homeless or very low-income people. They attend academic classes for 50 percent of the program time, mastering basic skills and preparing for their high school equivalency diploma. The program also includes individual counseling, peer support groups, driver's license training, recreation, and cultural activities. Major emphasis is placed on providing opportunities for young people to develop as leaders through making decisions affecting the program and its policies, through involvement in community life, and through leadership training. The original concept for YouthBuild grew out of a youth program in East Harlem. Congress passed the Youth Build Act as a subtitle to the Housing and Community Development Act of 1992, and there are currently 100 YouthBuild programs across the country.

YouthBuild attracts and serves a largely male, minority, and economically disadvantaged population. Roughly 85 percent of YouthBuild enrollees are male. Sixty-eight percent of YouthBuild enrollees are *African American*; 10 percent are Hispanic; 10 percent are Native American, Asian/Pacific Islander or multiracial; and 11 percent are white. More than half (57 percent) come from households with an annual income of less than $15,000; almost 80 percent have household incomes of less than $25,000. Thirty-six percent of the participants are parents. One in four enrollees reports having either a high school diploma (18 percent) or a Graduate Equivalency Degree (7 percent). Almost 18 percent report that they have not had a job since leaving high school, and 49 percent have held one to three jobs since they left high school. In short, the program is largely composed of inner-city poor and unemployed young people.

Not surprisingly, a significant number report undesirable neighborhood conditions. Seventeen percent say they do not feel safe in their neighborhood, 60 percent report that the lack of jobs is a major neighborhood problem; 41 percent maintain that drugs and drug dealing is a major problem and one-third report that gangs and violence are a big problem. One of four enrollees have been convicted of a felony; the same share have served time in jail. Almost one-third report some kind of criminal background, and 10 percent have been in treatment for drug or alcohol abuse.

Data collected early in the implementation of the program indicated that the sites have been successful in retaining most of the participants in the program for the full year, in placing many of them in college or in jobs and in helping those placed in jobs earn average hourly wages that are generally good for employment/training programs for poor urban youth ($7.53 an hour).

Qualitative data on YouthBuild programs indicates compelling evidence that participation in the program changes the lives of participants in positive ways.

These data also pointed to staff characteristics that help engender youth engagement in YouthBuild. These characteristics include respect; unsolicited demonstration of caring—patience, persistence, encouragement; openness about self and background; providing help when help is needed; honesty, good judgement, ability to handle confidentiality, and being a good listener. The evaluators found that once trust is established, role models—either counselors or peers who've had similar experiences-help youth believe change is possible, and facilitate their efforts to make that change.

The youth programs described above differ in the age groups with which they work and the program components they provide. They share in common the fact that they provide opportunities for participants to meet one or more of their basic human needs in positive and productive ways. They clearly contradict the popular view that "nothing works" for young people from our most disadvantaged communities. On the contrary, these evaluations provide evidence that when a youth development approach is incorporated into program activities and the way in which adults involved in the programs relate to the youth participants, young people can and do thrive.

## CHALLENGES AND OPPORTUNITIES

Youth services are faced with a number of challenges, in part due to the fact that it is not a field; rather, it is collection of discrete, program components typically focused on problems which lacks a common set of core principles, a system for training and developing the capacities of those who work with youth, rigorous evaluation of progress, and a national policy to support a developmentally focused approach. There is a growing consensus among youth serving professionals and youth-oriented organizations regarding the steps which must be taken to institutionalize a youth-development approach at the federal, state, and local levels. To improve the lives of youth in this country, particularly those from our most distressed communities, we must apply the knowledge from theory, research, and evaluation about youth needs and effective programming to the following activities:

• Establishing a coherent national policy which supports positive youth development. This would include the development of national goals and a core set of youth focused, developmental principles to guide practice, policy, and research.

• Specifing core outcomes—short-term, intermediate, and long-term—that we wish to help youth achieve, and the indicators of those outcomes.

• Developing the infrastructure necessary to operationalize policy, plan, coordinate, and implement effective youth services at the national, state and local level. This would include establishing an interconnected system for training and developing youth workers; making information about effective approaches easily accessible; creating a network of community supports for youth; insuring that such support exists in the areas of greatest need; establishing mechanisms for conduct-

141

ing ongoing evaluations to monitor progress; and appropriating sufficient, stable and long-term financial resources to support the infrastructure.

• Building the capacity of the systems in which youth spend much of their time-families, communities, schools – to provide the level and quality of support needed to promote positive youth outcomes.

There are encouraging signs that there is a window of opportunity to move forward a youth-development agenda. Youth development concepts are finding their way into the language, programs, and practices of federal agencies such as the Justice Department and the Department of Housing and Urban Development, and interagency working groups. At the local level, a number cities and counties have established task forces and initiatives focused on developing the capacities of youth. These localities are by setting a common vision based on youth development principles, coordinating policies and activities, and marshaling resources from various sources. At the same time, a number of local communities across the country have established comprehensive community initiatives which have the explicit dual goals of building community capacity and improving outcomes for children and families. The Young American's Act, passed by Congress in 1989, was designed to establish a national youth policy. During the 103rd Congress, the Youth Development Block Grant, a proposal that would authorize funds to expand community-based youth development programs, was introduced. This proposal was subsequently introduced during the 104th Congress as the National Youth Development Community Block Grant.

Simultaneously, there also reminders that we have much to do to address the challenges to making effective youth services available to all youth. Funds were never appropriated to implement the Young Americans' Act, nor were the youth development block grant proposals authorized.

Clearly, moving forward and institutionalizing a youth development approach on a broad scale is challenging, but it is not impossible. On the contrary, other developed countries have experienced success in this area. In a study of the youth policies of the United Kingdom, Australia, Germany, Sweden, and Norway, the author found that these policies tended to be developmental, broadly based, inclusive and participative. These countries have identified youth issues as a broad public responsibility, established a legal and organizational structure within which to carry out that responsibility, and appropriated funds at a significant level and on a stable basis to carry out youth policies and programs.

This country is well-poised to make programmatic approaches that focus on the developmental needs of youth available to all young people. We have legislation that provides a framework for such an agenda. We have a cadre of youth serving and youth-oriented organizations as well as youth who have themselves experienced positive outcomes resulting from their participation in developmentally oriented programs, which can be expanded and mobilized to extend the reach of effective program strategies to those who are underserved. We also have evidence and lessons from impact evaluations and qualitative research about effective approaches and the benefits that such approaches can yield, which provides a basis for action.

It does not make sense to continue down a path that has been shown to be ineffective, particularly when we have evidence that there is an approach and a set of practices that works. We have nothing to lose by adopting a broad-based, developmental approach to promoting positive youth outcomes. We have, however, lost much already by failing to act on the knowledge we have about effective youth-development approaches. This loss is evident in the unconscionable number of youth who are in distress. That we have much to gain is clear from the reports on young people whose lives have been improved noticeably because they were given an opportunity to meet their needs in positive and healthy ways. All young people deserve that opportunity.

## BIOGRAPHICAL SKETCH

Karen Fulbright-Anderson, a research fellow with the Roundtable on Comprehensive Community Initiatives of the Aspen Institute, manages the work of the Roundtable's Evaluation Steering Committee. She was formerly Director of Research for the Vera Institute of Justice, and a Program Officer at the Ford Foundation and at the Commonwealth.

Dr. Fulbright-Anderson earned a bachelor of arts degree from Wellesley College, a master of city planning degree and a doctorate degree in Urban Studies and Planning from the Massachusetts Institute of Technology (MIT).

# THE PARADOX OF URBAN POVERTY

By
Timothy Bates

# ABSTRACT

Living costs in urban areas are held down by the presence of low-wage service industries that draw heavily upon a ghetto labor force. Particularly in cities with thriving central business districts, labor-intensive service industries are critically important to maintaining the quality of life for the urban elite working in the managerial and professional occupations. In an environment of declining government enforcement of laws regulating working conditions and wages, low-wage service workers are increasingly slipping into poverty. Growing informalization in labor markets generally is tending to reduce wages and fringe benefits compensation for a vast stratum of the labor force nationwide. While black Americans are disproportionately hurt by these trends, the road to reform calls for support to a broad class-based agenda to reverse the decline of the institutionalized power of labor.

## Poverty in Central Cities

When U.S. Department of Housing and Urban Development (HUD) Secretary Henry Cisneros calls upon local governments to improve their business climates by "lowering operating costs, reducing unreasonable regulatory burdens..." his objective is job creation generally, but achievement of that objective may entail increasing the ranks of the urban poor (Cisneros, 1995, p.5). Rising poverty in urban America is increasingly rooted in the fact that officially sanctioned economic-development policies are working. Understanding why this is true is a precondition for formulating pragmatic political-economic strategies for attacking the causes of this tragic situation.

The nature of expanding poverty is most apparent in central cities that have experienced substantial central business-district growth in the past 30 years. America's major urban areas benefit from the presence of a large labor force employed at low wages. Metropolitan area industries can be sorted into three broad groups. First, export industries provide the raison d'être for the regional economy. They are oriented toward national and international markets — autos in Detroit, financial services in New York, motion pictures in Los Angeles. The second major industry group complements the export industries by selling them the goods and services used to produce the exported products. Both of these groups tend to be dominated by large firms utilizing high-technology production processes. A third group of industries supplies the local economy with food, shelter, clothing, recreation, education, and the like. Many are low-wage industries dominated by small businesses, and this is the sector most likely to employ central-city minority residents.

An inherently exploitive relationship is established (Fusfeld and Bates, 1984). Living costs in the metropolitan area are held down by the presence of low-wage service industries. Costs of production in the export industries and their supplier firms are limited because the services they buy are provided, in part, by low-wage workers. The low wages paid to ghetto residents are embedded in the prices of products and services that the entire community relies upon. If one large city (or state) were to undertake a serious effort to eliminate ghettos and the poverty found there, base costs of the area's export industries and their complements would increase. Higher government expenses, rising distribution costs, and more expensive services would increase the cost of living for those employed in the export and complementary industries. Rising living costs would necessitate higher wages in order to attract appropriately skilled managers and professionals to the region.

Higher costs could reduce the region's comparative advantage (relative to other metropolitan areas), thereby slowing local economic growth. Maintaining the poverty inherent in low-wage industries is an important component of regional viability, and this is particularly true in America's emerging global cities. If worker incomes increase in the low-wage industries, then the cost of living will rise for affluent, white-collar workers and their standard of living will fall. The observation that "someone has to clean the floors" reflects the widespread realization of the need for a ghettoized, impoverished subsector within a healthy urban economy.

Preferences of highly educated women to pursue managerial and professional careers interact with the high cost of living in corporate-headquarters cities, such as New York and Los Angeles, producing a rise of affluent one- and two-earner households that voraciously consume an array of services. Often lacking sufficient time to cook their own meals, clean and press their clothes, raise their children, clean their houses, and so forth, these affluent households rely heavily upon the services forthcoming from the low-wage sector. The result is a vast infrastructure of restaurants, gourmet food stores, domestic services, messenger services, laundries, dog walkers, child-care centers, and the like. The resultant low-wage jobs in the labor-intensive service industries are critically important to maintaining the quality of life for the urban elite working in the managerial and professional jobs that are proliferating in the expanding CBDs.

The new urban labor aristocracy requires the presence of a vast low-wage labor force because they purchase more and more of the consumer services that, in earlier generations, would have been produced within the household, often by housewives. Work that was previously internal to the household — raising children, cooking meals — is increasingly done by low-wage workers in the major corporate headquarters cities of America. In this context, "immigrants represent a desirable labor supply because they are relatively cheap, reliable, willing to work on odd shifts, and safe," (Sassen-Koob, 1981, pp. 28-29). Providing the "large cohort of restaurant workers, laundry workers, dog walkers, residential construction workers, and the like," immigration helps to lower the cost of maintaining the elite lifestyle of the new urban labor aristocracy (Feagin and Smith, 1988, p. 15).

Why is poverty rising? Why are real wages falling for a broad stratum of workers in the U.S.? How are these trends related to educational attainment? To worker productivity? Practices adopted by employers, not trends in worker productivity, are increasingly responsible for rising poverty that is rooted in declining compensation and job security. Discussions about poverty's causes are dated and increasingly irrelevant to the realities of life in urban America.

## Our Badly Dated Paradigms of Poverty's Causes Must be Radically Rethought and Reconstructed

A powerful thread of American culture holds that economic success and material wellbeing are attainable to all who diligently pursue these goals. Poverty is thusly viewed as evidence of personal defects, such as sloth, lack of character, immorality. When particular subgroups of the population lag far behind the mainstream, society's response has been split. Such groups are often viewed as victims of discriminatory social, economic, political processes — Jim Crowism, for example. Their prospects and progress are seen as stifled by discriminatory barriers such as racist hiring practices. Simultaneously, many in the dominant society see certain demographically defined groups — African Americans, Latinos, Native Americans — as laggard because of widespread personal deficiencies, including laziness, defective culture, criminal inclination, even genetic deficiency.

Among employed men with less than a high school degree, 25 percent of all African Americans and 41 percent of Hispanics nationwide in 1989 were earning poverty-level earnings, far above 1979 levels of working poverty (Acs and Danziger, 1993). Thirty years ago, the dominant society would have interpreted such statistics as evidence of the need for improvements in the educational system, higher minimum wages, laws outlawing discrimination in employment, and the like. Today, the pendulum is swinging in the other direction.

Changing relations in America's workplaces are not narrowly restricted to employers that hire poor people. Broad-based trends typifying major corporations as well as small businesses are reshaping the workplace for low-wage workers.Many of America's high-wage employers are downsizing the corporate labor force and contracting out to low-wage suppliers work that was previously done in-house. A nationwide employer offensive to cut labor costs, combined with government's failure to act decisively on labor's behalf, is changing labor relations. Problems facing black workers are rooted, in part, in the fact that they are in a weaker position than white workers to defend themselves from modern-day employer practices (Bates, 1995). A narrow preoccupation with worker productivity and skill levels can divert attention from the critically important need to revitalize and expand the institutions that protect labor across the race, ethnicity, and gender spectrum.

Defenders of the severe earnings inequality that typifies the U.S. labor market invariably abstract from all of this and cite, instead, the following generalization to justify the status quo.

## Generalization #1:

Labor market outcomes are determined by the abilities of workers and potential workers. The better qualified applicant gets the job; the more productive employee receives higher compensation than the less productive employee; advancement opportunities, similarly, accrue to the most highly qualified workers. Since ability determines outcomes, those seeking to get ahead had better hone their abilities: acquiring more education and skills are pragmatic strategies for those who desire to compete successfully in today's labor market.

No one disputes the large element of truth in this generalization. Critics have traditionally pointed out, rather, that the meritocracy justification for earnings inequality ignores important realities about the labor process. Particularly when simplistic meritocracy arguments are put forth to justify the lower earnings, higher unemployment rates, and lower labor-force participation rates of African Americans as opposed to whites, critics rightly claim that discrimination skews labor market outcomes in ways disadvantageous to black workers. Discrimination applicable to labor market outcomes appears in many forms, but the following generalization captures the crux of the discriminatory processes.

## Generalization #2:

Labor-market opportunities are shaped by employer attitudes. An employer who believes that blacks generally are less reliable workers than whites will prefer to hire whites when applicants appear to be equal in every respect other than race. Such an employer may hire black workers if 1) a suitable supply of white applicants is unavailable, or 2) blacks can be hired at lower wages than similarly qualified whites. Due to these discriminatory employer attitudes, African Americans will tend to suffer from restricted job access and lower wages than similarly qualified white workers. Employer attitudes must be altered before the meritocracy argument cited above is accepted as valid.

Variations of generalization #2 implicate whites who refuse to work side by side with blacks, or white consumers who refuse to shop in environs where black employees are numerous, as further causes of discriminatory labor market outcomes. According to these variants, the culprit responsible for maintaining black disadvantage in the labor market is white attitudes.

Generalizations #1 and #2 are not mutually exclusive. Indeed, progressive labor market policies popularized in the 1960s were an amalgam of these generalities: black/white inequality would be fought by 1) upgrading education and skill levels, particularly among young African Americans, and 2) putting legal pressure on employers to abandon their discriminatory attitudes.

Generalizations about employee productivity and employer attitudes still provide some insight into understanding the causes of earnings differentials, but the world has moved on and powerful new forces have emerged that are heightening inequality, both within and across racial groups. Growing polarization typifies the labor force generally. In a society where the rich are getting richer and the poor are getting poorer, impacts upon African Americans partially reflect their underrepresentation in the ranks of the rich and their overrepresentation in the ranks of the poor.

Generalizations about solutions to poverty transcend concerns about discriminatory attitudes and worker productivity. Probably the dominant solution embraced by policy makers since the early 1960s is to seek more rapid economic growth for the U.S. economy, thus pulling the underemployed to higher wage and employment levels: as President John F. Kennedy asserted, "a rising tide lifts all boats."

But the rising tide generated by rapid Gross National Product (GNP) growth has become a paradoxical tide over the past two decades: the yachts are rising but many of the rowboats are getting swamped.

## Generalization #1 for understanding rising poverty:

Large corporations and growing numbers of small firms operating on the technological frontier increasingly produce goods and services by combining skilled labor with technically advanced equipment (Bound and Johnson, 1992). In this technologically advanced sector, capital per worker is typically high and increasing, wages are often high, and rapid increases in worker productivity are the norm. Firms therefore often find it possible to expand their output of goods and services *without any corresponding expansion in employment opportunities for less skilled workers.* Indeed, growing firms may actually reduce their employment of blue-collar workers over time, replacing them with an expanded stock of sophisticated capital equipment staffed by growing numbers of engineers, systems analysts, and the like. As blue-collar workers are displaced from these high-wage sectors of the economy, they flood the sectors that do utilize their labor — low-wage small-business employers, most commonly. Growth in the high-technology, capital-intensive businesses (large corporations, most commonly) simultaneously produces a rising Gross National Product (GNP) and a growing surplus population seeking work in the small-business sector, where they depress wage levels. This pattern of economic growth is properly viewed as a long-run cause of (not a cure for) falling real wages and a rising incidence of working poverty among less-skilled workers. *Economic growth in modern-day America increasingly is the cause of labor-force polarization and growing poverty.* In a very real sense, success causes failure.

Beyond the fallacious view that GNP growth effectively alleviates working poverty and underemployment across-the-board, myths rooted in generalizations about immigrant experiences in the labor force have attracted policy makers in recent years. Consider one popular latter-day Horatio Alger — the Korean grocer — who can flourish selling wares in America's poorest urban areas. Certainly the immigrant Korean merchant validates American culture's premise that this country is still the land of opportunity for those who work hard. As immigrant groups have established businesses serving low-income inner-city districts, the question of why local residents (including African Americans) did not take advantage of these business opportunities has become a popular line of speculation. What about the poor, the unemployed, and the welfare recipients: why did they not seize the opportunities exploited by the Koreans? Was it because of aversion to hard work, lack of initiative, or related cultural deficiencies? Alternatively, is it because the local poor often lack college educations, white-collar work experience, and financial resources possessed by many of the immigrant Korean entrepreneurs? In fact, the median immigrant Korean business owner is a college graduate who possesses significant personal wealth. Most are overqualified to run mom and pop retail stores, but they are stuck in these low-yielding lines of self-employment by limited fluency in the English language (Bates, 1994). Quite simply, they are underemployed.

## Generalization #2 for understanding rising poverty

Immigrant experiences in the U.S. are shaped by barriers and opportunities that are routinely misinterpreted by the media and most other Americans. The misinterpretations conveniently tend to rationalize a status quo of growing urban poverty, and they overlook the fact that centers of urban immigrant population typically are doing poorly. Sustained high levels of both job creation and immigration, for example, typified Los Angeles County during the 1970s and 1980s, with the incidence of working poverty growing substantially. Between 1969 and 1987, the proportion of male, year-round, full-time (YRFT) workers in L.A. County earning less than $10,000 annually (in 1986 dollars) doubled, rising from 7 percent to 14 percent of YRFT workers. Whereas only 6 percent of L.A. manufacturing jobs were low-wage (defined in conjunction with the poverty level) in 1969, over 20 percent were low-wage in 1987 (Schimek, 1989). Low-wage workers "increased in total numbers from 114,000 in 1969 to 467,000 in 1987, a rate of growth 16 times that of the total population of Los Angeles County" (Soja, 1992, p. 364). The illegal immigrants working in the informal economy that did not respond to applicable government population surveys are not counted in these figures, but their presence increased poverty levels well beyond official estimates. According to those official estimates, Los Angeles County, while experiencing substantial economic growth in the 1969-1987 period, went from a situation of below-average poverty (1969) to above-average poverty (1987) relative to the country as a whole.

Analyses of low-wage employment growth in cities like New York and Los Angeles often confuse the symptoms of working poverty with its causes. For example, the informal economy is portrayed as a sweatshop revival phenomenon: destitute people work in off-the- books enterprises concentrated in immigrant population centers. A common-sense definition of the informal economy is a set of small-scale business activities conducted in a manner that evades government regulation and taxation. The rise of the informal economy is not principally associated with the illegal employment of poor immigrants. Opportunities for generating income in evasion of prevailing government rules and regulations are widely available throughout society. A true understanding of why such evasion has been expanding in recent decades sheds light on the causes of the indecently low wages, declining benefits, and loss of job security that typify a rising share of America's employment opportunities.

## The Informal Economy: Apparition Today, Mainstream Tomorrow

Sociologist John Kasarda's observation that "virtually all of New York's employment expansion was concentrated in white-collar service industries," (1985, p. 65) is based upon standard statistical series reported by federal government agencies. His skills-mismatch hypothesis — that central-city net job growth was found solely in occupations that demanded college credentials, while minority job seekers disproportionately were high school dropouts — seemed out of sync with trends in global cities. If job opportunities for the unskilled really were shrinking rapidly, as the official statistics suggested, why were immigrants continuing to pour into New York City from places like the Dominican Republic and China? Why were sweatshop manufacturing industries growing rapidly (Waldinger, 1986)? Departure of working- class whites from the central city was creating some opportunities for immigrants and indigenous minorities to enter New York City's work force, but rapid growth of the informal economy was widely seen as creating jobs for unskilled workers. These jobs are often invisible to agencies that compile employment statistics (Waldinger and Lapp, 1993).

This view of the informal economy tends to focus attention on the misfeasance of the immigrant-entrepreneur sweatshop owners and the tax-evading dog walkers among the urban poor. Viewing the informal economy thusly serves to divert interest and attention from the broader role being played by wealthier and more powerful groups that are promoting "legal employment at indecently low wages and in abhorrent conditions" (Waldinger and Lapp, 1993). What is that role?

There is a disenfranchisement under way, of the institutionalized power captured by labor over the past century in the U.S.: the rise of the informal economy is a *symptom* of the decline of labor, not a cause. The informal economy is a specific form of relations of production embedded in a specific historical context: the context is an attenuating system of institutionalized regulation. This system includes a set of laws and rules enforced by active intervention of government into the private employment realm. It encompasses established relations between employers and employees nationwide embedded in union contracts, normal employment practices of non-union employers, custom, and workplace tradition. It is the social contract.

*The social contract is being substantially rewritten. The rise of the informal economy is a reflection of fundamentally changing political-economic processes at the core of society. Immigrant entrepreneurs may benefit from such changes, but do not cause them.* Although informal activities may be periodically harassed by the state, the "informal sector as a whole tends to develop under the auspices of government tolerance" (Castells and Portes, 1989, p. 27). Decline in enforcement and subsequent rise in minimum-wage law violations, for example, was a serious problem by the early 1970s (Levitan and Belous, 1979), well before the growth of the informal economy was observed. Immigrant entrepreneurs were quick to realize that declining government enforcement of an array of worker health, safety, wage, and similar regulations provided them with a foot in the door, a comparative cost advantage in certain small-business sectors (Bonacich and Light, 1988). Reaping cost savings from "lax enforcement of wage and sanitary provisions of the labor code" (Light and Rosenstein, 1995, p. 77), Korean-owned small businesses became dominant in small-scale retailing in Los Angeles county in the 1970s and 1980s, a development that went far beyond mere creation of off-the-books firms. Having a desperate, often destitute immigrant labor pool to draw upon (partially due to government tolerance of illegal immigrant workers), of course, facilitated exploiting the advantage conveyed by the de facto demise of enforcing laws protecting workers in Los Angeles. As the personnel director of an Asian-owned fast-food chain described the Los Angeles labor market, "The Latinos in our locations, most are recent arrivals. Most are tenuously here and here on fragile documents. I see them as very subservient." Blacks, by contrast, were "far more aware of the regulatory system and far more aware of remedies if they've been wronged" (Waldinger, 1996, p.282). This firm employed a work force made up largely of immigrant Latinos.

## Race and Class: A 1990s Perspective on Inequality

Men and women often concentrate in different labor market niches, and their experiences as employees differ profoundly. For reasons of brevity, the rest of this chapter focuses largely upon male workers.

Steadily rising levels of educational attainment have typified young African Americans nationwide in recent decades (Carter and Wilson, 1995). Steadily rising, as well, is the incidence of subpoverty-level earnings. Particularly among young *African American* males lacking college degrees, labor-force participation rates are on a downward trajectory, and black-white unemployment rate differentials are rising. What is causing these dangerous trends?

Nationwide, 72.6 percent of African American males 20 to 24 years old were employed in 1973, but the employed share of this group had fallen sharply — down to 63.9 percent — by 1988. The largest drop was concentrated in highly industrialized Midwestern states — Michigan, Illinois, Ohio. To understand the declining employment prospects facing such heavily-impacted groups as young high school-graduate adults, we need to place the black job seeker in a broad context: focusing upon class rather than race provides a good starting point.

Declining earnings typify the least-educated workers most commonly, and this trend has coincided with very large increases in earnings inequality nationwide (Levy and Murnane, 1992). Changes in real weekly earnings for full-time, year-round male workers (all races) nationwide from 1979 to 1989 indicate polarization by worker education levels:[1]

| Education level | percent change in earnings, 1979-1989 |
| --- | --- |
| less than high school degree | -19.6% |
| high school diploma only | -11.3% |
| college: 1-3 years | -2.8% |
| college: 4 plus years | +4.9% |

Declines in real wages, labor-force participation, and growth of working poverty were particularly pronounced in the peak de-industrialization years of the 1970s and early 1980s. Between 1969 and 1984, for example, the share of black men aged 25 to 55 earning less than $10,000 — an amount insufficient to maintain a family of four above the poverty threshold — grew from 25 percent to 40 percent, measured in 1984 constant dollars (Jaynes and Williams, 1989). The early 1980s, in particular, were recessionary years. In contrast to past business cycles, however, earnings rebounded only for highly educated workers. The return of prosperity failed to generate earnings recovery for blue-collar workers.

## Undermining Organized Labor

Proliferation of maquiladoras along the Mexican border reflects the same political-economic dynamics that produce a growing informal sector in Manhattan. Both patterns of business growth reduce the costs of labor substantially. Informalization in the labor market tends to reduce wages, but the greatest savings occur from non-payment of fringe benefits and employee-related payments to government. The power of labor is falling in all spheres: bargaining with employers, social organization, and political clout. "Undeclared, unprotected labor, small units of production, networks rather than socialized labor processes, homework rather than factories, unstable relations of production, multiple intermediaries between workers and capital, segmentation of labor along age, gender, and ethnic lines, dependence of the job on the absence of legal control" — all of these factors are contributing to the de-collectivization of the labor process, the decline of the labor movement as an organized force (Castells and Portes, 1989, p. 31).

Declining ability to compete in the labor market is nonetheless blamed entirely upon the deficiencies of individuals: they need to acquire more education and skill so that they will be more productive workers. Although the link between high worker productivity and high earnings has prevailed throughout most of the 20th century, it is increasingly being severed. In the U.S. durable-goods manufacturing sector, for example, average output per worker rose 37.2 percent over the 1982-1991 period, but this greater productivity coexisted with declining real hourly compensation for manufacturing workers nationwide. (U.S. Bureau of Labor Statistics, 1992). The automotive assembly auto-parts industries in the U.S. cut their ranks of low-skill workers dramatically over the 1975-1990 period while, simultaneously, *low-wage* employment grew substantially. (Howell, 1994).

Sources of rising inequality lie less and less in individual worker deficiencies and more and more in the evolving productive forces that are reshaping the global economy. The material forces reshaping America and the global economy are not hidden or subtle. They are manifested most clearly, as speaker Newt Gingrich points out, in the rapid and accelerating rate of technical advancement that is reshaping the workplace. The microchip and the other assorted products of scientific discovery continually alter the composition of the labor force, the urban landscape, the products we consume — indeed, the content of life.

Twenty years ago, bureaucratic trade unions represented most of the nation's manufacturing production workers. In the durable-goods manufacturing areas, particularly where large corporations were most dominant, labor and corporate America coexisted in relative harmony. The crux of the social contract in manufacturing was that unions:

1) Permitted management to have complete control over production;
2) Accepted increased worker productivity as a key goal; and
3) Kept workers on the job.

In return, the large manufacturers provided high and gradually increasing wages for their workers (O'Conner, 1974). When productivity gains occurred, they were not ordinarily passed on to the customers in the form of lower prices; instead, they were retained to support higher wages and profits. This social contract between labor and capital had evolved in the post-World War II period. The deal began to unravel in the 1970s.

Increased international competition is often blamed for undermining corporate America's social contract with its work force. Key unionized sectors, such as autos and steel, lost market share to foreign rivals in the 1970s, and the profits of the impacted companies often suffered. International competition, however, was only part of a more fundamental phenomenon that was remaking corporate America. In a world of rapid technological advancement, some entrenched firms adopt and prosper, while others lag behind and experience rising costs and or falling market share (hence, falling profits). Sometimes an entire industry lags, as did steel. New, more innovative competitors — foreign and domestic — move in to replace the industry laggards: thus, newcomer Nucor Steel is a giant today, while industry giants of the 1970s like Republic Steel have been cut back and merged out of existence.

Rapid technological change has helped to spur growing competition — both domestic and international — and many of corporate America's giants have had to cut costs and innovate to remain competitive. Innovation has often meant less reliance upon unionized blue-collar workers. The previous era of corporate giants sharing monopolistic profits with unionized workers has been replaced by a modern era in which the high-wage costs of unionized labor have become a prime target for corporate cost cutters.

Former Secretary of Labor Ray Marshall captured the spirit of corporate America's new attitude towards blue-collar labor when he noted that "Since the early 1970s, U.S. companies have been competing mainly through reducing domestic wages and by shifting productive facilities to low wage countries" (Marshall, 1992).

Fraying of the social contract between corporate America and its work force has produced dramatic uncouplings of historical relationships between worker productivity and compensation. A $15 per hour unionized job with General Motors is a prime candidate to become a $6 an hour non-unionized job with a small manufacturing firm: the same worker may be working at the same machine in the same building; the wage reduction reflects the altered labor relations of the 1990s. Worker productivity changes did not produce the $9 per hour wage cut. Rather, the $15 per hour wage was rooted in the social relations of production of a bygone era; the $6 wage reflects the emerging reality of blue-collar manufacturing work in the 1990s.

Strategies for converting high-wage jobs into low-wage jobs include:
1. Downsizing the corporate labor force and contracting out to low-wage suppliers work that was previously done in-house;
2. Relying more heavily upon part-time and temporary workers, while not providing traditional fringe benefit coverage to these employees (Appelbaum, 1992);
3. Playing hardball with the existing work force, reducing their wages and fringe benefit compensation;
4. Shifting operations to low-cost sites, both within the United States as well as globally (Howell, 1995).

This transformation in the relations of production has been greatly facilitated by government's promarket ideological climate. The Reagan revolution and ensuing events at all levels of government have produced an array of government policies favoring corporate America's push for revamped employment and employee compensation practices. America's institutional arrangements for protecting workers — labor unions, labor laws, minimum wage levels — have eroded severely, freeing corporate employers to rewrite their social contract with labor (Goldfield, 1987; Appelbaum and Batt, 1994).

What began most commonly as a corporate attempt to reduce their reliance on high-cost, unionized, blue-collar employees has become, in the 1990s, an all-encompassing revision of the relations between labor and capital in U.S. society.

## Rising Urban Employment Increasingly Coexists with Rising Poverty

The dominant political-economic conventional wisdom today suggests that the U.S. must increase its ability to compete globally. This entails decreasing government regulation of business, government sanctioning of corporations shifting productive facilities to low-wage areas such as Mexico, declining influence of labor unions, and a host of related polices. The common denominator is that these policies serve to reduce the costs of labor substantially. Not all workers are equally impacted.

Earlier in this article, urban industries were divided into three groups — export firms, suppliers to the export firms, and firms serving the local economy. Downsizing, contracting out, and the like are strategies whereby the export firms cut their reliance on expensive white-collar employees and unionized blue-collar workers. Many of these jobs continue to exist, but they are now found in group two, the complementary firms that serve the export industries. Payrolls of America's largest industrial companies, the Fortune 500 for example, have declined predictably. The Fortune 500 companies created 4.5 million net new jobs in the U.S. during the prosperous 1960s; total employment numbers stood at 14.6 million in 1970, or 20.6 percent of all non-farm employment. The *Fortune 500* companies destroyed 3.5 million jobs during the prosperous 1980s: their U.S. employment fell from 15.9 million in 1980 to 12.4 million in 1990, which was 11.3 percent of all non-farm employment (Kemper Financial Services, cited in the *Wall Street Journal*, August 10, 1992). Their employee ranks have continued to shrink in the 1990s.

The net effect of contracting out and downsizing for the large export firms has been to cut costs. The displaced workers are often re-employed at lower wages, sharply reduced fringe benefits, and lessened job security. Intense pressure imposed by the export industries upon supplier firms to cut costs forces them to squeeze their employees: wage cutting, relying increasingly upon part-time and temporary workers, and slashing fringe benefits are common responses. The complementary supplier firms, in particular, are moving away from institutionalized employment practices emulating large corporations, and toward laissez-faire employment practices. Laissez-faire practices have always been the norm in the informal economy. Among the group-three firms — those serving the local economy — small businesses are widespread, unions are weak, and protection of workers depends heavily upon government enforcement of legally mandated employment safety standards. It is in this sector that the lines between the informal economy and above-ground economy are blurring. The movement to lessen government regulation of business has its greatest impact on workers employed in the small retail and service businesses that serve the local economy.

How can inner-city ghetto areas attract employers and strengthen their economic base in the prevailing political-economic milieu? The consensus seems to be shifting toward acceptance of the Reagan Administration's initial conception of enterprise zones. The crux was that a reduction of government presence within the inner-city zones would create fertile grounds for indigenous entrepreneurial activity. This reduced public presence would be achieved by largely eliminating government regulation within the zone, in conjunction with tax relief. As James Johnson notes, the federal government under Reagan made substantial progress towards this laissez-faire ideal when it "aggressively relaxed environmental regulations and reduced the budgets and slashed the staffs of governmental agencies that were charged with enforcing laws governing workplace health, safety, and compensation, as well as hiring, retention, and promotion practices" (p. 152, 1995).

The informalization of a growing share of America's small business (and big business) is the expression of new forms of social control being imposed on America's workers, often with the acquiescence of the state. A political consensus in Washington calls for increasing global competitiveness of America's businesses and reduced regulatory burdens. In practice, these goals often manifest themselves as declining job security, falling wages, plummeting fringe benefits, poor working conditions, failure to enforce worker employment, health, and safety regulations; in the inner-city context, this increasingly causes working poverty. There is nothing on this list of consequences that is upsetting to the large corporations that make up the export base of America's large cities. The broad-based lowering of labor costs coexists with an expanded supply of low-wage service workers to clean houses, cook meals, raise children, and walk the dogs of the managerial and professional elites that run these large corporations. Challenges to this emerging status quo, if they are forthcoming, will arise when younger generations of workers put forth a class-based agenda to reverse the decline of the institutionalized power of labor.

## Reform Agenda for the Working Poor

A coherent strategy for upgrading the economic status of black Americans solidified in the 1960s. Broadly, the plan was to open jobs to blacks by eliminating barriers to employment and advancement. Key components included upgrading education and skill levels, while pressuring employers to recruit aggressively the very black workers who had traditionally been barred from a wide range of skilled blue- and white-collar jobs.

The equal opportunity strategy has produced significant employment gains for black Americans in government, educational institutions, the professions, and business enterprise. Yet these expanded opportunities have coexisted with declining labor-force status and persistent poverty, particularly among black male workers who are not college educated. The equal opportunity strategy is in the American tradition of individual achievement. Yet the limitations of this approach are starkly apparent in America's declining inner-city minority communities. Coexisting with widened opportunities is the growing gap between the haves and the have-nots.

The ideology of individualism and equal opportunity increasingly provides a rationale for not attacking the roots of the problems of declining labor-force status. In subtle ways, widened opportunities support the very economic processes that preserve low-wage work, the urban ghetto, and poverty in America. The reality of expanded opportunities has drawn millions of intelligent and capable black Americans into the economic mainstream, with its wider opportunities and greater rewards. As they contribute to the advancement of the dominant society, the isolation of the ghetto they leave behind and the drains of its talent and capital only grow worse. Some become fully committed to the ideology of individual advancement, even to the point of attacking the very efforts that pressured employers to recruit and promote black workers. Meanwhile, those who remain caught in poverty are told that the fault is theirs, that if they had the initiative and ability to seize opportunities, they too could have been affluent.

Providing equal labor-market opportunities to minorities is a useful objec-

158

tive to strive for, but this policy, by itself, is simply not addressing the root causes of working poverty and underemployment that plague so many of the black Americans residing in major urban centers. Much more is needed.

Big cities have aggressively pursued development and job creation strategies that concentrate on central business district expansion. When these policies work, they create more white-collar managerial and professional jobs in fields such as finance and information technology. Downtown jobs for workers who are not college educated derive from complementary development policies boosting the convention trade and the central business district entertainment complex. If successful, lots of low-wage service jobs are forthcoming in hotels, restaurants, convention centers, and the like. Note that these development policies, when they work, most often contribute to the polarization and the proliferation of low-wage work discussed earlier in this article. Central business district growth is a cause of, rather than a cure for, the growth of the urban low-wage labor force. It is the *success* of urban development policies, not their failure, that is generating growing working poverty in major cities like New York.

Public policy needs to address the problems of the low-skill work-force toiling in labor-intensive low-wage industries — often small business dominated — if the growth of urban poverty is to be checked. A fundamental change in the low-wage labor market requires that government enforce living wages for employees. An immediate increase to a $6 per hour minimum wage, followed by a 1997 increase to $8 per hour, would be a powerful step in the right direction. The standard for a revised and extended minimum wage could be the wage that provides an income at or just above the poverty line for an urban family of four, indexed to consumer prices, when one member of the family is employed full time. Coverage should be extended to all workers and enforcement must be strengthened considerably by imposing much stronger sanctions against employers that evade the law. The notion of a living wage, as defined above, is exactly how Australia's minimum wage legislation is written. A serious minimum wage is the quickest way to alleviate the poverty inherent in proliferating low-wage service employment.

Simplistic application of static economic theory supports the folklore that the minimum wage has adverse effects on employment. But the dynamics of a higher base wage level are not simplistic: higher employer wage costs also mean increased aggregate demand when wage earners spend their higher incomes. Higher wage costs trigger increased use of capital equipment, which causes, in turn, rising worker productivity. In fact, the long-term effects of rising wages can have positive dynamic effects on the economy (Porter, 1983).

A more substantive objection to payment of living wages is that higher wages pass through to higher prices, i.e. a minimum wage increase is inflationary. A serious program that enables many of the working poor to earn a living wage indeed is likely to cause higher income groups to pay more for the products and services of the present low-wage industries. A significant shift in income to the poor leaves others worse off: the prices of restaurant meals often rise; sending shirts to the dry cleaners becomes more costly. The crux of the matter is that society stands to lose some of the tangible benefits derived from a status quo of maintaining the poverty inherent in low-wage industries. Thus, higher income groups may oppose payment of living wages to the working poor. They may opt, instead, to maintain the present ghettoized, subsector within the urban economy.

Inner-city ghettos lack the strong economic base from which political power might emerge. A program aimed narrowly at paying a living wage to the urban working poor is unlikely to prevail, since the envisioned gains come at the expense of more powerful groups. This is why any successful attack on the roots of growing urban poverty are likely to be part of a broader working-class coalition addressing the decline in the institutionalized power of labor broadly. The agenda of such a coalition would be to strengthen America's institutional arrangements for protecting workers. Reform of the minimum wage is apt to be substantive if it is part of a broader political struggle for expanded worker well-being and security. Laws governing a wide range of interrelated issues — expanded unemployment coverage, worker training opportunities, enforcement of safe working conditions, higher minimum wages, greater access to medical care, and so forth — need to be strengthened so that all of America's workers can share the fruits of technological progress and economic growth. The narrower race-based agenda that emerged from 1960s activism needs to merge into a wider working-class agenda for political action if the problems of impoverished black Americans are to be addressed effectively in the 21st century.

1.Labor-force statistics on earnings, labor-force status, and worker educational background are drawn from the *Current Population Survey* (CPS), which is compiled by the U.S. Bureau of Labor Statistics.

# REFERENCES

Acs. Gregory, and Sheldon Danziger, "Educational Attainment, Industrial Structure, and Male Earnings through the 1980's," *The Journal of Human Resources* (Summer 1993).

Appelbaum, Eilien, "Structural Change and the Growth of Part-Time and Temporary Employment," Virginia duRivage, ed., *New Policies for the Part-Time and Contingent Workforce*, (Armonk, N.Y.: M.E. Sharpe, 1992).

_____, and Rosemary Batt, *The New American Workplace* (Ithaca, ILR Press, 1993).

Bates, Timothy, "Individual Skill Levels and Labor Force Status Among African American Males," *Journal of Negro Education* (Summer 1995).

_____, "Analysis of Korean-Immigrant-Owned Small Business Startups with Comparisons to African-American and Nonminority-Owned Firms," *Urban Affairs Quarterly* (December 1994).

Bonacich, Edna, and Ivan Light, *Immigrant Entrepreneurs: Koreans in Los Angeles* (Berkeley, University of California Press, 1988).

Bound, John, and George Johnson, "Changes in the Structure of Wages in the 1980's: An Evaluation of Alternative Explanations," *American Economic Review* (June 1992).

Carter, Deborah, and Reginald Wilson, *Minorities in Higher Education* (Washington, D.C.: American Council on Education, 1995).

Castells, Manuel, and Alejandro Portes, "World Underneath: Origins, Dynamics, and Effects of the Informal Economy," *The Informal Economy,* A. Portes, M. Castells, and L. Benton, eds. (Baltimore: Johns Hopkins University Press, 1989).

Cisneros, Henry, "Urban Entrepreneurialism and National Economic Growth" U.S. Department of Housing and Urban Development essay (September 1995).

Feagin, J., and M. Smith, *The Capitalist City* (New York: Blackwell, 1988).

Fusfeld, Daniel, and Timothy Bates, *Political Economy of the Urban Ghetto* (Carbondale: Southern Illinois University Press, 1984).

Goldfield, Michael, *The Decline of Organized Labor in the United States* (Chicago: University of Chicago Press, 1987)

Howell, David, "The Collapse of Low-Skill Male Earnings in the 1980s: Skill Mismatch or Shifting Wage Norms?," unpublished manuscript, 1994.

_____, "Collapsing Wages and Rising Inequality," *Challenge*, (January/February 1995).

Jaynes, Gerald, and Robin Williams, *A Common Destiny* (Washington, D.C.: National Academy Press, 1989).

Johnson, James, "The Competitive Advantage of the Inner City: Comment," *Harvard Business Review*,(July-August 1995).

Kasarda, John, "Urban Change and Minority Opportunities," *The New Urban Reality*, Paul Peterson, ed. (Washington, D.C.: Brookings Institution, 1985).

Levitan, Sar, and R. Belous, *More than Subsistence: Minimum Wages for the Working Poor* (Baltimore: Johns Hopkins University Press, 1979).

Levy, Frank, and Richard Murnane, "U.S. Earnings Levels and Earnings Inequality: A Review of Recent Trends and Proposed Explanations," *Journal of Economic Literature* (September 1992).
Light, Ivan, and Carolyn Rosenstein, *Race, Ethnicity, and Entrepreneurship in Urban America* (New York: Aldine De Gruyter, 1995).

Marshall, Ray, "The Future Role of Government in Industrial Relations," *Industrial Relations*, (Winter 1992).

O'Conner, James, *Fiscal Crisis of the State* (New York: St. Martin's Press, 1974).

Porter, Michael, *The Competitive Advantage of Nations*. (New York: Free Press, 1983).

Sassen-Koob, S., "Exporting Capital and Importing Labor: the Role of Caribbean Migration in New York City," Center for Latin American and Caribbean Studies Occasional Paper, New York University (1981).

Schimek, Paul, "Earnings Polarization and the Proliferation of Low-Wage Work," (Graduate School of Architecture and Urban Planning, UCLA, 1989).

Soja, Edward, "Poles Apart: Urban Restructuring in New York and Los Angeles," *Dual City: Restructuring New York*, J. Mollenkopf and M. Castells, eds. (New York: Russell Sage Foundation, 1991).

U.S. Bureau of Labor Statistics, *Productivity and Costs* (Washington, D.C.: U.S. Department of Labor, 1992).

_____, *Current Population Survey* (Various Issues).

Waldinger, Roger, *Through the Eye of the Needle: Immigrants and Enterprise in New York's Garment Trades* (New York: New York University Press, 1986).

_____, "Who Makes the Beds? Who Washes the Dishes? Black/ Immigrant Competition Reassessed," *Immigrants and Immigration Policy*, Harriet Duleep and Phanindra Wunnava, eds. (Greenwich: JAI Press, 1996).

_____, and Michael Lapp, "Back to the Sweatshop or Ahead to the Informal Sector," *International Journal of Urban and Regional Research*, vol. 17 (1993).

*Wall Street Journal*, (August 10, 1992).

## BIOGRAPHICAL SKETCH

Timothy Bates is Professor of Labor and Urban Affairs at Wayne State University. He is a consultant for the U.S. Department of Justice Civil Rights Division, the U.S. General Accounting Office, and the Small Business Administration. Professor Bates is presently writing a book on small-business ownership among Asian immigrants in the United States.

# DEVELOPING BLACK AND LATINO SURVIVAL STRATEGIES: THE FUTURE OF URBAN AREAS

**James B. Stewart**

# ABSTRACT

This analysis explores implications of economic developments anticipated by "futurists" for the economic well-being of blacks and Latinos in urban areas. The principal focus is on the effects of expanding linkages of various urban areas to the global economy on labor market outcomes for blacks and Latinos. The deleterious national employment status of blacks and Latinos related to overrepresentation in declining sectors is mirrored in most cities. The examination of specific developments in selected sunbelt cities reveals that more extensive linkages to the international economy are generally associated with less equitable labor market outcomes for blacks and Latinos. Unequal access to employment opportunities is related to both residential segregation and existing community development policies. Recommendations for improving educational delivery systems and housing and community development policies are offered that can serve as part of a comprehensive strategy to achieve greater equity in labor-market outcomes as linkages of urban economies to the international economy continue to expand.

This analysis explores the implications of the economic and social developments predicted by "futurists" for the prospective status of blacks and Latinos in the United States. Particular attention is focused on the likely impacts of the ongoing global economic transformation on urban areas. Given the high level of urbanization of black and Latino populations, the transformation of urban areas will have critical effects on the well-being of both groups in the 21st century. Thus the paper is also a call for the development of black-Latino coalitions to advocate for urban policies capable of empowering both groups to play a major role in the world of the next century.

The analysis begins with an overview of selected frameworks used by futurists. Futurists' perspectives range from the "optimistic," highlighting increased potential for individual freedom, to the more "pessimistic," focusing on the growing dominance of human lives by global corporations and the destruction of the traditional work culture and employment bases. The implications of the predictions for urban areas are also considered specifically.

These perspectives are juxtaposed with the realities of the overall labor market experiences of blacks and Latinos in the contemporary global economy in the third section. This discussion focuses not only on employment status per se, but also on the effects of programs designed to improve labor-market outcomes. The linkages of several specific urban areas to the global economy are then examined, focusing specific attention on how the employment status of Blacks and Latinos are affected by the extent of international connections in each city. Additional information about housing patterns and policies in three cities is provided to illustrate how residential location affects access to growing segments of urban economies. The concluding section discusses the policy implications of the study, with particular emphasis on the need to improve school-to-work transitions and retraining programs and the possible role of community-development corporations in fostering greater equity in the employment and housing arenas, as well as overall quality of life.

## Alternative Views of the Future

In the world envisioned by the optimistic futurists, disembodied technological change is the driving force shaping the future. The new possibilities created by these technologies are seen as human-liberating, primarily at the level of the individual. To illustrate, John Naisbitt and associates have presented present future scenarios in the form of so-called "megatrends," i.e. "directions transforming our lives" (Naisbitt,1982). These directions, according to Naisbitt, include a declining significance of traditional patterns of association, racial/ethnic and national identity. However, it is clear from recent events including the O.J. Simpson trial, the Million Man March, the battle over Proposition 187 in California, and the efforts to pass "English-only" legislation in several states, that conflicts surrounding race, ethnicity, and language are increasing, not decreasing. In fact, recent polls suggest that, at least for black and white Americans, there is greater polarization than ever regarding perceptions of the significance of discrimination, the usefulness of policies like Affirmative Action, etc. The key question is whether this is a short-term transitional phenomenon or a signal of a long-term escalation of conflict related to demographic changes that portend a future in which the traditional majority status of whites vanishes.

While the optimistic futurists acknowledge the major transitions underway in the global economic order, they are viewed as much less problematic than by their more pessimistic counterparts. As an example, Naisbitt suggests that there is a movement away from "forced technologies" toward high tech/high touch solutions that presumably involve developing a balance between physical and spiritual needs in ways that prevent raw technology, per se, from dominating human lives. Naisbitt also touts the de-emphasis of highly centralized institutions in favor of decentralized approaches to problem solving. Examples include the decline of the importance of the federal government and the erosion of labor unions. Optimistic futurists also celebrate the movement away from seeking solutions through traditional institutions in favor of self-help, exemplified by the resurgence of interest in entrepreneurship and the growing interest in independent schools.

For present purposes, it is important to highlight the fact that the positive developments foreseen by Naisbitt are generated from a mindset that restricts attention to a small segment of American society. To illustrate, blacks and Latinos are only mentioned in the context of the idea that population growth among other identifiable populations will alter the traditional focus of domestic social policy from black/white relations, thereby increasing the marginalization of blacks, creating increased potential for intergroup conflict.

There are many negative consequences correlated with Naisbitt's megatrends that are of critical importance to blacks and Latinos, and that are implicit in the writings of those futurists who use changes in the economic arena as their point of departure.

The work of Alvin and Heidi Toffler has recently received widespread media attention, in part because their latest book, *Creating a New Civilization, The Politics of the Third Wave*, contains a foreword written by Newt Gingrich, Speaker of the U.S. House of Representatives. The Tofflers' central notion is that three major waves of technological advance have and are shaping major transitions in global civilization and they employ what is described as "social wave-front analysis" to examine the patterns of transformation. According to the Tofflers, social wave-front analysis "looks at history as a succession of rolling waves of change and asks where the leading edge of each wave is carrying us" (Toffler and Toffler,1995;21). The Tofflers further indicate that social wave-front analysis "begins with the very simple idea that the rise of agriculture was the first turning point in human social development and that the industrial revolution was the second great breakthrough. It views each of these not as a discrete, one-time event but as a wave of change moving at a certain velocity" (Toffler and Toffler,1995;22)

For the Tofflers, a critical force shaping the future is the emergence of a global Third Wave economic system based on the accumulation and manipulation of information. One consequence of this development is the increasing marginalization of societies with economies heavily dependent on industrial and/ or agricultural production.

As noted in the introduction, we are particularly concerned with the implications of the global economic transformation for urban areas. As noted by Abbott (1993,184), "the effects of the globalized information economy have been uneven across nations, regions and cities." Abbott suggests that there are two competing hypotheses regarding spatial distribution tendencies. The first, characterized as the "world city" hypothesis, "suggests that specialized domestic transactions and international services concentrate in a few comprehensive metropolises that organize national or even international economies" in ways similar to the financial sector (Abbott,1993;184). The second hypothesis suggests that administrative and information activities are free to locate wherever the configuration of amenities is optimal (Abbott,1993;184). Particular types of amenities are necessary to attract "knowledge workers." Knight (1989,238) maintains that "the quality of educational, cultural, recreational, and medical services available becomes a critical factor in recruitment and hence in locations of knowledge-intensive activities."

Abbott (1993,184) indicates that uncertainty regarding the spatial imperatives of the global transformation "has invited attempts to design urban development policies that capitalize on the increasing importance of international exchange and information."

Pressman (1985,359) suggests it is likely that a "constellation of relatively *diversified and integrated* cities" will develop embodying "a high degree of subregional integration, allowing particularly for people to live near their places of employment." He argues further that a new system of "virtual" cities will emerge "with functions quite different from traditional, historic cities," that encompass "communities, campuses, laboratories and corporate offices" dispersed geographically but connected electronically, relatively independent of the parent city (Pressman,1985;359). Pressman cautions, however, that the pace of change will be slow, constrained by existing spatial configurations, physical plant, and social organization.

Knight (1989,238) asserts that "the educational infrastructure is especially important in the knowledge-based city" and that "the educational system must provide all residents with the option of pursuing careers as knowledge workers." However, it is clear that this expectation is inconsistent with developments in the global workplace. In contrast to the privileged position of knowledge workers, Rifkin (1995,xvi) insists that "fewer and fewer workers will be needed to produce the goods and services for the global population - moving toward a near workerless world." It is predicted, for example, that 35 percent of the workforce will be comprised of contingent workers by the year 2000. Aside from the fact that contingent workers do not receive benefits, these predictions are troubling because part-time workers earn 20-40 percent less than full-time workers.

Knight (1989,239) insists that "if cities are to act as development poles in the global society, they must also be able to manage locally so they do not become socially polarized and divided cities." He maintains that divided cities are not inevitable, rather they are created by default by allowing market forces and technology to dictate development. The alternative, according to Knight, is to "shape development through the civic process and secure a future in the global society" (Knight,1989;239-40). In a similar vein, the Tofflers predict that "the globally competitive race will be won by the countries that complete their Third Wave transformation with the least amount of domestic disruption and unrest" (Toffler and Toffler,1995;34). However, achieving such a tranquil transformation constitutes a major challenge both for the society at large and in particular for urban areas. As the Tofflers observe:

"In the United States—and in many other countries—the collision of Second and Third Waves creates social tensions, dangerous conflicts and strange new political wave fronts that cut across the usual divisions of class, race, sex or party. This collision makes a shambles of traditional political vocabularies and makes it very difficult to separate progressives from reactionaries, friends from enemies. All the old polarizations and coalitions break up." (Toffler and Toffler,1995;24)

The foregoing discussion provides a useful foundation for the examination of the overall situation of Blacks and Latinos in the emerging world order and, in turn, variation in the effects of the global transformation across specific urban areas.

## Blacks, Latinos and the World of Work—An Overview

Despite some quantitative differences in employment status, occupational distributions and earnings, the qualitative dimensions of the employment picture facing blacks and Latinos in the future are very similar. This parallel trajectory results from comparable contemporary labor-market experiences.

The precipitous decline in manufacturing employment has been a major factor affecting the employment status of blacks. Several studies indicate that while manufacturing employment accounted for only about 20 percent of total employment in the mid-1980s, about 50 percent of all workers displaced as a result of plant closings and relocations had been employed in manufacturing. Blacks have been significantly overrepresented among displaced workers (see, for example, Jacobson, LaLonde, and Sullivan, 1993). Latinos have also been adversely affected by the "skills mismatch" created by the ongoing economic transformation. To illustrate, Ortiz's study of Latino employment patterns in New York and Los Angeles found that African Americans, Puerto Ricans and even Mexican-Americans, to some extent, had all experienced similar patterns of job loss as a result of the decline of manufacturing and the growth in the service sector (Ortiz,1991). It is important to recognize that even though the service sector now far outstrips manufacturing as an employment base in the American economy, it is also vulnerable to international competition. Black and Hispanic men employed in the service sector share the experience of being much more likely to be employed in those industries with the largest employment losses (Armah,1994).

Despite the significant growth in service-sector employment blacks and Latinos continue to be underrepresented in white-collar occupations and overrepresented in blue-collar occupations. Blacks tend to be overrepresented among union members, and although black union members earn less than white union members, the gap is less than is the case for non-union workers. In contrast, Gonzalez and Gray (1984) maintain that the most powerful industrial unions have historically excluded Puerto Ricans from important positions and that civil service unions have also been a barrier to Puerto Rican economic mobility. The status and visibility of the United Farm Workers, founded by Cesar Chavez, began to decline in the 1980s with the increasing urbanization of Mexican-Americans (Skerry,1993). Given that unions have had some positive impacts on employment and earnings, the projections of futurists that unions will be less influential in the decades to come do not portend well for blacks and Latinos.

The employment outlook for blacks and Latino women is no more positive than for men. Futurists such as Aburdene and Naisbitt (1992) predict that opportunities for women will be expanding in the future. It is true that non-Cuban Latino women have been more successful than Latino men in making gains in professional, managerial and technical occupations, a pattern similar to that occurring among blacks (Montgomery,1994). However, black and Latino women continue to share the burden of the dual barriers of race/ethnicity and gender. The circumstances facing Latina professionals have not been studied as systematically as that of black women, with representative studies of the latter group including those of Simms and Malveaux (1986) and Sokoloff (1992). More generally, it appears that Latina women have a lower labor force participation rate than Black women (Segura,1992). These various patterns suggest that Black and Latina women will lag in benefiting from the developments forecast by futurists.

It is important to examine how employment prospects differ across sectors. Considering the public sector first, futurists prognosticate that the federal government will continue to decline in significance as a direct employer. The question remains as to whether these employment losses will be offset by gains at the state and local levels. Blacks are more likely than Latinos to be employed in the public sector. This is true for all levels of government (Edwards, Thomas and Burch,1992; Reimers and Chernick,1991; Stafford,1991). One exception to this pattern exists in the San Antonio, Texas local government; Mexican-Americans have had employment parity since the 1960s (Skerry,1993). In general, blacks and Latinos tend to be concentrated into relatively low-paying agencies and occupations

(Reimers and Chernick,1991; Idson and Price,1992).

One question of particular interest to this investigation is whether the growth in employment in high-tech industries offers any significant counterbalance to the trends cited above. As a starting point, it is critical to note that growth does not occur monotonically in any industry. All industries are subject to general business cycles, and the highly volatile character of some high-tech industries has the potential for creating relatively greater patterns of employment volatility. Several high-tech industries, most noticeably semiconductors and aerospace, have already experienced major shake-outs. Mar and Ong reported that in the wake of the 1985 sectoral recession in Silicon Valley's semiconductor industry, only 43 percent of black workers had been rehired two years later compared to 60 percent of White workers and 65 percent of Hispanic workers (Mar and Ong,1994). Ong and Lawrence (1995) found, using 1989 and 1992 data, that African-American and Latino workers bore a disproportionate share of the employment losses associated with defense cuts in California's aerospace industry. Much of the employment growth in the last decade has occurred in small to medium-sized firms associated with high-tech and service, many not covered by existing non-discrimination legislation.

In addition to these losses based on state-by-state estimates, Williams (1994) reports that blacks lost approximately 158,000 military and defense-related jobs between 1991 and 1996. According to Williams, this represents 12 percent of anticipated defense-related job losses as a result of the military downsizing, compared to an approximately 9 percent representation of blacks in the civilian labor force. Although specific estimates were not generated for Latinos, it is likely that this population is experiencing disproportionate effects in some states where blacks also experienced disproportionate losses, specifically California and Texas. Unlike blacks, Latinos are underrepresented in the armed forces (Rosenfeld and Culbertson,1992). As a consequence, the direct impacts of the ongoing military downsizing affect blacks more directly.

The overrepresentation of black and Latino males in correctional institutions and under other types of criminal justice system control is another problem related directly to the ongoing global transformation. This phenomenon reflects, in part, the marginalization of black and Latino males from emerging labor markets and the thinly disguised pattern of constructing correctional institutions in rural, impoverished white communities to provide alternative employment to that lost by the decline in manufacturing, mining, and agriculture. The high degree of urbanization of blacks and Latinos precludes any direct employment benefits from accruing from the large federal and state expenditures on new prison construction.

There is a widespread perception that the issue of job losses due to restructuring and/or international competition experienced by blacks, in particular, are exacerbated by competition from immigrants. While there is some research which suggests that prior to the mid-1970s black male workers were disadvantaged by competition from women and recent immigrants (Hyclak and Stewart,1986), evidence based on 1980 data suggests that black native-born men have in fact benefited from the increase in immigration. The major impacts of immigration have been on other immigrant groups. To illustrate, Borjas (1986;15) reports that "increases in the supply of the various Hispanic groups — Mexicans, Puerto Ricans, Cubans and other Hispanics — have small effects in (sic) the earnings of non-Hispanics, but sizable effects on the earnings of the groups themselves."

The important question of the effectiveness of retraining programs for displaced workers must also be addressed. Generally, researchers have not found widespread reduction in earnings following dislocation, although a significant proportion of workers do experience significant earnings losses. As an example, Swaim and Podgursky (1991) found that about 30 percent of re-employed full-time blue collar workers and 25 percent of re-employed white-collar and service workers received wages that were more than 25 percent below predislocation levels. Earnings losses and re-employment probabilities differ across socio-demographic groups. Jacobson, LaLonde and Sullivan (1993) report most studies find that gender is not a very important determinant of earnings losses. There do appear, however, to be significant differences across racial groups. Kletzer (1991) found that both blue and white-collar non-white men and women had lower probabilities of re-employment and lower post-displacement earnings than whites. Swaim and Podgursky (1991) found longer unemployment durations for blacks than whites.

The design of training programs significantly affects re-employment and earnings outcomes. Seitchik and Zornitsky (1989) claim that relatively modest investments in remedial education, entry-level job training, and job-search assistance can be potentially valuable for many groups, and in particular, for workers from the lower half of the wage age salary distribution. Leigh's (1990) review of the literature produced the following conclusions: (1) classroom training does not appear to generate additional benefits beyond job search assistance alone; (2) on-the-job training has a larger net impact than classroom training, but does not yield consistently positive effects on earnings; (3) the net benefits from training appear to be larger for men than for women; (4) there is little difference in the benefits between blacks and whites; and (5) workers under 45 years old benefit more from training than older workers.

The assignment of participants to specific training activities differs by gender and across racial groups. These patterns may reflect group differences in educational attainment and work experience, but must be taken into account in assessing training outcomes. In general, women are more likely to be assigned initially to occupational classroom training and less likely to be assigned to on-the-job training and work experience. In a recent study of the earnings and employment outcomes of participants in Job Training Partnership Act Title III programs, it was found that Hispanic men and women were disproportionately assigned initially to work experience. Black men were more likely than their white and Hispanic counterparts to be assigned to occupational classroom training and less likely to be assigned to on-the-job training. Black women were the most likely to be assigned to job-search assistance/direct placement. Blacks were more likely to complete training than members of other groups (Stewart,1995).

One of the findings of particular interest to this investigation is that rates of economic growth in a participant's geographical locale were associated, to a limited degree, with an increased likelihood of program completion. This raises the possibility that as individual cities respond differently to the global economic transformation, the degree of vulnerability of blacks and Latinos and the available options to ameliorate poor labor market outcomes will also vary.

## Urban Areas and the Global Economic Transformation

As suggested previously, the global economic transformation can be expected to have differential effects across urban areas and on different population groups within urban areas. Abbott (1993) has analyzed the urban response to the global economic transformation focusing specifically on the sunbelt region. He argues that, "international and informational opportunities have helped many of the Sunbelt's major cities break out of a one-dimensional relationship with a previously dominant national core and emerge as centers of change in their own right" (Abbott,1993;184-5). Abbott specifically examined the change in international connections and information functions in 30 cities between 1960 and 1980. Indices were developed for each city for both categories, with a maximum possible point assignment of 10 for each index. Internationalization scores were based on six criteria: foreign-born population, foreign trade, international information center role, international banking activities, foreign investment, and importance of foreign markets to local enterprises. Information economy scores were based on four criteria: white-collar employment, employment in financial services and corporate administration, presence of major corporate headquarters, and activities as a federal administrative center.

For present purposes, a subset of those cities will be examined for which supplemental information is available about the relationship between changes in employment across and within sectors and the unemployment rates of different population groups. The cities of particular interest are Atlanta, Dallas, Denver, Houston, Los Angeles, Miami, San Diego, San Francisco, and Washington, D.C.

Focusing first on the general pattern of linkages to the global economy and employment shifts, relevant data are presented in Table 1. In evaluating the changes in international linkage and information functions between 1960 and 1980, it is important to recognize that these changes are layered on top of a pattern of significant variation in the level of international linkage and information functions existing in 1960. To illustrate, San Francisco and Los Angeles had relatively well-developed international linkages in 1960, while Atlanta and Denver had virtually no such connections. In a similar vein, San Francisco, Washington, Dallas and

Los Angeles had well-established international information functions in 1960 while this function was underdeveloped in Miami.

TABLE 1
**Indicators of International Activities and Job Turnover**
**Selected Urban Areas 1960 - 1984**

| Area | (1) Change in International Role Index Points 1960-1980 | (2) Change in Information Function Index Points 1960-1980 | (3) Gross Job Turnover 1980-1984 as a Percentage of 1980 Jobs | (4) Percentage Turnover Occurring Within Same Sector | (5) Percentage Turnover Occurring Across Sectors |
|---|---|---|---|---|---|
| Atlanta | 4.0 | 4.0 | 18.7 | 61.46 | .14 |
| Dallas | 4.0 | 3.0 | 26.0 | 68.91 | .49 |
| Denver | 0 | 2.0 | 19.6 | 69.58 | .22 |
| Houston | 1.5 | 3.0 | 22.3 | 76.40 | 0 |
| Los Angeles | 6.0 | 3.0 | 6.5 | 71.77 | 1.63 |
| Miami | 6.0 | 3.0 | 3.0 | 70.63 | 5.77 |
| San Diego | 3.0 | 1.0 | 20.0 | 75.38 | .02 |
| San Francisco | 3.0 | 2.0 | 26.2 | 62.19 | .81 |
| Washington | 4.5 | 4.0 | 20.4 | 70.52 | .48 |

Source:
Columns 1 and 2 - C. Abbott, "Through Flight to Tokyo: Sunbelt Cities and the New World Economy, 1960-1990," in A. Hirsch and R. Mohl, (eds.) *Urban Policy in Twentieth-Century America* (New Brunswick, NJ: Rutgers University Press,1993), Table 6.4, p. 193.

Columns 3, 4 and 5 - T. Hyclak and J. Stewart, "Racial Differences in the Unemployment Response to Structural Changes in Local Labor Markets," *The Review of Black Political Economy* 23 (4), (Spring,1995), Table 1, pp. 34-35.

With the exception of Los Angeles and Miami, all of the urban areas in the sample experienced high rates of job turnover in the magnitude of 20 percent or greater between 1980 and 1984. The vast proportion of this turnover involved job changes between firms within the same sector rather than individuals moving into other industries. Thus, whatever momentum was associated with changes in international roles and information functions over the period 1960 to 1980, it did not catalyze significant employment shifts across sectors with the possible exceptions of Los Angeles and Miami. However, it should be recalled that these two urban areas experienced the lowest rates of job turnover overall during this period.

Table 2 contains average unemployment rates for blacks, Hispanics and whites for each of the urban areas over the period 1981 to 1984. In general, these data indicate that Blacks had higher unemployment rates than either Hispanics or whites. The areas with the highest ratios of black-to-white unemployment rates are Washington, Atlanta, and Dallas. Blacks in Los Angeles and Miami had the lowest black-to-white unemployment ratios. It will be recalled that these were also the areas with the lowest overall job turnover rates.

TABLE 2
**Average Unemployment Rates for Blacks, Hispanics and Whites**
**Selected Urban Areas 1981 - 1984**

| Area | (1) Black Rate | (2) Hispanic Rate | (3) White Rate | (4) Black Rate/ White Rate | (5) Hispanic Rate/ White Rate |
|---|---|---|---|---|---|
| Atlanta | 11.3 | n.a. | 4.0 | 2.83 | n.a. |
| Dallas | 10.8 | 5.8 | 3.9 | 2.77 | 1.49 |
| Denver | 11.5 | 12.0 | 5.4 | 2.13 | 2.22 |
| Houston | 14.9 | 8.7 | 5.6 | 2.66 | 1.55 |
| Los Angeles | 14.3 | 11.2 | 7.8 | 1.83 | 1.44 |
| Miami | 14.6 | 9.9 | 7.7 | 1.90 | 1.29 |
| San Diego | 17.8 | n.a. | 7.6 | 2.34 | n.a. |
| San Francisco | 16.9 | n.a. | 6.8 | 2.49 | n.a. |
| Washington | 10.7 | n.a. | 3.5 | 3.06 | n.a. |

Source:
n.a. - not available

Source:
Columns 1-3 - Bureau of Labor Statistics, *Geographic Profile of Employment and Unemployment*.

The urban areas discussed above were also examined as part of a larger study of racial differences in the relationship between unemployment rates and structural changes in local labor markets over the period 1981-1984 (Hyclak and Stewart,1995). The cities in this study included both other Sunbelt urban areas and various northern and midwestern cities. The study found that black unemployment rates were significantly more responsive to differences in aggregate demand growth and wage flexibility than are white and Hispanic unemployment rates. The study also found that black unemployment rates were affected more by structural changes in labor demand than was the case for white and Hispanic unemployment rates.

More detailed analysis of the results from this study reveals that the model used to generate the findings in fact significantly underpredicts black, and to a lesser extent Hispanic, unemployment rates for most of the cities discussed above. This underprediction may well be related to the relatively high degree of international linkage and information functions in this particular subset of urban areas compared to the others in the complete sample. In many cases the magnitude of the underprediction is substantial as documented in Table 3.

TABLE 3
**Comparisons of Predicted and Actual Average Unemployment Rates of Blacks and Hispanics.  Selected Urban Areas 1981 - 1984**

| Area | (1) Actual Black Rate | (2) Predicted Black Rate | (3) Actual Hispanic Rate | (4) Predicted Hispanic Rate |
|---|---|---|---|---|
| Atlanta | 11.3 | 10.2 | n.a. | n.a. |
| Dallas | 10.8 | 8.3 | 5.8 | 1.7 |
| Denver | 11.5 | 8.0 | 12.0 | 14.9 |
| Houston | 14.9 | 15.5 | 8.7 | 6.4 |
| Los Angeles | 14.3 | 12.8 | 11.2 | 11.5 |
| Miami | 14.6 | 13.4 | 9.9 | 9.3 |
| San Diego | 17.8 | 17.0 | n.a. | n.a. |
| San Francisco | 16.9 | 18.6 | n.a. | n.a. |
| Washington | 10.7 | 7.8 | n.a. | n.a. |

Source:
Columns 1 and 3 -Bureau of Labor Statistics, *Geographic Profile of Employment and Unemployment*

Columns 2 and 4 -Computed from results presented in T. Hyclak and J. Stewart, "Racial Differences in the Unemployment Response to Structural Changes in Local Labor Markets," *The Review of Black Political Economy* 23 (4), (Spring,1995).

The principal implication emerging from the preceding discussion is that interventions designed to improve the labor-market outcomes for blacks and Hispanics in urban areas must be sufficiently flexible to address differences in local labor-market dynamics and variations in the manner and extent to which specific cities are linked to the evolving international economic order.

As noted previously, the spatial configuration of job opportunities and residential enclaves can influence the extent to which different groups can benefit from linkages to the international economy and information functions. This can be illustrated by examining recent trends in housing markets and housing policy in three of the cities in this study. It will be recalled that Pressman (1985) suggested that in some international/information cities, people would increasingly be living nearer to their place of employment. Pressman (1985) also observed that this internationalization process had the potential to produce "divided cities."

Such an "internationalization-related" pattern of division would, however, necessarily feed upon existing patterns of residential segregation and housing policies. In the case of Atlanta, between 1980 and 1988 employment in the city grew by an average of 1.5 percent per year compared to 6.05 percent for the whole Atlanta area region (Robinson,1992). By 1989 blacks and other racial minorities accounted for 70 percent of the city's residents, but only 26 percent of the total region population. One innovative effort to develop a stronger linkage between the city's housing market and the job market involved creation of the Atlanta Housing Enterprise Zone Program, an outgrowth of the Atlanta Urban Enterprise Zone Act of 1983. The goal of this program was to encourage private investment in housing construction and rehabilitation in selected areas of the city using techniques similar to those employed to encourage private employers to locate in inner-city neighborhoods The program was not focused exclusively on housing for low and moderate income residents, but designated zones had to be located in a census tract with either high unemployment and/or poverty rates, or a population less than 1,000. As of 1990, only two projects had been developed (in two census tracts), and the beneficiaries consisted primarily of middle- and upper-income households (Robinson,1992). This scenario constitutes an example of what Knight (1989) described as policies that provide amenities targeted at those workers most directly linked to the processes of internationalization and information function expansion. Unfortunately, in this case the result was increased rather than decreased racial division.

A somewhat similar pattern occurred in Los Angeles. Between 1980 and 1988 the city's international linkages and information functions grew substantially. International trade-related jobs expanded to 10 percent of the total employment base and 140 banks from thirty-five nations had established offices within the urban area (Grigsby and Hruby,1992). Grigsby and Hruby (1992) found that residents in predominantly black neighborhoods did not benefit significantly from this growth pattern and, in fact, continued to be underdeveloped relative to the rest of the city. Paralleling the scenario in Atlanta a public entity, the Community Redevelopment Agency (CRA), developed a targeted program to spur housing development in black and Latino communities. This agency was, in fact, responsible for producing 10 percent of all new housing units constructed in Atlanta between 1980 and 1988. Twenty percent of the CRA-sponsored units were constructed in predominantly black and Hispanic communities. This amounted to 50 percent of all new units built in black communities during this period. Also, similar to developments in Atlanta, the principal beneficiaries of this program were not the original neighborhood residents. Grigsby and Hruby (1992,237) reported that much of the housing has been constructed in conjunction with the University of Southern California, and that "students and persons associated with the university are the beneficiaries of this housing, and not local residents seeking a place to live."

Houston presents a case where constraints on the suburbanization of blacks has limited opportunities to benefit from internationalization and information function expansion. Bullard (1992) reports that the representation of blacks in the suburbs of Houston actually declined between 1960 and 1980, from 12.9 percent to 6.2 percent. Although the overall degree of segregation declined somewhat during this period, Bullard (1992,177) indicates that black suburbanization often entailed "an extension of the segregated housing pattern that has typified the central city." Bullard (1992,177-8) also notes that "in other cases, older black suburban enclaves . . . have been encircled by new residential and commercial construction with few of the new amenities benefiting the nearby black residents."

Two basic conclusions emerge from the preceding discussion. First, there is a need for an expanded and area-specific approach to the preparation of workers to function in globalizing cities. Consistent with the perspective advanced by Knight (1989), particular attention must be placed on equalizing access across population groups to schooling, apprenticeship, and retraining programs most directly relevant for knowledge work. Second, efforts to position urban areas to take advantage of opportunities created by the global economy must be linked to neighborhood development and housing policies that promote a high degree of parity across geographical subareas. Without such policies, it will be impossible to equalize spatial and demographic access to occupations linked to international functions and residential habitats providing a high quality of life.

## Policy Implications

Preparing future and current black and Hispanic workers to meet the challenges of globalizing urban labor markets is severely compromised by patterns of segregation and underfunding in urban public school districts. This problem derives, of course, from the manner in which public education is currently funded, which penalizes areas with eroding property tax bases. Some examples of the disastrous consequences of underfunding public education in selected cities, including East St. Louis, New York City and San Antonio, are documented poignantly in Kozol (1991). The conditions documented by Kozol and others reflect the fact, as noted by Jones-Wilson (1991), that urban school improvement programs targeted at the "disadvantaged" are no longer a national priority. As an example, in the last session of Congress, efforts were made to eliminate 43 education programs and reduce spending in more than a dozen others including the Title I compensatory education program (Pisch,1995).

On the positive side, Congress passed the School-to-Work Opportunities Act (STWOA) in 1994, aimed at improving the productivity and competitiveness of the U.S. labor force and preparing young people for rewarding work lives (Office of Technology Assessment,1995). The objectives of this legislation are to be accomplished by coordinating the creation of comprehensive statewide and local networks to facilitate school-to-work transitions. At the local level, partnerships of educators, employers, employees and students will be the driving force behind activities supported by this legislation. The legislation mandates that projects be coordinated with other education and training activities receiving federal support. Thirty-six grants were made to local areas in 1994 (Office of Technology Assessment,1995). Many of these grants were awarded to smaller urban areas, but the potential exists for expanded activity in this arena in larger cities with stronger linkages to the international economy.

Proposals in the 1996 U.S. Congress to consolidate over 100 federal education, job-training, and employment-assistance programs into single block grants to states are currently stalled. The proposed legislation would require that state and local governments spend 35 percent of the block grant on adult job training, 20 percent on vocational education, 15 percent on programs for at-risk youth, and 5 percent on adult education and literacy, with the balance available for distribution at governors' discretion (Burd,1996). While this consolidation may eliminate some unnecessary duplication, the overall levels of spending in key areas like vocational and adult education would be decreased significantly.

Efforts to convert support for many existing programs into block grants does not bode well, based on experiences in Chicago with Community Development Block Grants (CDBG) reported by Rich (1989). Rich (1989,346) notes, in part:

On paper, CDBG appears to be an ideal tool to address the physical development needs of distressed neighborhoods. Cities can use their block grant funds for a wide variety of activities, including both physical development and human services. Yet, without external constraints on local choices regarding program uses, block grant funds tend to be spread widely, and often include less pressing improvements in relatively well-off neighborhoods.

In general, there is a need to create a seamless relationship among elementary, secondary, post-secondary, and adult educational systems. A relevant example identified by Toffler as early as 1970 include a planned experimental college in New York's Bedford-Stuyvesant District, that "would disperse its facilities throughout the stores, offices and homes of a 45 block area, making it difficult to tell where the college ends and the community begins." Toffler (1970;406-7) suggests that in this type of setting "students would be taught skills by adults in the community as well as by regular faculty." This type of approach to the preparation of new labor-market entrants as well as retraining experienced workers displaced by the global transformation is absolutely critical if urban areas are to avoid becoming "divided cities." A comprehensive and coordinated strategy for developing urban human resources is required to address what appears to be an inevitable increase in the rate at which knowledge becomes obsolete in the face of accelerating technological innovation. But the development of such an approach and the redesign of existing educational and training processes to meet the challenges of preparing workers to compete in a global economy will require more, not fewer resources.

As suggested previously, there is a need to coordinate housing-development and employment-location policies. The experiences in Houston and Los Angeles, discussed previously, indicate that sole reliance on governmental authorities responsible for promoting housing development and enforcement of antidiscrimination legislation is insufficient to promote reasonable spatial parity of employment opportunities created by the internationalization of urban economies. Community-based organizations must be empowered to become active players in influencing the spatial distribution of employment and housing developments in the urban areas of the 21st century.

Handy (1993,50) has described various initiatives that are designed to provide this type of community-based momentum. To illustrate, he suggests that there is significant potential for Community Development Corporations (CDCs) "to act as developers, financial packagers, and in some cases operators of retail shops and industrial parks." Handy also proposes that "some CDCs may act as, work closely with, or actually become quasi-public economic development corporations in local jurisdictions (Handy,1993;50). Handy (1993,50) further observes that there has been an "increased use of local-housing partnerships whose members include city officials, bank and insurance representatives, local development corporations and housing organizations as a partnership forum." He also advocates the creation of "pooled partnership syndications to generate equity funds to leverage federal, state, and bank funds and local Community Development Block Grants" along with "tax credits for socially responsible investments" (Handy,1993,51).

Undertaking the type of programs suggested above will not solve independently the problem of employment dislocation created by the evolution of the global economy. As noted previously, current trends point clearly to future reductions in traditional employment arenas relative to the size of the labor force. As a consequence, there will be a growing need to expand the scope of activities for which paid compensation is provided. The Tofflers (1995,53) argue, for example, that:

"The jobless desperately need money if they and their families are to survive, and it is both necessary and morally right to provide them with decent levels of public assistance. . .

"As . . . new jobs are not likely to be found in what we still think of as manufacture, we will need to prepare people through schooling apprenticeships and on-the-job learning for work in such fields as the human services."

The Tofflers further maintain that:

"if . . . wages are low in the service sector, then the solution is to increase service productivity and to invent new forms of work-force organization and collective bargaining. Unions, primarily designed for the crafts or for mass manufacturing, need to be totally transformed or else replaced by new-style organizations more appropriate to the super-symbolic economy." (Toffler and Toffler,1995;53)

In a similar vein, Aronowitz and DiFazio (1994;256-58) claim there is a need for society to provide subsidies in the form of tax deductions for shadow wages for voluntary community service work.

Finally, the design of creative approaches to income maintenance must go hand-in-hand with policies designed to generate more equitable outcomes in the arenas of employment creation, training; and housing development. Progressive income-assistance policies should be seen as an appropriate mode of maintaining the local economic infrastructure necessary to prevent the types of social tensions associated with "divided cities."

Particularly difficult problems are likely to arise in urban areas where new populations seeking to benefit from the global transformation are perceived by previous residents as limiting their opportunities to adapt to changing circumstances. Kotkin (1993,254) suggests, for example, that "Many older, more established communities—both *African-American* and Anglo—will feel themselves overwhelmed and in some sense displaced by the energetic newcomers, both in the marketplace and, over time, in the political arena." More generally, the Tofflers (1995,24) observe that:

"In the United States—and in many other countries—the collision of Second and Third Waves creates social tensions, dangerous conflicts and strange new political wave fronts that cut across the usual divisions of class, race, sex or party. This collision makes a shambles of traditional political vocabularies and makes it very difficult to separate progressives from reactionaries, friends from enemies. All the old polarizations and coalitions break up."

The type of policy agenda proposed in this analysis can become a foundation for establishing a basis for building new coalitions devoted to creating habitable and vibrant cities for all citizens in the next century. The guidelines that should be kept in mind in pursuing equitable development trajectories in our urban areas have been aptly stated by Rich (1989,346):

"Place-oriented programs that attack some of the fundamental causes of poverty, forces manifest in the physical decay of distressed neighborhoods—disinvestment and abandonment of residential and commercial buildings, loss of employment opportunities, aging infrastructure, lack of public facilities such as schools, health clinics, and recreation centers—are also needed in tandem with programs that focus on education and training, health care, nutrition, alcohol and drug abuse treatment, and the like. Places do matter, and their condition does have an impact on the well-being of their residents."

# REFERENCES

Abbott, C. (1993). "Through Flight to Tokyo: Sunbelt Cities and the New World Economy, 1960-1990," in A. Hirsch and R. Mohl, eds. *Urban Policy in Twentieth Century America*. New Brunswick, N.J.: Rutgers University Press, pp. 183-212.

Aburdene, P. and Naisbitt, J. (1992). *Megatrends for Women*. New York: Villard Books.

Armah, B. (1994) "Implications of Trade on Service Employment: Implications for Women and Minorities, *Contemporary Economic Policy*, XII, pp. 67-78.

Aronowitz, S. and DiFazio, W. (1994). *The Jobless Future, Sci-Tech and the Dogma of Work*. Minneapolis, Minn.: University of Minnesota Press.

Borjas, G. (1986). *Immigrants, Minorities, and Labor Market Competition* Working Paper No. 2028. Cambridge, Mass.: National Bureau of Economic Research.

Bullard, R. (1992). "Housing Problems and Prospects for Blacks in Houston," in W. Leigh and J. Stewart, eds. *The Housing Status of Black Americans*. New Brunswick, N.J.: Transaction Publishers 175-194.

Burd, S. (1996). "Logjam in Congress Hinders Effort to Revamp Job-Training Programs," *The Chronicle of Higher Education*, (May, 31), A22.

Edwards, J., Thomas, M. and Burch, R. (1992). "Hispanic Representation in the Federal Government: Lessons From the Navy's Equal Employment Opportunity Enhancement Research Program," in S. Knouse, P. Rosenfeld, A. Culbertson, eds. *Hispanics in the Workplace*. Newbury Park, Calif.: Sage Publications, pp. 231-245.

Gonzalez, E. and Gray, L. (1984). "Puerto Ricans, Politics and Labor Activism," in J. Jennings and M. Rivera, eds. *Puerto Rican Politics in Urban America*. Westport, Conn.: Greenwood Press, pp. 117-126.

Grigsby, J. E. and Hruby, M. (1992). "Recent Changes in the Housing Status of Blacks in Los Angeles," in W. Leigh and J. Stewart, eds. *The Housing Status of Black Americans*. New Brunswick, N.J.: Transaction Publishers, pp. 211-240.

Handy, J. (1993). "Community Economic Development: Some Critical Issues," *The Review of Black Political Economy*, 21 (3), 41-64.

Hyclak, T. and Stewart, J. (1986). "The Effects of Immigrants, Women, and Teenagers on the Relative Earnings of Black Males," *The Review of Black Political Economy*, 15 (1), pp. 93-101.

Hyclak, T. and Stewart, J. (1995). "Racial Differences in the Unemployment Response to Structural Changes in Local Labor Markets," *The Review of Black Political Economy*, 23 (4), pp. 29-42.

Idson, T. and Price, H. (1992). "An Analysis of Wage Differentials by Gender and Ethnicity in the Public Sector," *The Review of Black Political Economy* 20 (3), pp. 75-98.

Jacobson, L., LaLonde, R. and Sullivan, D. (1993). *The Costs of Worker Dislocation*. Kalamazoo, Mich.: W.E. Upjohn Institute for Employment Research.

Jones-Wilson, F. (1991). "School Improvement Among Blacks: Implications for Excellence and Equity," in W. Willie, A. Garibaldi, and W. Reed, eds. *The Education of African Americans*.Westport, Conn.: Auburn House, pp. 72-78.

Kletzer, L. (1991). "Earnings After Job Displacement: Job Tenure, Industry, and Occupation," in J. Addison, ed. *Job Displacement, Consequences and Implications for Policy*. Detroit, Mich.: Wayne State University Press, 107-135.

Knight, R. (1989). "City Development and Urbanization: Building the Knowledge-Based City," in R. Knight and G. Gappan, eds. *Cities in a Global Society*. Urban Affairs Annual Review, Vol. 35. Newbury Park, Calif.: Sage Publications, 223-242.

Kosters, M. (1986). "Job Changes and Displaced Workers: An Examination of Employment Adjustment Experience," in Philip Cagan, ed. *Essays in Contemporary Economic Problems: The Impact of the Reagan Program*. Washington, D.C.: American Enterprise Institute.

Kotkin, J. (1993). *Tribes, How Race, Religion, and Identity Determine Success in the New Global Economy*. New York: Random House.

Kozol, J. (1991). *Savage Inequalities, Children in America's Schools*. New York: Crown Publishers.

Leigh, D. (1990). *Does Training Work for Displaced Workers, A Survey of*

*Existing Evidence.* Kalamazoo, Mich.: W.E. UpjohnInstitute for Employment Research.

Mar, D. and Ong, P. (1994). "Race and Rehiring in the High-Tech Industry," *The Review of Black Political Economy* 22 (3), pp. 43-54.

Mauer, M. (1994). "A Generation Behind Bars: Black Males and the Criminal Justice System," in R. Majors and J. Gordon, eds. *The American Black Male, His Present Status and His Future.* (Chicago: Nelson-Hall Publishers), pp. 81-94.

Montgomery, P. (1994). *The Hispanic Population in the United States: March 1993.* Current Population Reports, Population Characteristics, Series P20-475. Washington, D.C.: U.S. Government Printing Office.

Naisbitt, J. (1982) *Megatrends, Ten New Directions Transforming Our Lives.* New York: Warner Books.

Ong, P. and Lawrence, J. (1995). "Race and Employment Dislocation in California's Aerospace Industry," *The Review of Black Political Economy* 23 (3), pp. 91-102.

Ortiz, V. (1991). "Latinos and Industrial Change in New York and Los Angeles," in E. Melendez, C. Rodriguez and J. Figueroa, eds. *Hispanics in the Labor Force, Issues and Policies.* New York: Plenum Press, pp. 119-134.

Pitsch, M. (1995) "House Panel Approves $1.7 Billion in Cuts to 1995 Education Program," *Education Week* XIV (23) (March 1).

Pressman, N. (1985). "Forces for Spatial Change," in J. Botchie, et al., eds Technological Change and Urban Form. New York: Nichols Publishing Company, 349-361.

Reimers, C. and Chernick, H. (1991). "Hispanic Employment in the Public Sector: Why Is It Lower Than Blacks?" in E. Melendez, C. Rodriguez and J. Figueroa, eds. *Hispanics in the Labor Force, Issues and Policies.* New York: Plenum Press, pp. 135-158.

Rich, M. (1989). *Federal Policymaking and the Poor, National Goals, Local Choices, and Distributional Outcomes.* Princeton, N.J.: Princeton University Press.

Rifkin, J. (1995). *The End of Work, The Decline of the Global Labor Force and the Dawn of the Post-Market Era.* New York: G.P. Putnam's Sons.

Robinson, C. (1992). "Racial Disparity in the Atlanta Housing Market," in W. Leigh and J. Stewart, eds. *The Housing Status of Black Americans*. New Brunswick, N.J.: Transaction Publishers, pp. 85-109.

Rosenfeld, P. and Culbertson, A. (1992). "Hispanics in the Military," in S. Knouse, P. Rosenfeld, A. Culbertson, eds. *Hispanics in the Workplace*. Newbury Park, CA: Sage Publications, pp. 211-230.

Segura, D. (1992). "Walking on Eggshells: Chicanas in the Labor Force," in S. Knouse, P. Rosenfeld, A. Culbertson, eds. *Hispanics in the Workplace*. Newbury Park, Calif.: Sage Publications), pp. 194-210.

Seitchik, A. and Zornitsky, J. (1989. *From One Job to the Next, Worker Adjustment in a Changing Labor Market*. Kalamazoo, Mich. W.E. Upjohn Institute for Employment Research.

Simms, M. and Malveaux, J., eds. (1986). *Slipping Through the Cracks: The Status of Black Women*. New Brunswick, N.J.: Transaction Publishers.

Skerry, P. (1993). *Mexican Americans, The Ambivalent Minority*. New York: The Free Press.

Sokoloff, N. (1992). *Black Women and White Women in the Professions*. New York: Routledge.

Stafford, W. (1991). "Racial, Ethnic, and Gender Employment Segmentation in New York City Agencies," in E. Melendez, C. Rodriguez and J. Figueroa, eds. *Hispanics in the Labor Force, Issues and Policies*. New York: Plenum Press, pp. 159-182.

Stewart, J. (1995). *An Analysis of Earnings and Employment Outcomes of JTPA Title III Program* Participants. Final Report submitted to the National Commission for Employment Policy, (September).

Swaim, P. and Podgursky, M. (1991). "The Distribution of Economic Losses Among Displaced Workers: A Replication," *Journal of Human Resources* 26(4), pp. 742-755.

Toffler, A. (1970). *Future Shock*. New York: Random House.

Toffler, A. and Toffler, H. (1995) *Creating a New Civilization, The Politics of the Third Wave*. Atlanta: Turner Publishing Co.

Torres, A. (1991). "Labor Market Segmentation: African American and Puerto Rican Labor in New York City, 1960-1980," *The Review of Black Political Economy* 20 (1), pp. 59-77.

U.S. Bureau of Labor Statistics (various years). *Geographic Profile of Employment and Unemployment*. Washington, D.C.: U.S. Government Printing Office.

U.S. Congress, Office of Technology Assessment (1995). *Learning to Work: Making the Transition from School to Work*, OTA-EHR-637. Washington, D.C.: U.S. Government Printing Office, (September).

Williams, R. (1994). "An Estimate of Black Gross Job Losses Due to Reduced Defense Expenditures," *The Review of Black Political Economy* 22 (3), pp. 31-42.

## BIOGRAPHICAL SKETCH

**James B. Stewart** is currently Vice Provost for Educational Equity and Professor of Labor Studies and Industrial Relations at Penn State University. He is the co-editor of the volumes Black Families: Interdisciplinary Perspectives, The Housing Status of Black Americans, Blacks in Rural America, and W.E.B. Du Bois on Race and Culture: Philosophy, Politics and Poetics. He is also the editor of the forthcoming collection entitled African Americans and Post Industrial Labor Markets and has published extensively in Economics, Labor Studies and Africana Studies professional journals.

Dr. Stewart is the former editor of The Review of Black Political Economy and former President of the National Economic Associations.

# U.S. HOUSING POLICY IN 1996:
# THE OUTLOOK FOR BLACK AMERICANS

by
**Wilhelmina A. Leigh, Ph.D.**

# ABSTRACT

This chapter evaluates the effectiveness for black Americans of various forms of federal housing assistance. Some housing assistance programs implemented in the past, such as Section 235, have been discontinued because of design flaws. Others, such as the Nehemiah Housing Opportunity Grants Program, were funded for so short a period of time that it was not possible to determine their worth. Still other currently operating programs (e.g., Low-Rent Public Housing and Section 8), which serve black Americans in a manner that might best be characterized as "separate but *un*equal," face threats to their continued existence posed by the twin desires to balance the federal budget and to reinvent government. The 1996 housing policy context is fully detailed in the chapter along with a discussion of how black Americans are likely to fare in this setting.

Although the U.S. Department of Housing and Urban Development (HUD), the agency with primary responsibility for housing assistance in urban areas, was not established until 1965, the federal government has intervened in the housing market to foster a variety of broad objectives since the 1930s. These objectives have ranged from providing countercyclical stimulus to the economy, to guaranteeing fair access to housing for all, to improving the housing of the poor, and have been achieved to varying degrees in the many federal housing assistance programs. Federal housing assistance has been funneled through states and localities, and through local housing authorities (LHAs) or public housing authorities (PHAs). It has included the construction and leasing of housing, subsidizing rents, subsidizing interest rates, guaranteeing and insuring mortgages, and supporting and regulating the secondary market for home loans.

Just as the wide ranging goals of federal housing policy have not been achieved to the same degree across programs, the extent to which black and white Americans have received benefits under these programs also has differed. From the 1930s through the 1950s and 1960s, the "separate but equal" doctrine was dominant throughout the nation and was reflected in program outcomes for blacks. "Separate but equal" in housing assistance programs often translated into "separate but *unequal*" locations of housing developments and quality of units. Today's entrenched patterns of rigid racial segregation and the associated lessened access to opportunities for schooling and employment for black Americans are the continued legacy of "separate but *unequal*" treatment by housing assistance programs. These patterns of separation between the races make it especially difficult both to achieve the objective of fair access to housing and to operate all housing programs to serve members of different racial/ethnic groups equitably.

This chapter describes the current housing assistance environment and evaluates the effectiveness of various forms of assistance for black Americans. It begins with an overview of federal programs, followed by details on the housing experiences of blacks. The final section characterizes the 1996 housing policy context and describes how black Americans and selected programs are likely to fare in this setting.

Housing policies and programs in the U.S. have been described as a "crazy quilt" of initiatives that seek to achieve numerous, often mutually exclusive goals. Although many might agree that the three primary objectives of federal intervention in the housing market are to encourage homeownership, improve housing for the poor, and enforce fair housing laws, conflicts arise in the implementation of programs to achieve these various ends. For example, programs to encourage homeownership that are effective primarily in suburbs often undermine the vitality of cities, where many of the poor and homeless are found.

The federal government intervenes in the housing market through programs funded both directly and indirectly. Appropriated monies appear in line items in HUD's annual budget for directly funded programs, while indirectly funded interventions are supported by revenues *not* collected by the federal government, a form of funding that usually does not receive the same scrutiny as department budgets. One example of an indirectly funded program is the deductibility of mortgage interest from individual income taxable by the federal government, which provides a powerful incentive for homeownership. In fiscal year (FY) 1994, this indirectly funded housing program accounted for $51 billion in tax subsidies (or revenues not collected), with over two-fifths (44 percent) going to the 5.2 percent of taxpayers with incomes above $100,000. The Low-Income Housing Tax Credit (LIHTC), first enacted in 1986 and made permanent in 1993, provides another such example. By allowing a deduction from federally taxable income for 10 years to investors in housing developments that serve low-income persons, the program stimulates the production of housing affordable to these persons. Either 20 percent of project units must be reserved for households with incomes less than 50 percent of the median income of the metropolitan area, or 40 percent of project units must be reserved for households with incomes less than 60 percent of the median income of the metropolitan area.

Direct housing assistance programs far outnumber indirect ones, although their total funding is less. Peak allocations for directly funded HUD subsidized programs ($32.3 billion) were made in FY 1978. Funding has fallen since then, while the number of programs for which HUD has statutory responsibility increased from 54 to just over 200 between 1980 and 1992. In addition, since 1990, Congress has created or substantially changed the mission of 67 HUD programs (of which 25 were not funded as of FY 1994).

In the appendix to this chapter the directly funded federal housing assistance programs are described in detail, along with the issues currently confronting each. The major programs and issues are noted below.

During the 1930s, the federal government intervened in the housing market by establishing the infrastructure for primary and secondary markets for mortgage loans, and by implementing a program to construct rental dwellings for low-income households. In the early years of the decade, a regulatory infrastructure was implemented to encourage lenders to make mortgage loans. Today, after modifications to this infrastructure, the Federal Home Loan Bank system operates an Affordable Housing programs under which each of the Banks advances funds to its member institutions to provide funds for mortgage loans or to develop rental properties. The Federal Housing Administration (FHA) (established in 1934) insures mortgage loans and thereby encourages financial institutions to make long-term, low-rate loans to home buyers in the primary mortgage market. Secondary mortgage market entities, which buy and resell or hold mortgage loans as a way to recycle funds to primary mortgage lenders, were established in the 1930s (Fannie Mae in 1938), in the 1960s (Ginnie Mae in 1968), and in 1970 (Freddie Mac).

Authorized by legislation passed in 1937 and known as Low-Rent Public Housing (LRPH), this program to house low-income families is the oldest, continuously operating federal housing program. Although the federal government currently provides grants for construction, it issued bonds to finance many of the older developments and owns these structures during the 40 years it makes debt service payments. After this period has passed, ownership of LRPH developments transfers to the LHAs/PHAs that have been the local operators and managers. The aging and disposition of more than 1.4 million units constructed under the LRPH program is an issue today.

The next decade for major federal housing program innovations was the 1960s, when programs combining interest-rate subsidies with mortgage insurance through the FHA were developed both for owners and renters. Both the Section 221-d-3 Below-Market Interest Rate (BMIR) program and the Section 236 program used these features to stimulate the construction by private sector entities of rental housing for low- and moderate-income families. Although these programs no longer fund new units, the potential change in ownership and the potential associated loss of these units from the inventory of low-rent dwellings have become policy issues. The continuing subsidies paid for units constructed under these programs in the 1960s and 1970s also are an issue in today's budget debates.

The Section 235 program, also established during the 1960s, used an interest subsidy along with FHA mortgage insurance to provide homeownership for low- and moderate-income households. Yet another innovation during the 1960s was the Section 312 Rehabilitation Loan program, which gives priority to low- and moderate-income applicants in targeted declining neighborhoods for loans to rehabilitate their residences. The Urban Homesteading program, authorized in 1974, also targets assistance to low-income residents of distressed neighborhoods by enabling them to buy at nominal cost federally owned properties for rehabilitation and residence.

Although the Section 8 program implemented in 1974 allowed for the new construction, substantial rehabilitation, and moderate rehabilitation of housing, in addition to providing rental assistance payments for households living in existing dwelling units, its major program components today are the Section 8 Existing-Housing Certificate program (authorized in 1974) and the Section 8 Voucher program (authorized in 1983). The Section 8 Certificate and Voucher programs both provide payments to landlords toward meeting the rents of low-income tenants. Tenants pay a *maximum* of 30 percent of income for rent in the Section 8 Certificate program, in which rent cannot exceed the amount set by HUD based on the size and location of a unit, or a *minimum* of 30 percent of income for rent in the Section 8 Voucher program, in which unit rent is not constrained by HUD standards. In FY 1994, approximately 1.3 million households received either Section 8 Certificates (1 million) or Vouchers (300,000).

In addition to the Section 8 Voucher program, the 1980s saw the implementation of self-sufficiency programs (such as Project Self-Sufficiency and Operation Bootstrap) and the Nehemiah Housing Opportunity Grant program. The self-sufficiency programs were developed as demonstrations to coordinate resources such as housing, education, training, and employment to enable low-income adults to move into the economic mainstream. In 1990, Family Self-Sufficiency was authorized as a permanent program to foster this goal. The Nehemiah program, authorized in 1987, stimulated the construction or rehabilitation of housing units concentrated in distressed neighborhoods by encouraging localities to reduce construction costs by donating land and giving tax breaks. At the same time, HUD provided interest-free second mortgages loans of $15,000 to low- and moderate-income homebuyers.

In the 1990s the HOME and HOPE (Homeownership and Opportunity for People Everywhere) programs were implemented. The HOME Investment Partnership program gives state and local governments the option to design their own housing assistance programs, consistent with plans submitted to HUD. The HOPE program, through its several components, finances the sale of various publicly owned dwelling units to low-income households. In addition, HOPE VI funds the comprehensive revitalization of distressed LRPH developments.

How are Black Americans housed today? The 32.5 million Black Americans, who were 12.5 percent of the 1994 population, are distributed around the nation and within metropolitan areas according to patterns that differ from those of White Americans. These differences apply for all Black Americans and for Black Americans who receive federal housing assistance; the two groups are discussed separately below.

## Housing of All Black Americans

The shares of the total black and white populations differ notably in all regions except the Northeast. The majority of black Americans (55 percent) resided in southern states in 1994, with nearly equal shares living in the Northeast (17 percent) and Midwest (20 percent), and the smallest share living in the West (8 percent). Only a third of whites (32 percent), on the other hand, lived in the South, with 27 percent in the Midwest, and 20 percent and 21 percent, respectively, in the West and Northeast.

Although white non-Hispanics comprise the majority of households in all regions and types of places (80 percent), their share among central city households is less than this, ranging from 63 percent of all central city households in the South, to 72 percent in the Midwest. Black households were only 20 percent of all central city households in the nation, in spite of the fact that the majority of the nation's 10 million households with a black householder—59 percent or nearly three-fifths—lived in central cities in 1990. A quarter of all Black households lived in suburbs.

Black households living in metropolitan areas are more likely to live in high-poverty neighborhoods than are other metropolitan area households. According to the 1990 Census, while only 4.5 percent of the entire metropolitan population lives in a high-poverty neighborhood (i.e., census tracts with a poverty rate of 40 percent or higher), such neighborhoods are home to 42 percent of the blacks in metropolitan areas and 60 percent of all poor black metropolitan residents. High-poverty neighborhoods in metropolitan areas are home to less than 8 percent of all whites and to 26 percent of all poor Whites.

The figures noted above suggest the spatial separation that exists among whites and Blacks throughout the nation. In 1990, among non-Hispanic blacks, 62 percent lived on blocks that were 60 percent or more black, and 30 percent lived in neighborhoods that were 90 percent or more black. At least 2 out of 3 white Americans lived in essentially all-white neighborhoods, and, in most major cities, more than 70 percent of the population would have to move to achieve block by block percentages of households by race/ethnicity equal to those for the metropolitan area overall. The 20 percent of the black population in the Midwest, for example, lives in the region with the five most highly segregated metropolitan areas in 1990—Chicago, Ill.; Cleveland, Ohio; Detroit, Mich.; Gary-Hammond, Ind.; and Milwaukee, WI. Over 80 percent of either all black or all white residents in these places would have to relocate to create the racial/ethnic distribution for the metropolitan area as a whole on each of the blocks in the locality. In Gary-Hammond, Ind., 90 percent of either all the black or all the white residents would have to move to achieve this end.

Given this evidence of "separate" residential locales for blacks and whites throughout the U.S., is there evidence of "equal" housing for the two races, consistent with the guiding policy principle (of "separate but equal") for the nation for more than half of this century? The short answer is "No," and, even more telling is the fact that the findings about the housing conditions of black Americans vis-à-vis white Americans in a 1975 report by the U.S. Commission on Civil Rights are still true today. This 1975 report found the following for the 1950-1970 period: although the gap between minority and white homeownership rates narrowed, it remained substantial; and although the condition of housing lived in by minority households improved over the period, it remained worse than that of whites. In 1994, the ownership rate for black households was 42.5 percent, while the rate for white households was 67.8 percent—still a substantial gap. The median value of owned homes among black households in metropolitan areas ($55,500) also fell short of the median value of owned homes among white households ($91,700) in 1990. In addition, according to 1989 national data, the overall incidence of housing problems for households at every income level was significantly higher for blacks than for whites, with 76 percent of blacks and 65 percent of whites reporting any. Excess cost was a problem for nearly two-thirds of black households (65.4 percent) and more than three-fifths (60.5 percent) of white households. Inadequacy of dwelling was a problem for over a quarter of black households (25.4 percent) but only for 10 percent of whites. Overcrowding was a problem for 6 percent of black households but only 2 percent of white households.

## Housing of Black Americans Receiving Federal Assistance

Little information is available about the race of beneficiaries of housing constructed as a result of tax subsidy programs. Tax return data do not provide race detail because tax forms do not collect this information. However, whites appear to benefit more than blacks from the deductibility of mortgage interest from taxable federal income because over 44 percent of this tax subsidy goes to taxpayers with incomes greater than $100,000, and the percentage of black households with incomes in that range is less than this percentage among whites. Although HUD is developing a data base for the LIHTC, another tax subsidy program, there are no current plans to include tenant characteristics in it. A comparison by the U.S. General Accounting Office of tax credit projects with LRPH developments in 9 locales found that, while serving smaller size households than LRPH, LIHTC developments were more likely to be located in predominantly low-income and minority neighborhoods than were LRPH developments.

### Rental Assistance.

Somewhat more race detail for benefits and beneficiaries for the directly funded federal rental assistance programs is available. Relative to their share of all households (11.6 percent), black households are overrepresented among very low-income renter households (26 percent), the target group for most federal rental assistance. Nationally, about 40 percent of the very low-income renter households receiving federal housing assistance are black, and 45 percent of them are white. In addition, in each of the four regions, the percentage of eligible black very-low-income renter households who get federal rental assistance exceeds the share among eligible white very-low-income renter households and eligible very-low-income renter households of other racial/ethnic groups.

The 40 percent average share for black households among recipients of federal rental assistance obscures significant differences in the racial/ethnic mix among the beneficiaries of the various programs, however. Blacks are more than half (53 percent) of the residents of LRPH but less than a third (30 percent) of the residents of private, project-based, subsidized developments. About a third of Section 8 certificate and voucher recipients were black in 1991.

### Low-Rent Public Housing (LRPH).

The qualitative residential experience of blacks and whites in LRPH developments varies by location, size, and type of development (elderly, family, mixed). The majority of African American residents of LRPH live in developments located in areas with concentrations both of poverty and of other African Americans; the majority of white residents of LRPH live in developments with much lower concentrations both of poverty and of African Americans. Census tracts with fewer than 1 percent African American residents have LRPH developments in which 71 percent of the residents are white, on average; census tracts in which 70 percent or more of the population is African American, have LRPH developments in which 92 percent of residents are African American. The poorest census tracts with LRPH developments (those with more than a 30 percent poverty rate) are almost exclusively African American (91 percent), while the non-poor census tracts containing LRPH developments (those with poverty rates less than 30 percent) have higher proportions of white tenants.

Minority representation varies with the size of the development, with larger developments (and the census tracts in which they are located) more likely to be predominantly African American. Large LRPH developments account for 38 percent of all units of LRPH but only 20 percent of all LRPH developments; these developments on average are 73 percent African American and are located in census tracts that, on average, are 45 percent African American. Although minorities (blacks, Hispanics, and others) made up 69 percent of the population of LRPH at the end of 1993, minority representation ranged from a low of 30 percent of those housed by LHAs/PHAs with fewer than 100 units, to a high of 90 percent of those housed by the largest PHAs (i.e., those with more than 2,500 units).

Family (and mixed) developments are predominantly African American, while elderly developments are predominantly white. Seventy percent of the African Americans in LRPH live in family units, and 52 percent of the whites in LRPH live in elderly units. When types of developments are evaluated separately, nearly two-thirds of the residents of family units (64 percent) and three-fifths (60 percent) of the residents of mixed units are African American. White households are 55 percent of the residents of elderly developments, with black households more than a third (35 percent).

**Sections 221-d-3 BMIR and 236.** Little tenant data is available for the properties assisted under these two programs. A 1970 calculation of the distribution of benefits under the 221-d-3 BMIR program reveals that whites had received 56 percent and non-whites 44 percent of program benefits at that time. When tenant data for these two programs in 1993 was combined with data for the Section 221-d-4 market rate program, the overall racial distribution for the three programs was 55 percent whites, and 35 percent blacks. The elderly are more than a third of the residents of these subsidized properties. In addition, these privately developed properties tend to be located in areas of extreme poverty, with an average of almost 40 percent of the area populations having very low incomes (i.e., less than 50 percent of the area median income). Over 80 percent of the tenants subsidized by these programs have incomes in this range, as well.

Section 8 Certificates and Vouchers. Eighty-seven percent of black Section 8 Certificate and Voucher recipients in 1993 were successful in finding a unit to lease that met program standards. Although the third of beneficiaries of the Section 8 Certificate and Voucher programs who were black in 1991 generally reside in neighborhoods that are less poor and racially concentrated than the neighborhoods surrounding LRPH developments, many minority Section 8 families continue to live in relatively segregated and economically distressed neighborhoods. Targeted mobility programs, such as the Gautreaux Assisted Housing Program, begun in 1976, in the Chicago, Ill. metropolitan area as part of a court settlement, have used Section 8 Certificates and Vouchers to expand residential options for minority households. In part because the numbers of households served have been so small as to not perceptibly alter the racial mix in the suburbs to which many Gautreaux families relocate, the program has been able to place about 5,600 low-income black families in neighborhoods with less poverty and distress. More than half of these new locales (with less poverty and distress) are predominantly white middle-class suburbs.

**Owner Assistance**

In virtually every year between 1976 and 1991, the year in which the FHA assisted approximately 345,000 low- and moderate-income families to become owners, minority borrowers (blacks and Hispanics) made up a greater proportion of all FHA borrowers than they did of all U.S. home buyers. The minority share of FHA borrowers fluctuated between a low of 11 percent in 1986 and a high of 29 percent in 1988, with the 1991 share 17 percent. The minority share of all home buyers increased by a third between 1976 and 1991, from 9 percent to 12 percent. The Section 203(b) One-to-Four-Family mortgage insurance program is FHA's major federal vehicle to assist households to become owners. During 1993, 81.8 percent of Section 203(b) insured mortgages were issued to white borrowers, and 7.3 percent were issued to African American home buyers.

Although no longer operating, the Section 235 mortgage insurance program targeted low-income buyers in many of the nation's cities during the 1960s and 1970s. A 1971 study on early program experience revealed the familiar "separate but *unequal*" pattern of residential location and unit quality. Most new Section 235 units were built in suburbs and were purchased by white buyers, while most existing Section 235 units were in central city neighborhoods and were purchased by minority buyers. When minority 235 buyers acquired suburban units, they usually did so in subdivisions whose occupants were predominantly minority. In addition, because minority 235 buyers tended to purchase housing that was older and less expensive than the housing purchased by whites, they received less in assistance payments—yet another inequity.

Blacks seem to be benefitting from the newer assistance programs—HOME and HOPE. Although Whites received the majority of HOME assistance of each type in FY 1993, as beneficiaries of over half (54 percent) of the funds for acquisition/construction/rehabilitation and 60 percent of rental assistance payments, blacks were nearly a third of the beneficiaries of these HOME-funded activities. They were 32 percent of the beneficiaries of the HOME programs for rental assistance and for acquisition/construction/rehabilitation; Black Americans were 29 percent of the beneficiaries of first-time homebuyer assistance. In addition, whites were beneficiaries of nearly half (49 percent) of the first-time home buyer assistance. In the HOPE III program, which provides grants to nonprofit organizations and co-operatives that purchase and/or rehabilitate single-family homes for sale to eligible low-income families at affordable prices, over half (52 percent) of the families assisted by implementation grants in FY 1993 were black; a third were white.

## 1996 Housing Policy Debate

The context for discussions about federal housing policy in 1996 is shaped by several facts and factors. Foremost is the fact that housing programs have never been funded at a level that can provide assistance to all eligible households; that is, housing assistance is not provided as an entitlement. The non-entitlement nature of HUD funding is reflected in the fact that out of 14.5 million low-income renter households eligible for housing assistance, only 4.1 million or 28 percent received it. The FY 1995 HUD budget of $25.6 billion was only 1.7 percent of the total federal budget, and appropriations are not likely to increase much over the next few years because of constraints imposed by the Budget Enforcement Act. Competition among HUD, the Department of Veterans Affairs, the Environmental Protection Agency, and the Nation Aeronautics and Space Administration for the funds available to the appropriations committee with jurisdiction for all these agencies is likely to be fierce. In this competition, the advocates for housing assistance may not be as effective as the supporters of veterans' programs or space exploration or the environment.

This lack of funding to fully meet the need for housing assistance, in combination with the fact that housing is costly and takes a long time to build has resulted in the use of numerous mechanisms, with a variety of budget impacts, to provide as much housing assistance as possible. For example, rather than being provided indefinitely, housing assistance is term-limited, with the lengths of terms ranging from 40 years (LRPH developments constructed before 1987; Section 221-d-3 BMIR; Section 236; and some Section 8 New Construction developments) to 5 years and less (e.g., Section 8 Vouchers). Although not guaranteed, renewability of assistance at the end of these terms often has been presumed by beneficiaries and advocates alike. The indirect funding of programs such as the LIHTC, through tax revenues *not* collected, is another example of a budget mechanism used to fund housing assistance. The LIHTC is funded without creating a line item in HUD's budget, and generating associated scrutiny. Devices such as these have been somewhat successful in increasing the amount of housing assistance provided, even as the long-term nature of housing construction itself has limited the success of selected initiatives. The fact that it takes years before groundbreaking for projects built with federal assistance has resulted in large sums of obligated but unspent housing funds reported in the federal budget. These funds first became targets for budget-cutters during the Reagan years and remain a target today.

The desire to devolve government assistance from the federal level to states and localities also has become a factor in HUD policies and programs. The HOME Investment Partnership program (1990) funds states and local governments to provide housing assistance to meet needs specified in plans submitted to HUD. In addition, HUD's Blueprints I and II (developed by Vice President Gore's Reinventing Government initiative) recommend consolidation of many programs into block grants and would transform HUD into a funds disburser to the states and cities, which would in turn use these funds with few strings attached. Finally, the proposed reform and decentralization of welfare assistance programs portends a major loss of revenue for LRPH, one of HUD's largest programs. In 1989, more than 60 percent of the households with children living in LRPH were receiving welfare assistance. Recipients who lose welfare eligibility and checks also lose the shelter allowance incorporated in these payments, which has become a stable source of revenue for the LRPH program.

Despite these contextual factors and growing housing problems today—perhaps most starkly reflected by homelessness and by the increased number of households with worst-case housing needs—housing was not a significant issue in the 1992 presidential election or the 1994 Congressional elections and may not be a high-profile issue during the 1996 presidential race. Why? There are many reasons, but one is the lack of a strong, well-organized, vocal constituency for programs that assist the poor.

In the face of these facts and factors, in 1996 and beyond, HUD will continue to grapple with three basic questions. First, how should it manage the housing it currently owns, finances, or otherwise assists, much of which is now deteriorating or at risk of loss from the inventory through statutory provisions? Second, what type of housing assistance should be provided in the future? Finally, how should future housing programs be administered? Each of these questions is discussed briefly below before discussing the position of blacks within the 1996 housing policy dialogue.

How should HUD manage its existing inventory of assisted units? The existing federal housing inventory consists primarily of units financed or constructed or with rents subsidized under the following programs: LRPH, Section 221-d-3 BMIR, Section 236, and Section 8. In each of these programs, the end of a rather lengthy term of assistance is approaching, raising both management and cost issues. The 40-year time frame is up for many LRPH developments, and the LHAs/PHAs that are becoming owners of these developments want to tear them down and are chafing at the 1-for-1 replacement requirement that HUD is, in many cases, unable to fund. In addition, although many in the housing sector believe that the program to preserve affordable housing constructed under the Sections 221-d-3 BMIR and 236 programs has been effective, government officials and some tenants are concerned about the high cost of incentives for owners, financed mainly with federal rental assistance payments. By 1995, $1.2 billion, or an average of

$19,152 per unit, had been spent for projects having completed the preservation process. Expenditures of this magnitude raise equity issues, since many households with incomes lower than those of the households assisted by these programs get no financial assistance to meet their housing costs. Finally, in selected instances, projects newly constructed under the Section 8 program may be converted to market rent levels after 20 years into their contract terms, a length of time that is approaching for many of the projects built in the mid-1970s. This, along with the need to renew the funding for Section 8 Certificates and Vouchers as they expire, generates another potentially sizable future financial obligation.

What type of housing assistance should be funded in the future? The answer to this question centers on the goals of federal housing policy and has imbedded within it an additional series of questions. For example, does the federal government want to continue both to increase homeownership—as the National Homeownership Strategy announced last year would suggest—and to improve housing for the poor? Or have housing objectives changed? Does HUD now want to serve only the poorest of the poor (or households with worst case needs), or to serve households that are both low-income and moderate-income? Does HUD want its housing programs to serve as an end unto themselves (i.e., merely provide housing to people), or to achieve other ends, such as economic self-sufficiency? Does HUD want to continue providing both rental assistance payments and interest subsidies within a single program? Does HUD want to fund only those programs with proven track records, or would HUD give funding priority to programs authorized in legislation but never funded? Would HUD rather give priority to programs that use federal dollars to leverage funds from other sources to provide housing assistance, or to programs that give the greatest amount of choice to the households served? Recent trends have been to move away from long-term assistance, away from project-based aid, away from developments receiving multiple subsidies, and toward tenant-based assistance targeted to the poorest of the poor. Whether these trends will continue in the future is critical to the nature and quantity of housing available for assisted households, both black and white.

The third issue how should HUD's programs be administered? was raised above in conjunction with the devolution of federal programs into block grants to states and localities. The reorganization and the dismantling of HUD have been discussed as well, to accompany the streamlining of program administration and fund disbursement associated with the use of block grants. Again, how should HUD's programs be administered is a question with many subquestions that do not have a single noncontroversial answer.

## Blacks and the 1996 Housing Debate

How do black Americans fit into the current housing policy debate? Although a third of blacks are poor and, thus, two-thirds are non-poor, the need for housing assistance cuts deeper into the population of non-poor blacks (than of non-poor whites) because of several things. During the eras of more generous federal spending, black Americans were shortchanged in access to program dollars because of the "separate but equal" policies that were the status quo. The legacy of "separate but equal" today is reflected among all blacks, poor and non-poor alike, in worse housing conditions (for both renters and owners), lower homeownership rates, and lower levels of household wealth attributable to owned homes than among whites. In addition, remedial programs of assistance (such as Section 235 and Gautreaux) have not provided full redress, either because of design flaws or inadequate funding.

Despite their greater need for housing assistance, blacks are most likely to be beneficiaries of the type of housing assistance at greatest risk of termination in the current wave of budget cutting and program devolution. LRPH is the housing assistance program in which blacks are most overrepresented relative to their need. Although blacks are only 26 percent of all very low-income renter households (i.e., renter households with incomes less than 50 percent of the median income in their locality), the main target group for federal assistance, they are 53 percent of the residents in LRPH developments. With the recent trend away from project-based assistance, the overrepresentation of blacks in LRPH could result in their being disproportionately affected by displacement, if funding is cut under this program or units continue to be lost from the inventory or the program is redesigned.

What steps can black Americans take in the current policy environment to get maximum benefit from existing or likely future programs? Phrased differently, what program initiatives are likely to benefit blacks the most, and which are likely to benefit blacks the least? The program initiatives discussed below are drawn from the history of housing assistance programs that have operated in this country for varying lengths of time and with varying degrees of success for both blacks and whites. All are not still funded. Pros and cons are noted for each as relevant to housing options and opportunities for blacks.

## Block Grants

As noted above, HUD has taken steps toward providing funds through a block grant for housing assistance via the HOME Investment Partnership program, which gives states and local governments the flexibility to design programs to work toward whatever goals they want to achieve (which have been approved in a plan submitted to HUD). In addition, a portion of HOME funds is earmarked for use by nonprofit organizations. Although the block grant design offers the promise of programs tailor-made for the communities served, programs funded via this mechanism will reflect the priorities and interests only of those included in the consensus building process leading to preparation of the program application. For instance, the top priorities identified in the Comprehensive Housing Affordability Strategies (CHAS) submitted by a sample of jurisdictions for first year funding under the HOME program, included addressing the needs of the low-income, end-ing homelessness, and improving affordability. Eliminating the causes of racial/ ethnic concentrations, developing self-sufficiency programs, and alleviating over-crowding—initiatives that could especially benefit *African Americans*—were the least frequently mentioned program strategies, included in 19 percent, 11 percent, and 11 percent of applications, respectively. A shift to the block grant mechanism to distribute funds and determine the nature of housing assistance challenges black Americans to take steps to insure that their interests are reflected in the application development process.

The performance funding concept, which has been suggested as a means to allocate bonus funds in the future world of block grants, also raises issues of concern to blacks. Under this concept, it may be difficult to measure performance and assess progress, especially when seeking to compare more distressed and less distressed environments. Which locality is more deserving of bonus funding—one that has farther to go to get to a non-distressed state but has made progress, or one starting out much nearer a healthy state and that can be expected to become non-distressed during a given funding period? Their relatively worse neighborhood conditions might place the low-income black Americans who would be eligible for federal housing assistance at a disadvantage under a performance funding system to allocate bonus money, if the system looks only at outcomes without looking at starting points and progress made beyond these.

### Rental Assistance

**Low-Income Housing Tax Credit (LIHTC).** One of the indirectly funded federal housing programs, the LIHTC stimulates the production of housing affordable to low-income persons. Its program rules are such, however, that developers find it easier to guarantee that they meet the minimum requirements for the share of low-income residents in their properties by renting their developments entirely to low-income persons. With little income mixing in developments, recent concerns about fraud in the determination of continued program eligibility, and some Congressional opposition to the program, in the future, the LIHTC could become stigmatized, and its developments could become distressed, in a manner similar to the current situation with LRPH. Its funding formula and its continued existence both could be challenged. Because 202∏- currently are beneficiaries of this program, a revision in its regulations, to foster greater income mixing among tenants, could contribute to future program viability.

**Low-Rent Public Housing (LRPH).** Net losses from the inventory of livable LRPH units may continue because HOPE VI funds to revitalize severely distressed developments may not keep pace with the volume of units removed from use, in need of repair or because they are located in buildings in which tenants refuse to live. Although proposals to terminate the LRPH program and give vouchers to its tenants were nixed in 1995, LRPH will not remain a viable housing choice without sizable cash infusions (for modernization, ownership conversion, etc.) that seem unlikely to be forthcoming in future budgets. Because black Americans are the dominant tenant population in LRPH, the trend away from project-based assistance and the financial hard times for this program portend future increases in homelessness among blacks (and others) who may be displaced from these developments. In the long run, training nonprofit organizations—including but not limited to resident management corporations—to take over ownership and management of LRPH could be one of the most fruitful uses of the currently scarce resources within this program. It might be one of the only ways to retain LRPH units for continued occupancy in the future.

**Section 8 with Portability.** Initiatives such as the Gautreaux Assisted Housing and the Moving to Opportunity for Fair Housing programs which have as their goal to expand residential options for low-income households, take advantage of the portability of Section 8 Certificates and Vouchers for use in jurisdictions other than the jurisdiction of issue. Although these programs have enhanced the life opportunities for many, their small scale (one of the reasons for their success) and a variety of other factors will keep them from being a comprehensive solution to the problems associated with poverty, racial concentration, and distressed neighborhoods. Section 8 portability, when not specifically channeled to racial/ethnic minorities as in these two programs, helps poorer white suburbanites access better suburban neighborhoods more often than it helps racial/ethnic minorities leave high-poverty neighborhoods. In addition, landlord preferences, tight rental markets, and Section 8 discrimination may continue to limit the options of racial/ethnic minority populations under targeted mobility programs.

Because Section 8-like tenant-based programs are likely to be the wave of the future for rental assistance, Black Americans should apply for and try to use them to their best advantage. However, threats of continued reductions in the terms of assistance or terminations after a given length of time, as means to shrink the HUD budget, do not guarantee that these programs will exist far into the future. Rental assistance may eventually be funded only as part of the HOME program, or as part of another block grant. In this case, black Americans would need to become involved in the citizen participation or consensus building process underlying the development of the block grant applications and the specification of funding priorities therein.

### Homeownership Assistance

**Section 312 Rehabilitation Loan Program.** Although Congress last appropriated new funds for Section 312 in FY 1981, it has continued to provide loans (with a cap of $33,500 per loan for residential and $100,000 per loan for nonresidential properties) to persons in targeted declining areas by using repayments and other program fees. The longevity of this revolving loan fund suggests how effective in revitalizing inner city neighborhoods a substantial initial endowment for a loan fund for a variety of housing purposes could be. Specifically, a revolving loan fund could provide the wherewithal to enable blacks living in distressed neighborhoods to improve their environs.

**Urban Homesteading.** The Urban Homesteading program (repealed by HUD as of FY 1992) offered the potential for low-income households to acquire vacant and unrepaired properties in the federal inventory to be rehabilitated and lived in by them as owners. Although the need for households that acquire Homesteading properties to get a loan to finance rehabilitation often proves problematic for black Americans, if this financing barrier could be overcome, a program such as this could offer yet another way to reclaim portions of distressed neighborhoods.

**Section 203 (k).** Potentially one of the FHA's most effective programs, the Section 203 (k) program provides insurance for loans to (1) finance rehabilitation of an existing property; (2) finance rehabilitation and refinancing of the outstanding indebtedness of a property; and (3) finance the purchase and rehabilitation of a property. This two-pronged mortgage assistance could go far to help homeowners in declining neighborhoods recoup their investments and could piggyback onto an "Urban Homesteading-like" program as a source of rehabilitation financing. In 1995, HUD created the Dream Builder program, which permits nonprofit developers to have access to the Section 203(k) program in cities with deteriorating dwellings and a scarcity of affordable housing. Under this program, a nonprofit could get a single mortgage loan to buy a house for 3 percent down, provide sufficient funds to rehabilitate the dwelling, and furnish a small developer's fee to defray the administrative costs of construction. Black Americans in declining neighborhoods both as individuals and nonprofits could benefit from the Section 203 (k) program.

**Nehemiah Housing Opportunity Grants Program.** Another initiative repealed by HUD, the Nehemiah program used a combination of mechanisms to reduce the cost of constructing houses, on contiguous parcels of land in certain distressed neighborhoods, to be purchased by lower- and moderate-income households. Nonprofits were eligible to construct the communities of new houses to be developed under this program. Black Americans in declining communities around the country could benefit by establishing initiatives similar to the original Nehemiah program run by a group of churches in Brooklyn, N.Y. which was the prototype for the federal program.

**Federal Home Loan Bank (FHLB) Affordable Housing Program.** The FHLB Affordable Housing program provides funds to subsidize interest rates on loans made through its member banks to facilitate the development of affordable housing. These loans can be used to finance both homeowner loans and the purchase, construction, or rehabilitation of rental housing in which a portion of the units are set aside for low-income households. Again, via nonprofits or as individuals, black Americans could seek out and apply for loans under these Affordable Housing programs in their respective bank districts.

**Ownership and Self-Sufficiency for Low-Income Households.** The HOPE subprograms provide grants to enable low-income persons to become owners of a variety of types of housing—LRPH units (to be owned by residents), other federally owned apartment buildings, and single-family homes owned by state and local governments. The evidence on LRPH ownership programs (before HOPE, which was established in 1990) reveals several problems, related to poor quality rehabilitation, costliness of conversions (from their current configurations to ones more suitable for ownership), and higher than anticipated staffing costs due to the need to educate and train tenants to become competent homeowners.

Despite this evidence, some tenant owners of LRPH developments, whose ownership was orchestrated through resident management corporations, tout it as the answer to many social ills and the means to economic self-sufficiency for low-income persons. If money were no object, perhaps homeownership for low-income households could be a major part of the solution to the problems of distressed neighborhoods occupied primarily by low-income persons with low skill levels, low employment rates, and beset by social problems. Per unit renovation costs of $130,000 at the Kenilworth-Parkside development converted to resident management and ownership in Washington, D.C. for example, raises equity issues with regard to allocating scarce dollars in a program that is not an entitlement.

The success of self-sufficiency programs (such as Project Self-Sufficiency and Family Self-Sufficiency) not linked to homeownership also depends on the availability of funds—for rental housing assistance, to train tenants for employment, to assist them in their job search, and to subsidize their child care costs— until they are truly self-sufficient. Until and unless adequate funding is made available for initiatives such as these, self-sufficiency programs may remain empty promises. Worse yet, if already operating self-sufficiency programs are terminated due to inadequate funding, new low-income owners may be left empty handed in, say, the 10th year of their 30-year mortgages, and nearly self-sufficient low-income renters may find their financial support gone at a critical moment for self-advancement.

Unless we reach the point where money is no object for federal housing programs, smaller scale and less expensive programs to enable low-income tenants to become owners, as in HOPE III (for low-income persons to become owners of single-family houses), may prove to be more practical. Programs such as this also are expensive and raise issues of equity in treatment among low-income households—those who become owners through HOPE III v. low-income households unable to be assisted by HOPE III v. moderate-income households ineligible for HOPE III but unable to become owners without some kind of financial assistance. Because of their share of the LRPH tenantry (53 percent) black Americans clearly will be affected by decisions related to the future of ownership assistance and self-sufficiency programs targeted on low-income households.

**National Homeownership Strategy.** On June 5, 1995, President Clinton and HUD Secretary Cisneros announced a program to raise homeownership in the U.S. to its highest level ever by adding 8 million new owners by the year 2000, as part of a National Homeownership Strategy. Many of these new owners are likely to be the low-income households targeted by the Section 235 program during the 1960s for assistance via a similar interest buydown mechanism. To help achieve this goal, HUD has enlisted 55 Partners for Homeownership, including entities such as the Federal Home Loan Bank system, Fannie Mae, and Freddie Mac. In addition, since 1992, to redress homeownership shortfalls among segments of the population, HUD has established targets for each fiscal year for Fannie Mae and Freddie Mac as a percent of the units they finance. For example, in 1996, 40 percent of the units financed by each of these secondary market entities must be occupied by low- and moderate-income households; 12 percent must be special afford-able housing (for very-low-income families and those living in low-income areas); and 21 percent must be for properties in geographically targeted locales (central cities, rural areas, and other underserved places). Fannie Mae also has established a series of Central Cities Initiatives/Partnership Offices to develop working relationships in selected cities (Baltimore, Cleveland, Denver, and Oakland) to enhance their ability to provide secondary market funding to fulfill their statutory goals. Although there is a continuing legacy of disproportionate lender denials of loans to minorities and for properties in selected neighborhoods, initiatives such as the National Homeownership Strategy combined with pressure from secondary market entities needing to purchase loans made in underserved areas to meet their affordable housing goals may make lenders more responsive and, therefore, homeownership more accessible to black Americans during the remainder of this century.

### Conclusion

Discussing housing alone and housing in urban areas primarily, as in this chapter, emphasizes a shortcoming in the analysis of urban problems. Problems of the "urbs" also are problems of the "suburbs," because the two are contiguous. For example, "*un*-fair" housing for blacks comes hand in hand with "*un*-fair" housing for whites because both blacks and whites are deprived of opportunities by residential racial segregation. In addition, housing is not a commodity valued for itself alone. Its type of construction and location have an immediate impact on community development and neighborhood quality, two associated topics equally as worthy of discussion as housing.

The linkages among these problems suggest that there need to be linkages among their solutions. Thus, it is my hope that this chapter becomes part of a much bigger initiative to enhance the quality of life for all Americans and to develop a synergy to allow us to create the kinds of urban and suburban environments in which we all would want to live.

Appendix
## Chronology of Federal Housing Assistance Programs

The federal role in the housing market has changed dramatically since the 1930s when the government first intervened to help move the economy out of the depression. The system of federally chartered savings and loan associations that had been established in 1933 to provide mortgage loans to stimulate the sluggish economy was abolished in 1989. The Federal Home Loan Bank system now operates an Affordable Housing program under which each of the Banks in its system makes advances to member institutions to subsidize the interest rate on loans for owner-occupied dwellings and for loans to finance the purchase, construction, or rehabilitation of rental housing, in which at least 20 percent of the units will be occupied by and affordable to very low-income households (i.e., those with incomes less than or equal to 50 percent of the area median).

During the 1930s, other financial intermediaries were established to stimulate homeownership and to foster the development of a secondary mortgage market. In 1934, the Federal Housing Administration (FHA) was established to insure payment on home mortgages made by lenders and, thereby, to expand the nation's pool of homeowners. Although various FHA loan funds have faced insolvency over the years and the demand for FHA loans has waxed and waned with the economy, the FHA single-family loan funds have become stalwarts of the market for home loans. As proof of its success, in FY 1994, the FHA reported the second highest volume of single-family loans in its 60-year history—1.3 million single-family loans including 450,000 to first-time buyers.

In 1938, the Federal National Mortgage Association or Fannie Mae was created to establish a secondary market for mortgage loans by buying them from primary market lenders (e.g., savings and loan associations) and thereby increasing the supply of funds for home loans. Originally restricted to buying only government-insured (i.e., by FHA or by the Department of Veterans Affairs) mortgages, Fannie Mae would either hold these mortgages in its investment portfolio or repackage them as mortgage-backed securities (MBSs) for sale to others. The Government National Mortgage Association or Ginnie Mae, established in 1968 as part of HUD, guarantees payments to investors from MBSs, thereby stimulating activity in the secondary mortgage market. Between 1970 and 1990, the Ginnie Mae MBS program provided the capital underlying the purchase of 13 million homes. The Federal Home Loan Mortgage Corporation or Freddie Mac, established in 1970 to buy and sell conventional (i.e., not government-insured) mortgages, is the other major secondary market actor. Fannie Mae and Freddie Mac both are quasi-private entities regulated by HUD, and both now buy and sell conventional and government-insured mortgages.

Also in the 1930s, the federal government established Low-Rent Public Housing (LRPH), the oldest extant directly funded program to improve the housing of the poor. Authorized by the U.S. Housing Act of 1937, the LRPH program provides reduced-rent publicly owned dwellings for families with incomes less than or equal to 80 percent of area median income (i.e., lower income) and for elderly, handicapped, and displaced individuals. The federal government finances both the construction and operation of these developments, which are administrated by LHAs or PHAs. After 40 years, when the tax-exempt bonds issued to finance construction have been paid off, ownership of LRPH developments built before 1987 transfers to the LHAs/PHAs. During FY 1994, the LRPH program served over 1.4 million households, accounting for about one-fifth of HUD's expenditures for housing assistance and 30 percent of all units subsidized by HUD.

Most of the LRPH developments standing today were built during the 1940s and 1950s, when other program initiatives operated to change the demographics of its beneficiaries. Beginning in 1949, the Urban Renewal program allowed localities to use the power of eminent domain to acquire properties, which were then razed, so the land could be sold to developers at reduced costs, to then lower the cost of constructing new developments. Households relocated by Urban Renewal, many of them black, were given priority to become LRPH tenants. Because the Section 202 program for the Elderly and Handicapped (established in 1959) created a residential alternative for households containing persons who are elderly or handicapped, many of the less poor elderly moved from LRPH into Section 202 developments in the 1960s.

Although LRPH had been the only program to serve low-income households for several decades, during the 1960s several additional programs were established, using a variety of mechanisms, to serve this population. The FHA combined mortgage insurance with interest subsidies to develop programs to serve both low-income owners and renters. The Section 221-d-3 Below Market Interest Rate (BMIR) program, implemented in 1961, stimulated construction of rental units for low-income households by insuring 40-year mortgages on apartments owned by nonprofit or limited-dividend corporations. Mortgage insurance was provided if the lenders agreed to issue the loans at below-market interest rates and if these lower rates (and associated limited profits) were translated into lower rents affordable by the poor. To induce private lenders to write BMIR mortgages, Fannie Mae bought these loans from their originators at the market rate or face value, in transactions which showed up as direct outlays in the federal budget. The large, up-front budget outlays associated with these transactions caused the 221-d-3 BMIR program to be short-lived, being replaced by the Section 236 program in 1968. In the Section 236 program, the federal government provides the interest subsidy through annual payments to the lenders throughout the life of the mortgage. These smaller annual payments in HUD's budget were politically more acceptable than the subsidy outlay for in the Section 221-d-3 BMIR program. Although both programs serve tenants with higher incomes than tenants of LRPH, the first rent subsidy program, the Rent Supplement program, was implemented for use with them. Under certain conditions, the terms of both the BMIR program and of Section 236, allow the limited-dividend developers to prepay their mortgages 20 years into the mortgage term.

The Section 235 program in its original form enacted in 1968, offered no-down-payment mortgage loans with reduced interest rates, for which low-income households paid only 20 percent of their monthly incomes. The difference between the mortgage note due each month and the owner's payment was made up by federal assistance. Later versions of the program included mandatory down payments, assistance for less than the full mortgage term, and owner payments greater than 20 percent of income.

Section 203 (b) is the largest of FHA's single-family programs, providing insurance for mortgages to finance home purchases and construction. Not specifically targeted to low-income households, this program helps meet the homeownership needs of anyone able to make the cash investment and mortgage payments, and meet the credit requirements. With the same eligibility terms and mortgage insurance mechanism as the Section 203 (b) program, Section 203 (k), also authorized in the 1960s, helps people buy and rehabilitate existing homes. Because of recent streamlining of the Section 203 (k) program, in FY 1994, 3,742 new loans were insured, an 11 percent increase over the previous year.

The final program to be noted from the 1960s is the Section 312 Rehabilitation Loan Program. Although Congress has appropriated no new funds for Section 312 loans since FY 1981, the program has used loan repayments, fees, premiums, and the recovery of prior year commitments to continue making loans to homeowners for 20 years at reduced rates for residential rehabilitation. In 1990, local governments processed 1,250 Section 312 loans and obligated $40.9 million. Priority is given to low- and moderate-income applicants, and dwellings must be in federally aided areas designated under the Community Development Block Grant (CDBG) or Urban Homesteading programs, two programs that target assistance to declining neighborhoods. Under the Urban Homesteading program, the inventory of federally owned properties in target areas is transferred first to local governments and then to residents at nominal cost. Low-income persons are given priority for properties. In FY 1990, Congress appropriated $13 million to acquire properties for homesteading, and 101 participating agencies obligated approximately $12.9 million of it to acquire 714 properties.

The 1970s became a decade of changes and innovation for federal housing assistance. The 1974 Housing and Community Development Act started federal housing activity again after the 1973 moratorium called by President Nixon. LRPH tenants had been able to purchase units that were separable from a larger development since 1965; the 1974 Act, however, authorized HUD to sell units to tenants while continuing to pay the long-term debt and the costs of rehabilitation. The LHA/PHA could decide to write down the sales price, although tenants had to obtain their own financing. Few tenants were financially able to take advantage of these purchase options. The availability of these provisions, however, reflected a growing awareness by the federal government of LRPH as an aging asset in need of modernization and repair. This was the first of many initiatives to provide LHAs/PHAs as many options as possible for the disposition of the developments they would ultimately own.

The major initiatives of the 1974 Act were the CDBG program (not discussed in this chapter) and Section 8. The original Section 8 Rental Assistance Program subsidized both very-low-income (income less than or equal to 50 percent of the area median income) and low-income (income less than or equal to 80 percent of the area median income) households to live in privately owned, newly constructed, rehabilitated, or existing units. Rental subsidy payments were calculated as the difference between the percent of income (now 30 percent) enrolled households were required to pay toward rent and the Fair Market Rent (FMR) established by HUD for units in given locations and of given sizes. Payments were attached either to the units (i.e., project-based, for newly constructed, substantially rehabilitated, and moderately rehabilitated units) or to the tenants (i.e., tenant-based, for existing units). Because activity under the project-based Section 8 programs has been channeled into other programs (e.g., Section 8 New Construction has become part of the Section 202 Program of Housing for the Elderly and Handicapped, and the Section 8 Moderate Rehabilitation program is now available only for Single Room Occupancy units for the Homeless), the major Section 8 programs operating currently are tenant-based—the Section 8 Existing-Housing Certificate program authorized in 1974, and the Section 8 Voucher program authorized in 1983. The major difference between the Section 8 Certificate and Voucher programs is the targeting of vouchers to tenants with incomes less than 50 percent of area median income and the lack of a ceiling on the rents that can be paid by voucher recipients for units. In FY 1994, approximately 1.3 million households received assistance through the two programs, with approximately 1 million households receiving certificates and nearly 300,000 receiving vouchers.

In the 1980s, other changes took place within the LRPH program. LHAs/PHAs removed 15,000 housing units, or about 1 percent of the total units from their inventories. This loss of units occurred at the same time that the number of LRPH housing units completed annually had declined—from 29,576 in 1981 to 2,603 in 1991—due to the reduction in federal funding. Although the limited new construction in conjunction with the removal of units from the existing inventory during the decade might have been expected to reduce the vacancy rate and the need for modernization funding for developments, it has done neither. Between 1984 and 1995, the national average vacancy rate in LRPH has climbed from 5.8 percent to 8 percent. In addition, despite the provision of almost $15 billion in modernization funding since 1981, the backlog of unfunded modernization today is at least $20 billion and continues to accrue. The requirement to replace each demolished LRPH units with another assisted unit (1-for-1 replacement) has slowed the rate of demolition, since adequate replacement funding is not available.

Also during the 1980s, HUD began to initiate programs to enhance the economic self-sufficiency of households eligible for federal rental housing assistance, including LRPH. In 1984, Project Self-Sufficiency was established as a demonstration program to coordinate resources (housing, education, training, and employment) in 155 communities to help single parents on Section 8 waiting lists move into the economic mainstream. To bolster tenant self-sufficiency or empowerment, in 1988, resident management corporations, which had existed on a small scale since the 1960s, were given statutory underpinnings and financing for technical assistance. Operation Bootstrap, the next self-sufficiency demonstration program, was implemented in 1989 and 1990 to serve both single-parent and two-parent families either awaiting or already receiving Section 8 assistance. Sixty-one communities received nearly 12,000 rental certificates under the program. In 1990, the Family Self-Sufficiency program was established to promote the development of local strategies to enable lower-income families to achieve economic independence and self-sufficiency. Although initially each LHA/PHA receiving funds for new LRPH units or additional Section 8 certificates or vouchers was mandated to operate a Family Self-Sufficiency program, in 1992, this mandate was softened to not penalize those LHAs/PHAs unable to operate a program because they lacked any of the following: the necessary supportive services for eligible families, funds for administrative costs, or the cooperation of state or local governments.

The loss of low-rent units through the prepayment of mortgage loans on Section 221-d-3 BMIR and 236 developments, now 20 years into their 40-year terms, became a concern, also during the 1980s. In 1987, a prepayment moratorium was established. In 1990, the Low-Income Housing Preservation and Resident Homeownership Act (LIHPRHA) was enacted to codify the revised terms under which developers could prepay their mortgages—only if federal funds were not available to provide incentives (in the form of higher rents) to developers to keep the project for low-income use, or if the current owner wished to sell but no buyer could be found who would maintain the low-income use of a project. As of September 30, 1995, the owners of 1,122 projects had filed with HUD notices of intent to extend affordability restrictions or to sell the properties to qualified purchasers. In addition, HUD estimates that if funds are not made available for preservation incentives during FY 1996, owners of at least 127 of the 223 developments already approved for preservation will have the right to prepay and end low-income affordability.

A final noteworthy program from 1987 is the Nehemiah Housing Opportunity Grants Program, similar to a local program of the same name developed and operated by a group of churches in Brooklyn, N.Y. Under the federal Nehemiah program, nonprofit sponsors would build or substantially rehabilitate a predetermined number of housing units concentrated in certain distressed neighborhoods and would receive HUD grants to provide interest-free second mortgages of up to $15,000 each to lower- and moderate-income buyers of homes. The down payment must equal 10 percent of the sales price of the home, and second mortgage loan repayments go into a revolving loan fund to assist additional households.

The major new programs of the 1990s are HOME and HOPE, along with portability demonstrations under the Section 8 program. The HOME Investment Partnership program and the HOPE (Homeownership and Opportunity for People Everywhere) program were created by the 1990 Cranston-Gonzalez National Affordable Housing Act (P.L. 101-625, November 28, 1990), a piece of legislation that introduced several themes that may carry over as housing policy into the next century. These themes include: decentralization of programs from the federal to state and local governments; emphasis on nonprofit housing sponsors; empowerment via linking housing with social services; and cost sharing between jurisdictions. The HOME Investment Partnership program reflects decentralization because it gives state and local governments the option to design their own programs. Fifteen percent of HOME funds also are earmarked for projects sponsored by community housing development organizations (CHDOs) or neighborhood-based nonprofit organizations. By November 1994, more than 100,000 units had received financial commitments under HOME. Appropriations for the program increased from $1.275 billion in FY 1994 to $1.4 billion in FY 1995.

The HOPE program has several components, which finance sales of various publicly owned units to low-income persons. One component finances sales of LRPH buildings to their residents (HOPE I), while another finances sales to low-income households of other apartment buildings owned by the federal government either through foreclosure or the failure of savings and loan associations (HOPE II). Yet another component finances the sales of single-family homes owned by state or local governments (HOPE III). The HOPE program for the Elderly combines social services with housing assistance for the elderly who otherwise would be unable to live independently. In addition, the HOPE VI program funds grant agreements to finance the comprehensive revitalization of severely distressed LRPH developments.

In 1992, a 5-year demonstration program called Moving to Opportunity for Fair Housing (MTO) was implemented in five cities—Baltimore, Boston, Chicago, Los Angeles, and New York. The MTO program would have provided approximately 2,000 families living in distressed inner-city neighborhoods with Section 8 rental certificates and vouchers, as well as counseling and other assistance to help them move to low-poverty areas. Although terminated in April 1995 because of opposition to the program in Baltimore, this residential mobility demonstration built upon the portability feature in the Section 8 program that allows beneficiaries to move to jurisdictions other than that of the LHA/PHA that issues the certificate or voucher.

# REFERENCES

Aaron, H. 1972. *Shelter and Subsidies*. Washington, D.C.: The Brookings Institution.

*Affordable Homeownership in New York City: Nehemiah Plan Homes and the New York City Housing Partnership*. 1994. Parts A & B (C16-94-1252.0 and C16-94-1253.0). Cambridge, Mass.: John F. Kennedy School of Government, Case Program, Harvard University.

*African Americans Today: A Demographic Profile*. 1996. Washington, D.C.: Joint Center for Political and Economic Studies.

Bogdon, A., J. Silver, and M. A. Turner, with K. Hartnett and M. VanderGoot. 1993. *National Analysis of Housing Affordability, Adequacy, and Availability: A Framework for Local Housing Strategies*. Washington, D.C.: The Urban Institute for the U.S. Department of Housing and Urban Development.

Burchell, R. W., D. Listokin, and A. Pashman. 1994. *Regional Housing Opportunities for Lower Income Households: A Resource Guide to Affordable Housing and Regional Mobility Strategies*. HUD-1501-PDR. Washington, D.C.: Rutgers University Center for Urban Policy Research for the U.S. Department of Housing and Urban Development, Office of Policy Development and Research.

Bureau of the Census. 1995. "Housing in Metropolitan Areas - Black Households." *Statistical Brief*. SB/95-5. Washington, D.C.: U.S. Department of Commerce, Economics and Statistics Administration.

Bureau of the Census. 1995. *Statistical Abstract of the United States: 1995*. (115th edition) Washington, D.C.: U.S. Department of Commerce, Economics and Statistics Administration.

Bureau of the Census. 1995. *USA Statistics in Brief 1995*. (A Statistical Abstract Supplement). Washington, D.C.: U.S. Department of Commerce, Economics and Statistics Administration.

Bureau of the Census. 1995. "What We're Worth - Asset Ownership of Households: 1993." *Statistical Brief.* SB/95-26. Washington, D.C.: U.S. Department of Commerce, Economics and Statistics Administration.

Casey, C.H. 1992. *Characteristics of HUD-Assisted Renters and Their Units in 1989.* HUD-1346-PDR. Washington, DC: U.S. Department of Housing and Urban Development, Office of Policy Development and Research.

Center for Housing Policy. 1994. *New Beginnings Project: A First Report.* Washington, DC: National Housing Conference.

Dreier, P., and J. Atlas. 1996. "U.S. Housing Policy at the Crossroads: A Progressive Agenda to Rebuild the Housing Constituency." *Working Paper.* Occidental College, The International and Public Affairs Center.

Fannie Mae. 1995. *Showing America A New Way Home.* 1994 Annual Report. Washington, D.C.: Fannie Mae.

"Glossary: Federal Housing Subsidy Programs." 1992. In W. A. Leigh and J. B. Stewart, eds., *The Housing Status of Black Americans.* New Brunswick, N.J.: Transaction Publishers, 253-265.

Goering, J., A. Haghighi, H. Stebbins, and M. Siewert. 1995. *Promoting Housing Choice in HUD's Rental Assistance Programs: A Report to Congress.* HUD-PDR-1543. Washington, D.C.: U.S. Department of Housing and Urban Development, Office of Policy Development and Research.

Goering, J., A. Kamely, and T. Richardson. 1995. *The Location and Racial Composition of Public Housing in the United States: An Analysis of the Racial Occupancy and Location of Public Housing Developments.* HUD-1519-PDR. Washington, D.C.: U.S. Department of Housing and Urban Development, Office of Policy Development and Research.

Guskind, R., and C. F. Steinbach. 1991. "Sales Resistance." *National Journal.* 23:798-803.

Hoben, J., and T. Richardson. 1992. *The Local CHAS: A Preliminary Assessment of First Year Submissions.* Washington, D.C.: U.S. Department of Housing and Urban Development, Office of Policy Development and Research.

Implications of the Prepayment Provisions in the Cranston-Gonzalez Housing Act. 1992. *CBO Staff Memorandum.* Washington, D.C.: U.S. Congressional

Budget Office.

Lazere, E. B., P. A. Leonard, and C. N. Dolbeare, et al. 1991. *A Place to Call Home: The Low-Income Housing Crisis Continues*. Washington, D.C.: Center on Budget and Policy Priorities and Low-Income Housing Information Service.

Leigh, W. A. 1992. "Civil Rights Legislation and the Housing Status of Black Americans: An Overview." In W. A. Leigh and J. B. Stewart, eds., *The Housing Status of Black Americans*. New Brunswick, N.J.: Transaction Publishers, 5-28.

Leonard, P. A., C. N. Dolbeare, and E. B. Lazere. 1989. *A Place to Call Home: The Crisis in Housing for the Poor*. Washington, D.C.: Center on Budget and Policy Priorities and Low-Income Housing Information Service.

Newman, S., and A. Schnare. 1994. "Back to the Future: Housing Assistance Policy for the Next Century." In *New Beginnings Project: A First Report*. Washington, D.C.: National Housing Conference, Center for Housing Policy.

Peterman, W. A. 1988. "Resident Management: Putting It In Perspective." *Journal of Housing*. 45:111-115.

"The Promise of Housing Mobility Programs." 1995-1996. *The Urban Institute Policy and Research Report*. 4-6.

Shlay, A. B., and King, C. E. 1995. "Beneficiaries of Federal Housing Programs: A Data Reconnaissance." *Housing Policy Debate*. 6:481-521.

Silver, H., J. McDonald, and R. J. Ortiz. 1985. "Background: Sales of Public Housing." *Journal of Housing*. 42:218-220.

Smith, R. 1991. "HUD Program Helps With Renovations." *The Washington Post*. (September 7, 1991).

Stegman, M. A. 1991. *More Housing, More Fairly: Report of the Twentieth Century Fund Task Force on Affordable Housing - Background Paper on the Limits of Privatization*. New York City: The Twentieth Century Fund Press.

Struyk, R. J., and J.A. Tuccillo. 1983. "Defining the Federal Role in Housing: Back to Basics." *Journal of Urban Economics*. 14:206-223.

U.S. Commission on Civil Rights. 1971. *Home Ownership for Lower Income Families: A Report on the Racial and Ethnic Impact of the Section 235 Program*. Washington, DC: U.S. Government Printing Office.

U.S. Commission on Civil Rights. 1975. *Twenty Years After Brown: Equal Opportunity in Housing.* Washington, D.C.: U.S. Government Printing Office.

U.S. Department of Commerce and U.S. Department of Housing and Urban Development. 1995. *American Housing Survey for the United States in 1993.* Current Housing Reports H150/93. Washington, D.C.: U.S. Government Printing Office.

U.S. Department of Housing and Urban Development. 1989. *Congressional Justifications for 1990 Estimates.* Part 1. Washington, D.C.: U.S. Department of Housing and Urban Development.

U.S. Department of Housing and Urban Development. 1992. *Annual Report 1990.* HUD-329-PA (19). Washington, D.C.: U.S. Department of Housing and Urban Development.

U.S. Department of Housing and Urban Development. 1992. *Family Self-Sufficiency: HOPE (Homeownership and Opportunity for People Everywhere).* HUD-1331-PDR (1). Washington, D.C.: U.S. Department of Housing and Urban Development.

U.S. Department of Housing and Urban Development. 1994. "Residential Mobility Programs." *Urban Policy Brief.* Washington, D.C.: U.S. Department of Housing and Urban Development.

U.S. Department of Housing and Urban Development. 1995. *Congressional Justifications for 1996 Estimates.* Part 2. Washington, D.C.: U.S. Department of Housing and Urban Development.

U.S. Department of Housing and Urban Development. 1995. *A Place to Live is the Place to Start: A Statement of Principles for Changing HUD to Meet America's Housing and Community Priorities.* Washington, D.C.: U.S. Department of Housing and Urban Development.

U.S. Department of Housing and Urban Development. 1995. *Rental Housing Assistance At A Crossroads: A Report to Congress on Worst Case Housing Needs.* Washington, D.C.: U.S. Department of Housing and Urban Development.

U.S. Department of Housing and Urban Development, Office of Fair Housing and Equal Opportunity. 1995. *1993 Consolidated Annual Report to Congress on Fair Housing Programs.* HUD-1531-FHEO. Washington, D.C.: U.S. Department of Housing and Urban Development.

U.S. General Accounting Office. 1993. *Public and Assisted Housing: Some Progress Made in Implementing HUD's Family Self-Sufficiency Program.* GAO/RCED-93-78. Washington, D.C.: U.S. General Accounting Office.

U.S. General Accounting Office. 1993. *Public Housing: Low-Income Housing Tax Credit as an Alternative Development Method.* GAO/RCED-93-31. Washington, D.C.: U.S. General Accounting Office.

U.S. General Accounting Office. 1994. *Housing Finance: Characteristics of Borrowers of FHA-Insured Mortgages.* GAO/RCED-94-135BR. Washington, D.C.: U.S. General Accounting Office.

U.S. General Accounting Office. 1994. *Public Housing: Housing Agency Officials Want More Flexibility in Replacing Deteriorated Housing.* GAO/T-RCED-94-159. Washington, D.C.: U.S. General Accounting Office.

U.S. General Accounting Office. 1995. *Housing and Urban Development: Public and Assisted Housing Reform.* GAO/T-RCED-96-25. Washington, D.C.: U.S. General Accounting Office.

U.S. General Accounting Office. 1995. *Housing and Urban Development: Reforms at HUD and Issues for Its Future.* GAO/T-RCED-95-108. Washington, D.C.: U.S. General Accounting Office.

U.S. General Accounting Office. 1995. *Multifamily Housing: Issues and Options to Consider in Revising HUD's Low-Income Housing Preservation Program.* GAO/T-RCED-96-29. Washington, D.C.: U.S. General Accounting Office.

U.S. General Accounting Office. 1995. *Public Housing: Funding and Other Constraints Limit Housing Authorities' Ability to Comply With One-for-One Rule.* GAO/RCED-95-78. Washington, D.C.: U.S. General Accounting Office.

Weicher, J. C. 1979. "Urban Housing Policy." In P. Mieszkowski and M. Straszheim, eds. *Current Issues in Urban Economics.* Baltimore, Md.: The Johns Hopkins University Press, 472-483.

Yinger, J. 1995. *Closed Doors, Opportunities Lost: The Continuing Costs of Housing Discrimination.* New York City: Russell Sage Foundation.

## BIOGRAPHICAL SKETCH

Wilhelmina A. Leigh, a senior research associate at the Joint Center for Political and Economic Studies, holds a Ph.D. in economics from the Johns Hopkins University. Her research interests are in housing policy and health-care policy, and she has published in both areas.

# THE CALL: UNIVERSAL CHILD CARE
## AN ELUSIVE BUT COMPELLING NATIONAL GOAL

**Evelyn K. Moore**

# ABSTRACT

The formative years of early childhood are crucial to the lifelong development of human beings, but parents, mothers in particular, are home far less than they were two decades ago because of their increased participation in the work force and thus cannot care for children full-time. They need child care.

While there are a variety of quality child-care programs which deliver excellent, developmentally appropriate care for young children and school-age children across the country, frequently not within reach of the great majority who need them. In fact, the gap is rapidly expanding between those children who have quality child care and those who do not. In 1993, more than 5 million American children under the age of three were in the care of adults other than their parents (United States Department of Health and Human Services, 1996).

In 1990, the National Child Care Survey found that more than 26 million children from birth through age 12 spent part or all of their day in child care. Ten million children ages 0-4 and 16 million ages 5-12 were in child-care arrangements. In addition, the survey estimates that the number of African-Americans in child care ages 0-12 is 4,432,938. This provides solid evidence that these numbers of children needing child care will increase with the growth of families with two, single-parent families, foster care, and welfare reform.

In light of these trends, this paper examines the current issues, problems, and promising practices in child care and advocates a universal child-care system which will assist all American families in balancing work, family life, and child care. A care system which protects and develops children in partnership with their parents would be stone in the steps to self-sufficiency.

## The Case For Child Care

It was over 25 years ago at the 1970 White House Conference on Children that child care was determined to be the number one priority for meeting the needs of children and families in America. Whether they are 0-3, whether they are preschoolers, or whether they are of school age, all children who need early care and education have a basic right to this service. While other countries in the industrialized world such as France have achieved this objective, working to achieve universal early care and education is an elusive but compelling national goal in the United States.

Child care, defined simply, is a regularly used arrangement in which children are physically in the care of someone other than their parents for a part of a 24-hour time period. Dramatic surges in the number of women who are in dual-career families, in single-parent households, or transitioning from welfare to work-coupled with the growing substitute parental forms such as kinship care or foster care-are illustrative of contemporary family life. These demographic, economic, and social changes have had a major effect on how we care for children.

For example, the percentage of American women with children under age 6 who work outside the home has increased to about 60 percent in 1990 from 10 percent in 1940. In addition, there has been a significant rise in mother-only families. In 1940, only 6.7 percent of children lived only with their mothers; in 1990, almost 25 percent did (United States Department of Health and Human Services, 1996). For families of all races and income groups, this change is due to the concomitant rise in divorce, separation and out-of-wedlock birth. The rise in mother-only families has become even more startling when we consider African-American families versus White families. About 80 percent of African-American children live in a mother-only family for at least part of their lives, compared with about 46 percent of white children (United States Department of Health and Human Services, 1996). But whatever the reason or race of the family, mothers have fewer options, less money, and greater need for quality child care than two-parent households.

In 1993, 9.9 million American children under age 5 were in need of child care while their mothers worked. Of that number, more than 5 million children under age 3 were in the care of adults other than their parents (United States Department of Commerce, 1995).

There is a significant differential in the race and ethnicity of families who can and do avail themselves of child care. In 1995, 79 percent of white children were in child care, 16 percent of African-American children, 14 percent of Hispanic children, 4 percent of Asian-American children and only 1 percent of Native Americans. This corresponds to the total ratio of American children by race and ethnicity: white 69.1 percent; African-American 14.7 percent; Hispanic 12 percent; Asian and Pacific Islander 3 percent; and Native American 1 percent. These child-care numbers probably represent an undercount when we consider the large numbers of children, particularly African-American, who are in informal arrangements and may not be reporting care arrangements. In terms of residences, the majority of African-American (56.7 percent) and Hispanic (50.6 percent) children live in metropolitan areas, whereas only 20.5 percent of white children live in cities (United States Department of Health and Human Services, 1996).

It is clear that contemporary mothers are less able to stay at home with their children as the need to work forces a new paradigm. For a brief period during the early '90s, fathers who mostly were casualties of corporate downsizing and fathers unable to get jobs took on the role of primary care providers. However, the trend was short-lived as many fathers regained employment. There are promising indicators that fathers are spending time, albeit limited, with their children (Pleck, 1996). Current estimates for paternal engagement time with young children is 1.9 hours for weekdays and 6.5 hours for Sundays.

It should also be noted that the extended family support network has experienced attrition, reflecting the growing number of aunts, grandparents, and cousins who are currently in the work force. For some children, grandparents are their substitute parents due to the death, illness, or abandonment of their biological parents. About 8 percent of children have a grandparent in the home. Only 3 percent of children in two-parent families live with a grandparent compared with 18 percent in mother-only families and 20 percent in father-only families (United States Department of Health and Human Services, 1996). The need for universal care resounds in the face of these circumstances.

## History of Child Care in African-American Communities

The struggle to provide quality child care has been a part of the African-American history since before the Civil War when care took the form of field nurseries for slave children (Dill, 1973). In the century following, the necessity to balance work and family life meant that child care was always an issue (Hill, 1972). Informal arrangements with extended families, neighbors, and church members were the predominant forms of care. But in the early part of the century and beyond, there were also organized efforts to provide care to enrich early childhood development, combined with programs to maintain children in custodial arrangements. The National Association of Colored Women, established in 1896, set up nursery schools. Churches had preschool programs. Black colleges offered courses in early childhood education and created laboratory schools for training practitioners (Hampton, Spelman, Tuskegee, Atlanta, and Howard universities). Dr. Flemmie Kittrrel, the first black early childhood development educator to receive a doctorate, was a prominent advocate for training and assisted in organizing college programs. Other African-American women in various cities were noted for the quality of their early childhood programs, such as Lucy Laney, who opened a nursery and day school in Augusta, Georgia; Dorothy Howard who operated Mrs. Howard's Nursery School in Washington, DC; and Oneida Cocrill who headed the Nursery School in the Rosenwald Garden Apartments in Chicago, Illinois. Unfortunately, little documentation is available on the programs or the costs of this earlier type of care.

Clearly, these efforts were exemplary, but limited, and did not begin to address the broader needs in communities across the country. Most families had to rely on informal arrangements with family members or friends, as they continue to do today.

The task is to structure a **universal,** quality child-care system in order to provide parents an opportunity to choose the desired child care arrangement, remove barriers and create opportunities to balance work and family responsibilities.

## Child Care as a National Issue

Organized child care in the United States has evolved from an unregulated, unconnected cottage industry to a multi-billion dollar business. It is loosely regulated by federal, state, and local entities. Parents in the National Black Child Development Institute's Parent Empowerment Program indicated that the search for quality child care is difficult, frustrating, and often nonproductive. There is little accurate, comprehensive information available in most jurisdictions. Parents indicate they have minimal choice in the price range they can afford, and they often must settle for poorer quality than they wish. Many parents are forced by circumstances into inadequate child-care arrangements, which results in time and effort expended searching for better care, and, most importantly, potentially jeopardizing the well-being of children.

The search for affordable, quality care presents a special hardship for African- American families. In the 1996 *State Survey on Child Care* published in *Working Mother*, June 1996, the following states emerged in the top 10: California, Colorado, Connecticut, Hawaii, Maryland, Massachusetts, Minnesota, Vermont, Washington and Wisconsin (Holcomb, B.). It is significant for African-Americans to note that none of these states represent geographical areas where there is a dense African-American population with the exception of Maryland. This points to the great need for African-American organizations and communities to become involved in the push for universal quality child care.

Although quality child care is a scarce commodity, particularly for infants and children with disabilities, incremental improvements have been made in recent decades. Head Start has to be credited with the paradigm shift in our program standards on early care and education. For young children, Head Start focused our attention on understanding that children need more than a classroom. Learning and development is connected to health, nutrition, social services, parent involvement, and parental empowerment.  Also, learning and development are vitally tied to the community, jobs, housing, and political action.  Therefore, child care in its broadest context is a child-development strategy, a parent-empowerment strategy, an economic-development strategy,  and a community-organizing strategy.

## Welfare Reform

Early in the Nixon administration, welfare reform was introduced and strategies were formulated to place children in custodial child care while requiring mothers to work.  As there was and continues to be a disproportional number of African- American families receiving Aid to Families with Dependent Children (AFDC), the proposal would have impacted millions of African-American children.  Currently, there are legislative efforts to require AFDC recipients to work.  The proposals do not provide adequate funds to ensure that children will receive quality child care.  While NBCDI believes that able-bodied adults should work and that work can build self-esteem and self-sufficiency, we cannot support any initiatives that threaten to warehouse African-American children.  What is needed is an infusion of dollars to support quality child care while mothers go to work, school, or job-training programs.

## Child Care as a Child Development Strategy

Quality child care is an intervention which promotes the physical, cognitive, social, and emotional development of children.  The single most important factor in child care is the relationship between the child and the care giver.  Children grow through relationships.  Children who are affirmed through affection, continuity, and age-appropriate care are more likely to develop trusting relationships with their care givers as well as with other adults. They learn confidence and feel safe in taking risks, a necessary quality for lifelong learning. (Kagan, Moore & Bredekamp, 1995).

Child care in the early years is a vehicle to provide children with a developmentally appropriate experience.  Developmentally appropriate experience has a fairly wide range of interpretations, but in general, it means that a curriculum should be child-centered with activities geared toward the age range and learning readiness of *each* child in the group—not toward the group as a whole.  This includes intellectually challenging teaching materials, of course, but it also means appropriate arrangement of materials and room equipment; sufficient choice of games and nonacademic activities; rest periods; food service; prominent display of child-generated artwork and other projects, availability of toys, books and games, acknowledgment and celebration of cultural diversity; and sufficient and appropriate physical activity.

Other attributes of a quality child-care environment:

- The physical plant meets all local regulations for structural soundness and fire safety;

- The water supply and sanitation facilities are adequate;

- The ratio of staff to children is acceptable;

- Bed linen, toys, and utensils used by the children are clean and safe;

- Group size should follow guidelines established by the National Association for the Education of Young Children;

- Food provided to children is plentiful and nutritious;

- Sufficient time is allowed for meals and bottle feeding; and

- The environment is bright, cheerful, and spacious.

There is new and exciting knowledge related to brain development and capacity in the early years of life and beyond which suggests that children need and thrive on appropriate stimulation from conception. It is imperative that an early start be given in infancy. The challenge before us is to ensure that young children are encouraged to engage in interactive learning experiences which provide opportunities for them to construct their own knowledge. These opportunities should include developing positive relationships with peers, parents, and other adults.

Of equal significance in using child care as a child-development strategy is the opportunity to identify, assess, and monitor the physical development and health status of the child. Early intervention can lead to good preventive habits (such as immunizations), early diagnosis, and treatment of conditions when needed.

**Types of Care**

Child care options in America exist on a continuum influenced by a seemingly infinite array of variables that determine whether care has a negative or positive impact on the development of a child. The value (negative vs. positive) placed on each situation depends entirely on the circumstances of the child, his family, and his community.

Research is mixed on types of care parents prefer. It is difficult to use utilization rate surveys because many families rely on informal child care arrangements. Statistics indicate that working parents rely about equally on informal care and market forms of care—usually defined to include licensed and unlicensed child care centers, preschools, Head Start programs, family child-care homes, and after school programs (U.S. Department of Commerce, 1995, P-70-53). The informal market is often invisible to the process. Strong findings from some studies suggest that while low-income families are more likely to use informal care, this pattern should not be interpreted as a preference (Meyers & Van Leuwan, 1992). Choice is frequently determined by availability and affordability instead of the arrangement that best meets the needs of the child.

Of the 5 million children under the age of 3 who are in the care of adults other than their parents, 30 percent were in a child care center, 32 percent were in family child care, 41 percent were cared for by relatives, and 22 percent had a non-relative in-home care provider (See Figure 1).

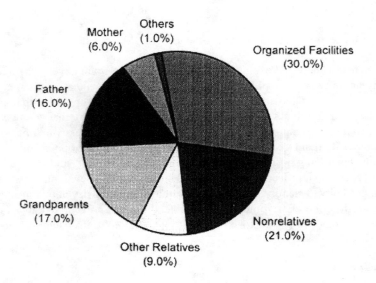

African-American families with the youngest child under age 5 are more likely to use center-based care than white or Hispanic families when the mother is employed. African-American families with school-aged children (5-12) are more likely to arrange care with relatives if the mother is employed (United States Department of Commerce, 1995, P-70-53).

Figure 2

## Primary Child Care Arrangement for African American Families
## When Youngest Child is Under Age Five and Mother is EMPLOYED

| TYPE OF CARE | % OF CHILDREN IN CARE | # OF CHILDREN IN CARE |
|---|---|---|
| Relative | 27 | 267030 |
| In-Home Provider | 0.1 | 989 |
| Family Day Care | 11 | 108790 |
| Center | 45 | 445050 |
| Other | 3 | 29670 |
| TOTAL | | 851529 |

## Primary Child Care Arrangement for African American Families
## When Youngest Child is Under Age Five and Mother is NONEMPLOYED

| TYPE OF CARE | % OF CHILDREN IN CARE | # OF CHILDREN IN CARE |
|---|---|---|
| Relative | 21 | 160230 |
| In-Home Provider | 1 | 7630 |
| Family Day Care | 2 | 15260 |
| Center | 8 | 61040 |
| Other | 8 | 61040 |
| TOTAL | | 305200 |

## Primary Child Care Arrangement for African American Families
## When Youngest Child is Ages 5-12 and Mother is EMPLOYED

| TYPE OF CARE | % OF CHILDREN IN CARE | # OF CHILDREN IN CARE |
|---|---|---|
| Relative | 42 | 476700 |
| In-Home Provider | 3 | 34050 |
| Family Day Care | 5 | 68100 |
| Center | 14 | 158900 |
| Self-Care | 3 | 34050 |
| Lessons | 6 | 68100 |
| Other | 0 | |
| TOTAL | | 839900 |

## Primary Child Care Arrangement for African American Families
## When Youngest Child is Ages 5-12 and Mother is NONEMPLOYED

| TYPE OF CARE | % OF CHILDREN IN CARE | # OF CHILDREN IN CARE |
|---|---|---|
| Relative | 22 | 100760 |
| In-Home Provider | 4 | 18320 |
| Family Day Care | 0 | 0 |
| Center | 8 | 36640 |
| Self-Care | 1 | 4580 |
| Lessons | 9 | 41220 |
| Other | 4 | 18320 |
| TOTAL | | 219840 |

Source: National Child Care Survey, 1990

* PLEASE NOTE-CHILDREN IN CARE % DOES NOT EQUAL 100. THE REMAINDER IS THE PERCENTAGE OF CHILDREN CARED FOR BY PARENTS.

Relative care is a practical and often preferred type of child care, particularly in the black community. Many African-Americans remember and know first hand the significance of the extended family as a child-care provider from their own experience.

It is clear from the statistics in Figure 2 that while a significant amount of child care is still provided by relatives, there is a mixed picture. When the mother is employed and the youngest child is age 5-12, 42 percent are in the care of a relative; when the youngest child is under five, only 27 percent of the children are cared for by a relative. The concern remains that the amount of informal care arrangements may not be captured by these statistics and may also be skewed because they do not disaggregate toddler care from preschool care.

## TYPES OF CARE

**Informal Care /**
**Relative Care**—refers to unregulated care arranged by parent and is invisible in the organized child-care system.

**Family Child Care**—refers to care provided in a private residence for a limited number of children by an unrelated care giver.

**In-home child care**—refers to care provided in a child's own home during a portion of a 24-hour day by a relative or non-relative adult other than the child's parent or guardian.

**Child Development Center\***—a facility which offers a child development program for more than five children between infancy and 13 years of age. The program may be full- or part-time and care for children before and/or after school.

**School-Age Child Care**—a program located in public schools which provides care for children ages 6-13 before and after school.

**Self Care**—refers to preschool and school-age children who are home alone before and/or after school

**Head Start**—A comprehensive child and family program which provides early childhood education services as well as social, health and parent involvement services for low-income children and families.

*Note: Center based care may include respite, employer-operated, emergency and drop-in care.*

**Types of Care**

### *Informal Care*

Informal care is child care arranged by the parent with the caretaker who may be a family member, neighbor, or friend. It is believed that this is the preferred choice of parents and that it is advantageous because the arrangement is convenient and the care giver is known by the parent. It is presumed that the adult-to-child ratio is favorable. It should be clear that these are assumptions without evidence, however. The fact is that this is unregulated care which may build on the strengths of the family and cooperative community networks. On the other hand, informal care may be inappropriate (i.e., inadequate care giving training, experience, age and condition of the care taker, etc.) and utilized by parents because they have no other options. Informal care is prevalent with African American families but little information is available on its characteristics.

### *Family Child Care*

Family child care includes non-parental paid care provided in a care giver's home. States may regulate the number of children in care, space requirements, space conditions, and care giver health status and training. Zoning regulations in a community may also be an issue in terms of location. With family child care, the adult-to-child ratio should be small, and family child care has the potential to provide nurturing interactive opportunities. This type of care is cited as preferred and especially appropriate for infants and toddlers because it tends to mirror the home environment and may be neighborhood-based.

### *Child Development Center Care*

Center-based child care is defined as a formal, organized entity or business whose purpose is to provide supervised care for young children in a non-residential facility. Centers may operate under various auspices including churches, YMCAs and corporations. Parents may pay a flat rate or payment may be based on a sliding-fee schedule. Many non-profit centers receive state, federal, and/or foundation support.

Employers may provide child care for their own employees on either a subsidized basis or on a sliding scale. Doing so supports workers in their parental roles and creates a more family-friendly work environment. This child-care arrangement is often preferred by parents with preschool children. This provides an opportunity to expose children to more experiences and allowing them to interact with peers.

## School-Age Care

School-age care operates before and after school for children ages 5-12. It may be under the sponsorship of school or community-based organizations including churches, community centers, recreation programs, as well as local affiliates of national organizations.

School-based care is provided before and after school for children ages 5-12. This form of care can vary in emphasis. Some programs focus on academic enrichment while others offer only recreational opportunities. School-based care programs are funded by a diversity of sources, including the government, local funding agencies, foundations, the United Way, corporations, and parents. Sliding-fee scales or discounts are sometimes offered to families with more than one child enrolled in a program. Quality varies widely but the hallmarks of school-based care are the protected environment of a school building, which must meet regulatory codes, the proximity to home, and the ability for a child to remain in familiar surroundings with appropriate supervision.

## In-Home Child Care

In this type of care, the child remains at home and the care giver, a relative or a non-relative, comes into the home to care for the child. Individuals are paid for providing this service. Generally, this type of care is expensive using market rates and it requires careful scrutiny of the care giver, who functions autonomously. In-home care can be beneficial for infants and toddlers, since there is a low care giver-child ratio. Children remain in the familiar surroundings of home and neighborhood. In addition, this form of care may be less stressful to parents, since they will not have to transport a child to care at a location outside the home, which may be less convenient and more time consuming.

## Head Start

Head Start is a comprehensive, community-based child and family program funded by the federal government and community resources. It is designed to enhance early child development and care for children in low-income families through the provision of a range of services including early childhood education, health, social, psychological, and nutrition services with a strong emphasis on parental involvement. Ten percent of the spaces in Head Start are allocated to children with disabilities. Up to 10 percent of families can have incomes over the poverty line. Most families have incomes at or below the poverty index. It is estimated that over 268,000 children in Head Start are African-American. Staff development and program quality are a current focus of attention.

Even though Head Start programs primarily enroll children aged 3-5, in 1995,

Early Head Start programs were established to serve families with children from birth through age 3. Historically, Migrant Head Start programs and parent and child centers have served infants and toddlers and their families.

Budget increases for Head Start have been sought and won over the years with support from every administration and both sides of the aisle. As in most early child-care programs, the need is far greater than the supply. Presently Head Start serves 40 percent of the eligible population. In 1995, 750,696 children were served; 268,749 were African-American children. It is likely that Head Start is the most well-known early childhood program in this country. It is widely acclaimed by policy makers, policy influencers, service providers, and consumers of child-care services. It has federal and community roots.

## Self-Care

In spite of national efforts to eliminate the problem of children being left alone to care for themselves, preschool children and school-age children, "latch-key kids," are caring for themselves while their parents work. These are probably not intentional neglect situations, but rather represent the dilemma of parents having to work to support themselves and their families with no options for child care. For these families, there is no informal support system, no money to pay for child care, or no available resources in the market-place. No community can afford the consequences of this horrible choice.

## Licensing, Regulation, and Safety Standards

Child advocate efforts to enact comprehensive federal regulations for child care have been largely unsuccessful. It is generally assumed that federal regulation places too high a cost on compliance for child-care centers. The consequences are that there is great variability related to standards for care and protection of children. Such crucial issues as types of care that are included in the regulatory process, facility inspections, staffing requirements, care giver qualifications, and training should not be left to chance. No community can afford a laissez-faire approach to child care.

A study conducted by a group of four prestigious universities in 1995 found that "... most child care is mediocre in quality, and sufficiently poor to interfere with children's emotional and intellectual development" (Study Team, 1995).

State regulatory definitions of what constitutes child care and the auspices of that care serve to exempt a number of programs from basic licensing and program requirements. For example, in some states, family child care may not be included in the regulatory process if there are fewer than three children in care in the home; part-day programs or church-run child care may be exempt and in-home care may only be monitored if public funds are used for payment. The importance of flexible comprehensive regulation for child care has been voiced by consumers and child-care practitioners. However, parents have a right to know about conditions in the facilities, the program content, and the background, qualifications, and health of the staff, including assurances of criminal background checks.

States with the most demanding licensing standards have fewer poor-quality child-care centers, and centers that comply with state regulations and guidelines provide higher quality services (Study Team, 1995). With this evidence, no community can afford to allow laxity in this area.

## Leadership, Education and Staff Development

Child-care programs are only as good as the staff that work in them. Research has confirmed that training and the qualifications of the care giver as the most significant factor-determining quality. The level of preschool teachers formal education and their special training positively affect children's development (Morgan, et al, 1993). Therefore, staff development and leadership development in the field of child care is crucial.

The quality of child care-training programs and the use of the funds to run them, must be held to the same high standards as other educational training programs. Some of the most pressing issues include: fulfilling career opportunities; incentives to pursue advanced training; inclusion of diverse populations in child-care staff recruitment; development of an appropriate and professional body of knowledge; establishment and consistent enforcement of standards of quality of care; and development of leadership programs in the African-American community.

The National Association for the Education of Young Children (NAEYC) has identified four early childhood professional development levels (Johnson & McCracken, 1989):

- Level I-successful completion of requirements for a Child Development Associate Credential (CDA) certificate and one year of work experience

- Level II-successful completion of an associate degree that conforms to NAEYC guidelines, plus two years of work experience

- Level II-successful completion of a baccalaureate degree that conforms to NAEYC guidelines, plus three years of work experience

- Level IV-successful completion of an advanced degree in a program meeting NAEYC guidelines, plus five years of work experience (The National Association for the Education of Young Children, 1989.)

**Federal Initiatives to Improve Training** (Carnegie Corporation of New York, 1994)

- The 1990 Head Start Reauthorization includes provisions for staff training and compensation. The law mandates, and funding has been appropriated, that every Head Start classroom has at least one teacher with a Child Development Associate credential, a state certificate that meets or exceeds CDA or an appropriate early childhood degree.

- Child Care and Development Block Grant (CCDBG) legislation requires that a state must spend at least 5 percent of its funds on quality improvement by upgrading compensation, training, resource and referral services, and licensing. CCDBG is one of the most significant ways in which the federal government has helped improve the quality and expand the supply of child-care. At least 40 states have used these funds to improve licensing and monitoring, which most states view as an essential element in ensuring quality. Almost every state uses CCDBG funds to invest in training for child care teachers and providers. Previously, nearly half the states made no attempt to help with training. Using CCDBG funds, states have developed mentoring programs, statewide resource centers, training clearinghouses, more intensive training for child-care programs; served more low-income children; used mobile vans to reach rural areas; and targeted efforts to work with special-needs and disabled children.

- The Care giver Personnel Pay Plan, begun in 1989, is a program within the military child-care system that links training of child-care professionals to pay increases in order to make salaries competitive with comparable professions within the military. This has resulted in decreased staff turnover.

## Staff Compensation and Leave Benefits

Child-care workers are one of the lowest paid of any essential industry in the United States. Nationally, the average wage for child-care center teachers is $6.80 per hour. Only 18 percent of these teachers have health benefits. There are no national statistics on family child-care providers, although it is conventional wisdom that many child-care providers do not receive benefits (Wayne, 1996).

The goal should be to establish pay levels that are reasonably competitive across professions that call for equivalent professional education, training and responsibilities. Staff also needs to receive usual employee benefits such as paid vacation, health insurance, sick leave, and disability.

In France, as well as other industrialized nations, there is appropriate compensation of staff and, in addition, maternity and early-care benefits available to parents. Infants' early experiences, actually from the moment they are born, are critical to their eventual development. Therefore, allowing plenty of time for a woman to recover from childbirth and for both parents to be with their new baby full time can give children and parents a head start. With very few exceptions, such as temporary disability insurance (TDI), parental leave from work is unpaid in the United States. The Family and Medical Leave Act is unpaid, which means that a parent of limited income cannot take advantage of not working without pay.

**Consumer Issues**

Efforts should be undertaken, in both the public and private sectors, to educate parents about the quality of child care, staff training and education and licensing requirements. Unless parents understand what high-quality child care is, they cannot be aware of the liabilities poor care poses to their children.

Providers of child care should be partners with parents in the child rearing process. Exemplary care givers share with parents a written plan of program activities, objectives and goals. This plan addresses educational, developmental, social, cultural, emotional and recreational needs and should be individualized to an appropriate degree. In addition, providers need to help parents understand how they guide behavior, help children take risks in a safe environment, teach them to make decisions, interact with their environment establish disciplinary measures, and help children achieve self-control.

In order to encourage parental participation in child care, parents and providers should meet in person on a regular basis to discuss how the child is meeting developmental and educational goals and to go over real and potential problems.

Currently, there is a growing national awareness for the need to establish formal associations in child care. There is an emerging organization, the National Association for Family Child Care, designed to provide state and local family child-care providers with support. However, few African-Americans are actively engaged as members or leaders.

Another significant organized effort is the National Association of Child Care Resource and Referral Agencies. It has a national office in Washington, D.C., and an active involvement of African-American leadership. Again, there still remains a need to involve more African-Americans in this association.

In order to work successfully, a child-care network must be locally developed and operated, coordinating services with a minimum of red tape. It must be comprehensive enough to encompass all available child-care providers and services (for-profit and nonprofit, for infants and toddlers, as well as older preschoolers) and include family-based, center-based, and other types of facilities. It should be located in an institution that is central to community activities. It is important that African-American families and child-care providers are active in these networks.

## Federal Funding

Even though federal programs are designed to serve specific populations, the rules often undermine the purpose. The Head Start Income Guidelines demonstrates the issue. It has been pointed out by the National Head Start Association that the "official poverty" line as determined by the Office of Management and Budget has denied many low-income children access to Head Start Services. Further, the Association points out that Head Start income guidelines are lower than the guidelines for Medicaid, Child Care Food Program, and Women, Infants and Children (WIC). As such, they exclude many of the working poor. In addition to the working poor, many middle-income families find themselves having to settle for poor quality child-care. Since publicly subsidized care is only provided for the poorest of families, there is a growing middle tier whose children might be at best left in precarious child care arrangements. Although these families want and deserve high-quality care, it is just not affordable for them. Studies have linked high-quality center-based programs to increased cost. (Study Team, 1995).

Child care operates in a mixed market of private nonprofit centers, publicly operated centers and those owned and operated for profit. The fact that different types of financing for these operations compete and co-exist in the same market can result in a wide range of differences in the cost and quality of services.

The majority of child care is paid for by the parents of children receiving the care. These parents, particularly single parents in low-income brackets, are paying a substantial portion of their income for child-care costs. Because African-Americans are disproportionately poor, the impact on their salaries is even greater. One of the most frequent concerns expressed by parents is the high cost of child care in relation to parental income. Employed parents with a child younger than five years spend approximately 10 percent of their income on child care, but families earning below $15,000 a year spend 23 percent of their total income on child-care costs (National Child Care Staffing Study). In fact, some parents have retreated from the labor force because they were unable to afford child care. Costs vary depending on geographic region. Working families spend on average $3,000 per year for child care. Good quality care costs between $5,000 and $8,300 per year, depending on staff salaries, staff, child ratios, and the type of care (Willer, 1990).

The largest federal income tax program that provides subsidies to working families to help pay for child care is the Child and Dependent Care Tax Credit. The Tax Credit helps working parents with a portion of their child-care expenses. Families with incomes up to $10,000 may claim 30 percent of allowable child-care expenses. Families with incomes above $28,000 may claim 20 percent of allowable child-care expenses. This tax credit is primarily used by middle-and upper-income families. Families with incomes over $50,000 are twice as likely to use this credit than families with incomes below $15,000

For families with low income or no income, several programs have been federally funded to pay for child care. The Family Support Act (1988) authorizes and requires states to guarantee child care to participants of the Job Opportunities and Basic Skills Training Program (JOBS) and employed recipients of Aid to Families with Dependent Children (AFDC) and a year of Transitional Child Care (TCC) after they become employed. The Family Support Act—At Risk Child Care Program provides child-care subsidies to working families who would be at risk of becoming eligible for public assistance without child-care assistance. The Child Care and Development Block Grant (CCDBG) provides direct child-care support to working families with incomes up to 75 percent of a state's median income without a state match requirement. In addition, CCDBG funds may be used to provide child-care assistance without regard to income to children who are in need of protective services in their own families or who have foster parents that are employed or in a job training or education program.

There are other federally funded programs which support child care and are not specifically targeted to low-income families. The Child and Adult Care Food Program provides meals for children enrolled in licensed child care and family daycare homes. Meals are subsidized at a set rate without regard to family income, therefore this program serves both low- and middle-income children. The Social Services Block Grant supports a wide range of social services. There are no requirements for how states should distribute these funds. However, some states do use this money to support child care. Since each state determines the eligibility requirements for this program, it is difficult to assess how much is spent on child care, estimates are in the 16 percent range (Besharov, 1996).

While these programs have provided some child-care assistance, the Government Accounting Office (GAO) in testimony in 1995 before the Senate Committee on Labor and Human Resources identified continuing problems in meeting child-care needs due to rigid distinct categories for service that did not reflect their interrelated causes and solutions, inadequate funding to pay actual cost of care, service gaps and supply shortages, particularly acute for infants, special-needs children, and before-and-after school (United States General Accounting Office, 1995).

The federal role in child care can be described as minimal at best. Head Start, for example, serves only 40 percent of the eligible population. Funding for child care is inadequate and limited to a few categorical initiatives each with its own eligibility criteria creating a bureaucratic maze of discrete, unrelated programs.

A summary of the current federal child care initiatives with specific allocated funding follows.

# FUNDING STREAMS

**AFDC/Job Opportunities and Basic Skills Training Program (JOBS) Child Care—** Funds totaling $655 million pay for child care guaranteed to AFDC recipients who are working or participating in education and job training. States must provide parents with vouchers if more than one form of legal child care is available. (These programs are authorized by the Family Support Act.)

**AFDC Transitional Child Care—**$200 million is allocated to provide states with funds to provide child care for families when parents become ineligible for AFDC because of employment, but need child care to continue working. (This program is authorized by the Family Support Act.)

**Title IV At Risk Child Care—**provides $297 million to states that provide child care for more than 200,000 children per month whose parents are not receiving AFDC but are at risk of going on welfare because of child-care expenses. (This program is authorized by the Family Support Act.)

**Child Care Development Block Grant—**This program provides $935 million to states for child care including before and after-school care, and for the development of early childhood education programs for over 750,000 children. Families must have incomes at or below 75 percent of their state's median income. Funds may also be used for children at risk of abuse or neglect.

**Child and Adult Care Food Program—**It's funded at $1.5 billion. This program is an open-ended entitlement that provides funds to states for meals and snacks served to almost 2 million children in licensed child-care centers and family day-care homes. All children enrolled are eligible for meal subsidies, although the amount of subsidy provided is based on need.

**Social Services Block Grant (formerly Title XX)—**Total funding for this grant is $2.38 billion. This grant provides support to states for a wide range of social services including child care. Estimates of the percentage of funds used by states for child care range from 14-16 percent.

**Dependent Care Tax Credit—**This tax credit of $2.8 billion helps working families claim a credit against taxes owed for 20 percent to 30 percent of their employment related expenditures for child care. The tax credit is calculated on a sliding scale based on income. Families without tax liability do not benefit from the tax credit since the credit is not refundable.

**Head Start—**It's the largest federally funded early childhood program. A budget of $3.7 billion provides services to 750,696 low-income children and their families. Over 268,000 head start children are African-American children.

# PROMISING DEVELOPMENTS IN CHILD CARE

**Early Head Start (EHS)**—In 1995 the Department of Health and Human Services established Early Head Start to provide quality services to low-income families with children from birth to age 3. Over 5,000 families in 68 EHS programs will receive comprehensive child and family services. While some programs have served families with infants and toddlers in the past, this is part of a new effort to make sure more children receive a head start as early in life as possible.

**Empowerment Zones**—There are nine empowerment zones in cities across the country and 95 enterprise communities. These communities use tax incentives and flexible grants to promote economic empowerment and private sector job creation in distressed communities. There are opportunities to include child care in the community assessment and mapping strategies, which examine availability, accessibility, and affordability of child care in the community. The potential role of child care in economic development may be examined also (Jeffries, 1996). The U.S. Department of Housing and Urban Development has provided $21 million to assist nonprofit organizations in providing early childhood development services for families living in public housing in these communities.

**National Association of Child Care Resource and Referral Agencies (NACCRRA)**—In 1994, nearly 1.5 million families used the services of child care resource and referral agencies (R&Rs). Of the 560 community-based R&Rs, 95 percent are part of NACCRRA. The Association trains 339,000 persons who work in centers, family child-care homes and school-age programs.

**The American Business Collaboration for Quality Dependent Care (ABC)**—In 1992, a consortium of more than 150 major U.S. corporations was launched to support the diverse dependent care needs of employees in order to attract and retain a productive, competitive work force. For a three-year period beginning in 1992, American Business Collaboration for Quality Dependent Care (ABC) invested $27 million in some 355 projects that serve more than 211,000 individuals in more than 45 communities. In 1995, the consortium launched its second phase, which seeks to identify and support replicable projects. Leading members of ABC, known as Champions, announced a $100 million commitment to exemplary dependent-care projects that they will fund over a six-year period. Champion members of ABC include Aetna Life & Casualty, Allstate, American Express, Amoco, AT&T, Bank of America, Citibank, Chevron, Exxon, GE Capital Services, IBM, Johnson & Johnson, Kodak, Mobil, Motorola, Price Waterhouse LLP, Texas Instruments, The Travelers Group, and Xerox.

**AT&T Child Care Initiatives**—AT&T established the Family Care Development Fund (Fund) to increase the supply and improve the quality of community-based child and elder-care services available to AT&T employees. From 1990 to 1995, the Fund granted $25 million to nearly 1,700 child- and elder- care projects and initiatives nationwide. The child-care grants have resulted in adding child care for nearly 13,000 children; improving care for more than 24,000 children; training 6,155 child care providers; and helping create an accreditation and national training program for school-age programs. AT&T has also developed an initiative designed to help employees balance their work and their lives outside the workplace. A component of this model initiative is a Child Care/Elder Care Reimbursement Account, which allows employees to set aside up to $5,000 a year in pre-tax dollars to pay for child- or elder-care expenses.

**Head Start Fellows Program**—In 1995, the Head Start Fellows program funded by the Department of Health and Human Services and administered by the Council for Early Childhood Professional Recognition began. This program provides public policy leadership opportunities to individuals in the Early Childhood field. Fellows will serve as special assistants to senior administrators within the Department of Health and Human Services or other federal agencies and have a mentor experience with a national organization involved with children and family issues. This program is part of a long-term quality-improvement initiative to enhance the skills of child-development and family-service workers.

**Council for Early Childhood Professional Recognition** has administered the **Child Development Associate,** a credentialing program which has provided a system for assessing the competence of early childhood caregivers since 1985. The Council works to improve the professional status of early childhood workers and is helping to meet the growing need for qualified child-care staff.

**National Association for the Education of Young Children (NAEYC) Accreditation Program**—The year 1995-1996 marked the 10th anniversary of the NAEYC Accreditation Program. This is a national voluntary accreditation system for early childhood programs. The process has two major goals: to help program personnel become involved in a process that will facilitate real and lasting improvements in the quality of the program; and to evaluate the program for the purpose of accrediting those programs that demonstrate substantial compliance with criteria for high quality.

**Child Care Bureau**—A single Child Care Bureau was organized during the Clinton administration for the first time in history to make sure programs funding child care are more consistent and coordinated. One of the initial activities of the bureau has been the launching of the Healthy Child Care Campaign coordinated with the Maternal & Child Health Bureau to improve the quality of child care through linkages with health services. The bureau has also launched the National Child Care Information Center, which disseminates child-care information to communities, policymakers, parents, programs, organizations, providers, and the public.

**States are Committed to Career Development for Early Childhood Professionals**—More than 40 states are developing comprehensive career development and training systems for practitioners working in all types of child care settings. This is extremely important because research has repeatedly confirmed that a key to quality and the prevention of harm in child care lies in the training and qualifications of the people who work with young children (Morgan, 1993).

**The National Black Child Development Institute** has an African-American Early Childhood Leadership Program. The goal is to increase the number of African-American leaders in the early childhood field by providing resources, improving access to information, and expanding opportunities for professionals to utilize and broaden their expertise.

**The National Institute for Early Childhood Professional Development** strives to improve the quality, consistency, and accessibility of professional preparation programs toward the goal of achieving a coordinated, articulated professional development system for the field of early childhood education. The Institute unertakes projects of standard setting, program review, leadership development, and information sharing through conferences and publications.

## CONCLUSION

America and the world will soon witness the birth of a new millennium and proudly proclaim this historic passage into the 21st century a new day. At the same time, millions of children will be born into a national child-care system that, if left unchanged, will fail to meet their needs. We cannot allow that to happen lest we imperil our future.

A nation that cares about children cares about child care. For decades, America has talked about the imperative to nurture the development of children. However, the rhetoric has outpaced action as evidenced by the increasing numbers of children who do not receive quality, affordable care. This issue is particularly acute for low-income and working- and middle-class families who cannot readily access the best possible care due to costs. As African-Americans are disproportionately poor and working class, while increasingly entering the middle class, they fall into the hardest hit categories. There are no federal programs and few private sector initiatives that address the child-care needs of the working and middle classes. These groups are overlooked by the current system. However, families with abundant resources have far greater and more desirable child-care options.

This country needs universal child care to ensure that all families have access to a quality child-care system committed to supporting the emotional, intellectual, social, and physical development of young children while their parents are at work, in school, or engaged in other self-help activities. In a democratic society, equal access should be available. Income should not disqualify participation. Government, in partnership with the private sector, can and should develop initiatives that promote universal child care. Other industrialized nations practice universality and are harvesting the fruits of their intervention in the results of well-adjusted children whose parents are empowered to work and provide a nurturing environment for their families. If nothing else, enlightened national interest should compel America to rehabilitate its inadequate system so that today's children are equipped to function and exhibit leadership in the next millennium. For all American children, quality child care should be a right and rite of passage.

# REFERENCES

Besharov, D. (1996). *Enhancing Early Childhood Programs*. Washington, D.C.: CWLA Press and the American Enterprise Institute.

Carnegie Corporation of New York (1994). *Starting Points: Meeting the Needs of Our Youngest Children*. New York.

Center for Research on Women and School-Age Child Care Project (1995). *Parents' Guide to School-Age Child Care*. New York: Child Care Action Campaign.

Dill, John. 1973. *"The Black Child and Child Care Issues," Child Care, Who Cares? Foreign and Domestic Infant and Early Childhood Development Policies*. Ed. Pamela Roby. New York: Basic Books.

Hill, R. (1972). *The Strengths of Black Families*. New York: Emerson Hall.

Hofferth, S., Broyfield, A., Deich, S. & Holcomb, P. (1990). National Child Care Survey.

Holcomb, B. (1996). *Child Care: How Does Your State Rate*. Working Mother, June.

Jeffries, J. M. (1996). *Expanding the Supply of Family Day Care in Upper Manhattan: Issues, Considerations and Recommendations*. New York: Columbia University Empowerment Zone Monitoring and Assistance Project.

Johnson, J. & McCracken, J.B., Eds. (1989). *The Early Childhood Career Lattice: Perspectives on Professional Development*. Washington, DC: National Association for the Education of Young Children and National Institute for Early Childhood Professional Development.

Kagan, S.L., Moore, E. & Bredekamp, S. (1995). *Reconsidering Children's Early Development and Learning*. Washington, D.C.: National Education Goals Panel.

Lombardi, J. (1996). Child Care Bureau, Administration on Children, Youth and Families. Telephone conversations. Washington, D.C.

Meyers, M.K. & Van Leuwen, K. (1992). Child care preferences and choices: Are AFDC recipients unique? *In Research on Children*. Buttrick, S. Ed., National Association of Social Workers. Washington, DC: NASW Press.

Morgan, G., Azer, S., Costley, J., Genser, A., Goodman, I., Lombardi, J., & McGimsey, B. (1993). *Making a career of it: The state of the states report on career development in early care and education.* USA: The Center for Career Development in Early Care and Education at Wheelock College.

National Association of Child Care Resource and Referral Agencies (1996). *Making Child Care Work: A Study of Child Care Resource and Referral in the United States.*

National Black Child Development Institute (1993). *Paths to African American Leadership Positions in Early Childhood Education.* Washington, D.C.

Pleck, J.H. (1996). *Paternal Involvement: Levels, Sources, and Consequences.* Presented at the Co-Parenting Roundtable of the Fathers and Families Roundtable Series, sponsored by the National Center on Fathers and Families.

Reisman, B. & Richardson, G. (1996). Child Action Campaign. Telephone conversation.

Study Team, (1995). *Cost, Quality, and Child Outcomes in Child Care Centers.* Denver: University of Colorado.

Taylor, H. (1996). Child Care Bureau, Administration on Children, Youth and Families. Telephone conversations. Washington, D.C.

United States Bureau of the Census (1995). *Income, Poverty, and Valuation of Non-cash Benefits 1993.* Current Population Reports, Series P-60, No.188. Washington, DC: United States Government Printing Office.

United States Department of Commerce, Economics and Statistics Administration Bureau of the Census (1995). *What Does it Cost to Mind Our Pre-Schoolers?* P-70-52. Washington, DC: United States Government Printing Office.

United States Department of Commerce, Economics and Statistics Administration Bureau of the Census (1995). *Who's Minding Our Pre-Schoolers?* P-70-53. Washington, DC: United States Government Printing Office.

United States Department of Health and Human Services (1996). *Trends in the Well-Being of America's Children and Youth: 1996.* Office of the Assistant Secretary for Planning and Evaluation. Washington, D.C.: United States Government Printing Office.

United States General Accounting Office (March 1, 1995). *Child Care: Recipients*

*Face Service Caps and Supply Shortages*. GAO/T-HEHS-9596. Washington, D.C.: United States Government Printing Office.

Wayne, C. (1996). National for Early Childhood Work Force. Telephone Conversation.

Whitebrook, M., Phillips, D., & Howes, C. (1989). *Who Cares: Child Care Teachers and the Quality of Care in America*. Oakland, CA: Child Care Employees Project.

Whitebrook, M., Phillips, D., & Howes, C. (1993). *National Child Care Staffing Study Revisited: Four Years in the Life of Center-Based Child Care*. Oakland, CA: Child Care Employee Project.

Willer, B. (1990). *Estimating the Full Cost of Quality,"* in B. Willer, ed., *Reaching the Full Cost of Quality in Early Childhood Programs*, Washington, D.C.: National Association for the Education of Young Children.

## BIOGRAPHICAL SKETCH

Evelyn K. Moore is executive director and a co-founder of the National Black Child Development Institute (NBCDI), a nonprofit organization committed to improving and protecting the quality of life of African-American children and families. Ms. Moore is the recipient of numerous leadership awards and currently serves on the boards of the National Council of Jewish Women Center for the Child, Child Trends, and Child Care Action Campaign.